T0358479

ROUTLEDGE LIBRARY EDITIONS: ENERGY ECONOMICS

Volume 4

HIGH-COST OIL AND GAS RESOURCES

HIGH-COST OIL AND GAS RESOURCES

JEROME D. DAVIS

LONDON AND NEW YORK

First published in 1981 by Croom Helm Ltd

This edition first published in 2018
by Routledge
2 Park Square, Milton Park, Abingdon, Oxon OX14 4RN

and by Routledge
711 Third Avenue, New York, NY 10017

Routledge is an imprint of the Taylor & Francis Group, an informa business

British Library Cataloguing in Publication Data
A catalogue record for this book is available from the British Library

ISBN: 978-1-138-10476-1 (Set)
ISBN: 978-1-315-14526-6 (Set) (ebk)
ISBN: 978-1-138-30371-3 (Volume 4) (hbk)
ISBN: 978-0-203-73080-5 (Volume 4) (ebk)

Publisher's Note
The publisher has gone to great lengths to ensure the quality of this reprint but points out that some imperfections in the original copies may be apparent.

Disclaimer
The publisher has made every effort to trace copyright holders and would welcome correspondence from those they have been unable to trace.

High-cost Oil and Gas Resources

Jerome D. Davis

CROOM HELM LONDON

© 1981 Jerome D. Davis
Croom Helm Ltd, 2-10 St John's Road, London SW11

British Library Cataloguing in Publication Data
Davis, Jerome D.
    High cost oil and gas resources.
    1. Offshore gas industry – North Sea
    2. Offshore oil industry – North Sea
    I. Title
    338.8'2   HD9581.N642

ISBN 0-85664-588-5

Printed and bound in Great Britain by
Redwood Burn Limited
Trowbridge and Esher

CONTENTS

Acknowledgements

Part One: Introduction
1. The Development Dilemma   11

Part Two: The Development Decision
2. The Development Decision — The Corporate Point of View   41
3. Governmental Regimes and the Development Decision   69

Part Three: The UK Offshore
4. 'Marginal' Fields — High-cost Fields in a British Policy
   Context   93
5. British Policy and 'Marginal' Fields: The Case of Oil   99
6. 'Marginal' Fields — The Case of Southern North Sea Gas   122

Part Four: The Danish Shelf
7. Denmark — The Development Decision in Absence of Policy   155
8. The Development Decision and Danish Oil   162
9. The Problems of Danish Gas   185

Part Five: Conclusion
10. High-cost Fields — Some Institutional Implications
    of the North Sea Contract   207

Technical Appendices
Technical Appendices to Chapter 1   237
Technical Appendix to Chapter 2   241
Technical Appendices to Chapter 5   243
Technical Appendices to Chapter 6   249
Technical Appendix to Chapter 7   252
Technical Appendices to Chapter 8   255

Index   261

ACKNOWLEDGEMENTS

The author is grateful to many people and several institutions for assistance in preparing this book. Mention should first be made of his colleagues at the Institute of Political Science, Åarhus University, in particular Ib Faurby and Ole Borre, Niels Bolvig from the neighbouring Economics Institute has also been very helpful. Comments made by Professor Peter Odell (Erasmus University) and Professor Edith Penrose (INSEAD) on earlier drafts were gratefully appreciated. Many who would wish to be unnamed both in industry and government have discussed high-cost fields with the author. The book has benefited immeasurably by their kind criticism and direction.

The Royal Institute of International Affairs placed facilities at the disposal of the author in 1974. Discussions there particularly with Susan Strange and Louis Turner were critical to setting this book in progress. Both the Institute of Political Science, Åarhus University, and the Danish Institute of International Affairs have advanced money to cover the inevitable travel expenses. Special acknowledgement of the Danish Oil and Natural Gas Company must be made. Seldom is a University Lecturer given a chance to study the intricacies of natural gas negotiations through actually 'learning by doing'. The author is therefore grateful to Bendt Agerliin Olsen and Director Gerhard Jensen for an interesting 18 months consultancy.

In the producing of this book, the author appreciates the patience of David Croom and the forbearance of his editor Melanie Crook. Thanks are also expressed to Jonna Kjaer, Anne Grethe Gammelgaard, Annie Dolmer Nielsen, and Anne Marie Christensen who have typed various versions of this manuscript, and to Lee N. Davis who has read it.

Jerome D. Davis
Åarhus, Denmark

PART ONE

INTRODUCTION

1 THE DEVELOPMENT DILEMMA

1.1. Introduction

It is a virtual truism that the hydrocarbon resources in the North Sea
will constitute a significant portion of that energy base on which
Western economies will depend in the next two decades. These resources
loom increasingly large in the European energy picture, at no time more
so than at the time of writing, in a period of spiralling oil prices and
trans-Atlantic and OPEC-OECD strife and dissension. Beginning with
the onshore 1956 Dutch Schlocteren discovery — a gas field so large
that the Esso New York management, unable to believe such a find,
flew to Holland to confirm its incredible size — the search for oil and
gas spread rapidly to the offshore areas of Europe. Gas was rapidly
discovered in the southern British North Sea; oil was found in small
amounts, first in Denmark and later in the British and Norwegian
sectors, becoming really significant with the finds of the Forties field
in the first area and the Ekofisk field in the second. The rest is largely
history. OPEC oil price increases led to a frenetic pace of activity in the
period 1973-80, particularly in the northern North Sea where finds of
enormous (but expensive) fields, Statfjord, Brent and Ninian, further
abetted exploration efforts. In 1977, for example, it was estimated that
a sizeable portion of the average multinational oil corporation's annually
budgeted sums for exploration and production would be in the North
Sea province.[1]

How important are these finds? Although the sum of the fields in
Table 1.1 (illustrated in Map 1.1) is small in overall global terms, it is
undeniably significant when seen from a European pont of view. The
yardstick of importance here is all too often overlooked. The question
is less one of how much oil and gas there is in comparison with other
oil and gas producing areas, and more one of the degree to which this
oil and gas be used in the shorter term to allow the Western economies
to buy time, adjust to global oil shortages, develop other more secure
sources of oil and gas, and introduce alternative sources of energy.
Fifteen billion barrels of oil, although only equivalent to one and a half
years of OPEC production, approximates almost six years of Saudi
Arabian production (at 7 million barrels a day). If anticipated ultimate
reserves are estimated at around 60 to 70 billion barrels of oil, this is
equal to 20-30 years of Saudi Arabian oil production. The same might

Table 1.1: North Sea Estimates — 1978

North Sea sector	Field name	Proven	
		Oil reserves (bbls. millions)	Gas reserves (ft^3 billions)
Northern British	Argyll	30	n.a.
	Auk	75	90
	Beatrice	156	n.a.
	Beryl A	400	520
	Brent	2,000	3,500
	Buchan	180	45
	Claymore	500	55
	Cormorant S	160	96
	Dunlin	586	94
	Forties	1,800	594
	Heather	150	95
	Montrose	150	105
	Murchison	360	180
	Ninian	1,100	418
	Piper	800	357
	Thistle	550	151
Southern British	Hewett	—	3,500
	Indefatigable	—	4,500
	Leman	—	10,500
	Rough	—	500
	Viking	—	2,900
	West Sole	—	2,200
Norwegian	Ekofisk Area	2,600	13,650
	Frigg	—	7,100
	Statfjord	2,700	2,200
	Valhall/Hod	390	1,450
Denmark	Dan	75	
	Bent	12	
	Cora	75	2,035*
	Gorm	140	
	Skjold	42	
Netherlands	NAM K/8, K/11, K/14, K/15-L/13, K/15B	n.a.	c. 3,730
	Pennzoil K/13		
	Placid L/10-11		
	Petroland L/7		
Grand totals		15,031	59,030

* Under contract

Map 1.1: North Sea Oil and Gas Fields and Discoveries to October 1976

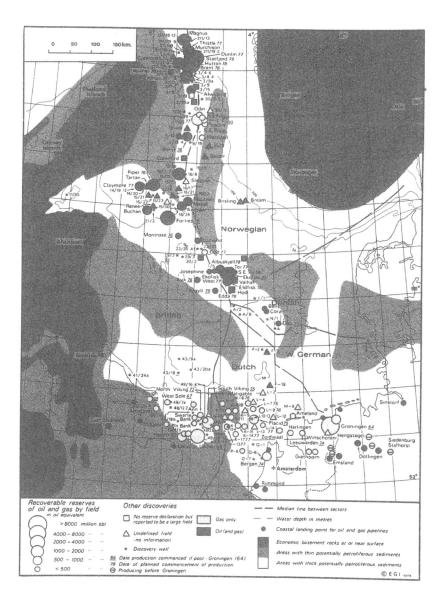

Source: P.R. Odell and K.E. Rosing, *Optimal Development of the North Sea's Oil Fields: A Study in Divergent Government and Company Interests and their Reconciliation* (London: Kogan Page, 1977), p. 30.

be noted with respect to natural gas reserves. Here, European consumption in 1973 was around 5.26 trillion cubic feet *per annum*. The gas reserves in Table 1.1 would cover European needs for another 15 years at this rate; ultimate reserves might cover European needs for twice that period. Although exact figures are hard to come by, North Sea gas reserves may be more significant in the long run than oil reserves.

As stated, however, the amount of oil and gas is highly important when it comes to questions of security and reliability of supply. In 1979, a year of spiralling oil prices caused by a shortfall of about four per cent in overall oil supplies, clearly the geographic location of the North Sea resources was of vital import to Europe. Intense European interest in the development of 'their' oil and gas reserves is very understandable.

Slightly different from 'European' interest in oil and gas reserves are the interests of the North Sea producing countries. Here the issue is not only one of self-sufficiency, but a more general governmental interest in maintaining economic growth, full employment and a positive balance in foreign trade during a period in which the world economy is experiencing a general downturn. Government spending, the rate of investment, and an increase of national exports all have important multiplier effects for general economic well-being. North Sea oil and gas, seen in these terms, is far more important than is often thought. Although offshore employment figures are low in overall economic terms, the impact on national gross capital formation, exports, and tax revenues is much more significant. Table 1.2 shows the percentage importance of the oil activities in terms of gross capital formation, per cent of exports and share of North Sea revenues in overall public expenditures for Norway and Great Britain.

Table 1.2 if anything, understates the situation. Exports of oil and gas do not include domestic market supplies (self-sufficiency). Tax revenues were just beginning to commence in 1978. (No Petroleum

Table 1.2: North Sea Activities in National Economic Perspective, 1978

	Norway	United Kingdom
		(% of national totals)
Gross capital formation	21.7	7.6
Exports	22.5	10.0
Tax revenues as % of gov't expenditures	6.2	3.4

Source: National statistics.

Revenue Taxes had yet been collected in the United Kingdom, for example.) The gross capital formation figure does not take into account the productivity of North Sea investment *vis-a-vis* the rest of the domestic national economy, a particularly important factor in the UK where productivity is low. In short, the effects of North Sea oil and gas on domestic economies are strongest in a period in which neither government policies with regard to balance of payments nor government policies on expenditure are liable to be major constraints on economic growth.[2]

Given the obvious exigency that everything economically viable should be extracted from the North Sea, it may come as a surprise that many of the oil and gas reserves known today may either never be developed, or will be developed only in the distant future. How can this be? As we will demonstrate, it does not always follow that when oil and gas are discovered and the return on investment is sufficient, the oil companies will eventually develop the resources. The process involved is complex. Oil companies must first lease the blocks, then conduct seismic surveys, drill exploratory wells, drill confirmation wells, examine the evidence, and then and only then make the decision, perhaps, to develop the field concerned. This final phase is known in the industry as the 'development decision'. We will define the development decision as the point at which a group of companies collectively decides to invest sums of money in a given oil or gas project. This decision takes place at Stage IV in Table 1.3, which illustrates the sequence of stages characterising offshore activities, and also outlines the initiating role of oil companies and the more passive supervisory roles of governments. The factors which enter into this decision are of critical importance, and include not only economic considerations, but also perceptions of risk, of the political environment, of the 'need' for the resources concerned, and so forth. With regard to high-cost fields — those fields with only a minimum of rent above the development cost — these considerations weigh rather more than for other types of fields. The problem is rendered more complicated due to the time lag involved in putting such fields into production. Even under optimal conditions many of the resources known to exist in the North Sea may well not be developed this side of the year 1990. (In the British sector, it takes an average of eight years from discovery of a field to actual commencement of production — and these are fields which with one or two exceptions pay extremely well.) The problem of timing is even more knotty regarding the higher-cost fields.

Most of the remaining resources in the North Sea undoubtedly

Table 1.3: The Development Decision in the Context of North Sea Activities

Stage	Government	Company
I. (preliminary surveys)	Government (1) grants company licence for surveys etc. (2) receives application for blocks (3) awards blocks	1. Reconnaisance 2. Bidding for blocks (with proposed work programmes for blocks desired)
II. (exploration drilling)	Government exercises control over drilling progress (environmental etc.) Also receives geological and other information	Exploration drilling
III. (appraisal drilling)	Same as in Stage II	Upon locating promising structure, company drills appraisal wells to ascertain whether field is economic
IV. (development)	Government grants approval to development programme prior to commencement of development	1. Development decision made 2. Contracting for project 3. Financing project 4. Establishment of platform and drilling of wells
V. (production)	Government supervises production to see that it is conducted in accordance with governmental guidelines	Commencement of production
VI. (reappraisal of depleting structure)	New plans for developing project require governmental approval. Abandonment of project requires government approval	Depleting field (1) leads to new appraisal and further development or (2) abandonment of field

Source: R.F. Hayllar and R.T. Pleasance, *UK Taxation of Offshore Oil and Gas* (London: Butterworths, 1977), pp. 3-5 provided the step-by-step procedure on which this table is based.

belong to this latter category. Large or otherwise promising fields remain to be discovered; but as companies exhaust the possibilities of one such structure after another, they are left with the less attractive prospects. Will these fields be developed? The answer to this question could have a critical bearing on whether Europe can rely on the North Sea to deliver a significant portion of the energy needed in the next two decades.

1.2. How Significant is the Problem? — The Reserves Involved

How many undeveloped fields are there in the North Sea? It has been authoritatively estimated that no fewer than 40 known British fields are in this category, a significant number of the fields listed in the Appendix to this chapter.[3] In Holland, as of June 1977, no fewer than 51 discoveries have been made, of which only six are currently being developed.[4] Only one of 14 Danish discoveries is developed, although development plans for another three fields are firm. There are some 23 undeveloped fields in Norway.

How much oil and gas is contained within these fields? A tentative impression of what these fields may contain is shown in Table 1.4. In this table the proved reserves (measured metrically) are the equivalent of the totals in Table 1.1. In contrast, the probable reserves are mostly from the undeveloped high-cost fields to which we have referred. The figures of 2,029 million tons of oil and 1,548 billion cubic metres of natural gas is a considerable amount — and this figure does not include further 'possible' reserves.[5] Figure 1.1, a classification system developed by the US Geological Service, perhaps indicates the dimensions of the problem better than does Table 1.3.

Two dimensions are presented in this figure, the economic dimension (vertical) and the certainty of discovery (horizontal). The reserves in Table 1.3 are essentially those in the upper left-hand corner of the figure. Whether they are developed in the future is a function of the price paid for the resources, of technology which reduces expense, and

Table 1.4: Proved versus Probable Reserves, North Sea, 1978

	Estimated proved reserves		Probable reserves	
	Oil (10^6 mt)	Natural gas (10^9 m^3)	Oil (10^6 mt)	(10^9 m^3)
United Kingdom	1,284	824.7	1,743	853
Norway	813	700	226	339
Netherlands	—	106	n.a.	260.9
Denmark	40	55	60	95
Totals	2,137	1,685.7	2,029	1,548

Sources: National Sources.

Figure 1.1: Resource Diagram

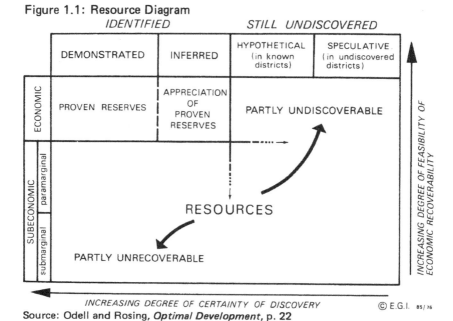

Source: Odell and Rosing, *Optimal Development*, p. 22

finally of increasing knowledge as to where the resources can be found. Many fields in the North Sea considered 'paramarginal' in 1978 could now be termed 'proven' due to price increases and the introduction of cheaper technology. In addition, reserves thought to be 'hypothetical', can now be considered 'inferred' due to increased knowledge of the North Sea province.

Fields which are just barely 'producible' in economic terms in this figure are sometimes rather misleadingly called 'marginal' fields. A semantic note would be in order at this point. 'Just producible' in Figure 1.1 means that the resources are produced at cost. No note is made of rent capture or other policies in this figure. In proper economic terminology, marginal means an absence of rent (in the case of the North Sea this rent is an oligopoly rent).[6] Much North Sea policy is aimed at capturing this rent element. Companies, in opposing such policies, have designated certain high-cost fields as 'marginal'. The term used in this sense has nothing to do with the presence or absence of rent. The fields in question are already subject to rent-capture legislation and must therefore, by definition, yield some rent. Rather, what the companies are driving at is that these fields are 'just producible' under certain rent-capture legislation, and that if any more rent-capture legislation is passed they will not be producible. These are high-cost — not marginal — fields. Since, however, in the proper economic sense of the term, these fields are frequently referred to as 'marginal fields' in policy discussions, we will use the term 'marginal' (in quotation marks) throughout this book to designate such high-cost fields, and to differentiate them from truly economically marginal fields.

The discovery and development of these high-cost fields is a dynamic of the interaction of geological and economic factors over time. Figure 1.1 both helps to define what high-cost fields are, and illustrates the geological-economic considerations underpinning policy on them.

1.3. The Policy Perspective

In the previous two sections we indicated that not only are high-cost fields important in the North Sea/European context, but that their future development is a function of geological and economic uncertainty. What remains is to put the problem in a policy perspective. As indicated by an interdisciplinary use of terms ('marginal' versus high-cost fields, for example), the policy focus is not wholly an economic focus. Also highlighted are the political problems involved in the development of these fields. To include such considerations, one must modify an economic approach. This is done in the next two sections. In these corporate behaviour is seen as 'bounded' by organisational, political, and licensing-contractual constraints. In this section, the economic aspects are 'centre stage'.

Economically, the development decision can be represented as a function of the following expression:

$$(1.1) \quad PV_0 = \sum_{t=0}^{T} \frac{OR}{(1+i)^t} - \sum_{t=0}^{T} \frac{DC}{(1+i)^t} - \sum_{t=0}^{T} \frac{EC}{(1+i)^t}$$

in which the present value of a high-cost project, PV_0, is seen in terms of future oil revenues, OR, net of taxes and royalties, development costs, DC, and costs of exploration, EC. The cash flows of these categories are discounted to the present at rate i. If one sets i equal to 15 to 20 per cent, and PV_0 approximates zero, one approaches the minimum return to enable active consideration of the North Sea resources involved.

OR, however, is an anticipated cash flow. In the wake of the 1973/4 and the 1978-80 OPEC price increases, a considerable oligopoly rent has accrued to North Sea projects. This can be represented as follows:

$$(1.2) \quad PV_0 = \sum_{t=o}^{T} \frac{OR}{(1+i)^t} + \sum_{t=o}^{T} \frac{OR'-OR}{(1+i)^t} - \sum_{t=o}^{T} \frac{DC}{(1+i)^t} -$$

$$\sum_{t=o}^{T} \frac{EC}{(1+i)^t}$$

in which OR' represents the actual income realised through general oil price increases. The rent element represented by OR'−OR has been the object of rent-capture legislation in virtually all North Sea nations.

All other variables have been held constant in expression (1.2), an assumption which clearly does not coincide with actual fact. In the real world, development costs and costs of exploration have both increased. Industry arguments have focused on such increases to argue that high-cost fields have been unfairly treated in the enactment of rent-capture legislation. Whatever the merits of these arguments (see Chapter 5 in particular), they have led governments to grant discretionary economic incentives to encourage the development of such fields. Here British policy is of particular note. To date, UK legislation includes such incentives as a discretionary remittance of royalty payments, the exemption of various quantities of crude from the Petroleum Revenue Tax, and a highly complex 'tapering provision' embodied in the Oil Tax Act of 1975.

If discretionary economic incentives are aimed at oligopoly/ Ricardian/uniqueness rents, another group of policies are directed towards 'scarcity rents'. Oil is an *in situ* depletable resource. What is produced today cannot be produced tomorrow at the same cost. The development decision consequently weighs the impact of current extraction on future profit. The future revenues in this manner are user costs or:

$$(1.3) \quad PV_{uc} = \sum_{t=o}^{T} \frac{OR_f}{(1+i)^t} - \sum_{t=o}^{T} \frac{DC_f}{(1+i)^t} - \sum_{t=o}^{T} \frac{EC_f}{(1+i)^t}$$

where PV_{uc} is the present value of the user costs concerned, OR_f

represents the foregone cash flows which might otherwise have accrued at a later point in time, and DC_f and EC_f the increased future costs of development and exploration. Assuming that there was a free market in 'just producible' high-cost North Sea fields, one such field would have a market value (MV) of:

$$(1.4) \qquad MV = PV_{uc} - PV_0$$

Here, PV_{uc} is the present value of future anticipated user costs, and PV_0, that present value which is the minimum required to put that resource into development now. If the market value (MV) is positive, it makes sense to wait to develop the field. The value involved, $PV_{uc} - PV_0$, is not only the 'market value', it is also defined as 'scarcity rent'.

These two concepts, free market and scarcity rent, are also of interest in a policy sense. One might argue that through appropriating anticipated scarcity rents, nations could encourage present development of high-cost resources. Unfortunately this is not the case. Although most North Sea nations enforce periodic rental payments for licensed areas, these payments are geared to the anticipated scarcity rents of the early 1960s. Since that time, scarcity rents have not been as much a function of the actual scarcity of crude oil and gas as of an oligopolistically enforced scarcity of these resources through the price leading behaviour of OPEC. 'Scarcity rent' in the North Sea context is more a function of anticipated increases in OPEC prices than of any depletion of oil and gas resources world-wide.

The concept of 'market value' implies that North Sea resources are freely exchangeable among firms. Such is not the case. The exchanging of resources in the North Sea involves reassigning licence shares – a closely regulated area. Furthermore, there is little incentive to exchange such shares. Periodic area payments are very low and, in most instances, possession of the resources involved is for periods of up to 50 years. This is unlike the US offshore areas where production must be commenced after a certain span of years. If such production does not begin, the area concerned reverts to Federal ownership.

One can very easily argue that 'scarcity rent' appropriation and market controls are supplements/alternatives to the discretionary economic incentives described earlier. In the context of this volume, such access provisions will be regarded primarily as an alternative to discretionary economic incentives.

What of the rate of activity, the major policy subject of this chapter and book? In the North Sea context, it is too often assumed that the oil firm 'sitting' on a high-cost field waiting for better prices or tax breaks as a function of OPEC behaviour or its own political lobbying has interests identical to the North Sea nation concerned. In fact user costs may be positive for the firms concerned, but negative for the nation. The reason for this is the very central place oil and gas have for government economic policy in general. For North Sea nations, getting high-cost fields into production ensures reliable energy supplies, encourages growth, eases policy restraints imposed by persistent balance of payments deficits and supplements existing government tax revenues. Due to the critical multiplier effects of these policy areas, non-development of high-cost resources have disproportionate effects on GNP growth.

For example, Norway is highly dependent on its North Sea activities. Let us assume that Norwegian policy can result in either of two future scenarios: a scenario which encourages the development of high-cost fields now; and one which postpones their development for up to ten years. We will call these alternatives Scenario A and Scenario B, respectively. Real growth in Gross National Product is assumed to be a function of the development/non-development of these fields. Non-development decreases real GNP growth from three per cent to two per cent. In contrast immediate development assures a real GNP growth rate of three per cent for the period 1978-89, followed by a two per cent *per annum* increase for the balance of the period to the year 2000; delayed development leads to a reverse pattern. (Table 1.5 specifies these GNP effects of development 'now' further.) To give these two scenarios meaning in present value terms, the differences in GNP growth will be discounted by six per cent — a not inappropriate social rate of discount.

The results of the two scenarios are summarised in Table 1.6. As can be seen, the GNP costs of not developing high-cost fields early on can be extremely high under the assumptions specified, a cost in 1978 real net present value terms of 273.5 billion Norwegian crowns. This is 71 per cent of Norwegian GNP in 1978 — and ultimately might be construed as a very good argument for public investment in high-cost fields.

Suppose Scenario B is chosen for reasons of conservation. In this case, due to the differing rates of growth, it will take 20 years before Norwegian GNP reaches parity with GNP under Scenario A. This, it could be argued, is a long time for public authorities to wait. Suppose the later production of the fields adds more than one per cent to GNP growth between the years 1990 and 2000? What rate of growth would

Table 1.5: Assumptions — Norwegian Scenarios A and B

Assumptions	Scenario A	Scenario B
High-cost fields	Developed immediately	Developed after ten years
GNP growth	3 per cent per annum 1978-89	2 per cent per annum 1978-89
	2 per cent per annum 1990-2000	3 per cent per annum 1990-2000

Table 1.6: Development of High-cost Norwegian Fields Reflected in a One Per Cent Change in Real Norwegian GNP Growth Rates[a].

	Scenario A Early dev't	Scenario B Late dev't	Different (A–B) Social Advantage of early dev't
		billions Nkr	
I. GNP Cash Flows			
1st 10 years	4920.9	4675.1	245.8
2nd 10 years	5766.3	5529.6	236.7
Totals	10,687.2	10,204.7	482.5
II. Present Value Disc. at 6 pct			
1st 10 years	3293.9	3127.8	165.1
2nd 10 years	2347.7	2240.3	108.4
Totals	5740.7	5368.1	273.5
III. GNP at end of 20 years	629.3	629.3	0

a. Based on a 1978 Norwegian Gross National Product of 384.2 billion Nkr. The social advantage of investing in high-cost fields is 273.5 billion Nkr. for this 20-year span or 71 per cent of the 1978 Norwegian GNP.

they have to contribute so that the 1978 present value of Scenario B equals that of Scenario A? For this to be the case, the Norwegian GNP growth would have to be the equivalent of 4.9 per cent *per annum.* Development of high-cost fields therefore — the figures in Table 1.6 reflect nothing else — would have to add 2.9 per cent *per annum* to real post-1990 GNP growth rates, surely a virtually impossible goal.

One can quarrel with the assumptions of this example. Non-development of high-cost fields might decrease Norwegian GNP growth by only 0.5 per cent, for example. One might additionally dispute the social discount rate and its impact on future generations. Yet the logic in the argument is unassailable: there are circumstances where it is in the Norwegian national interest to have high-cost fields developed. This may be recognised even more in Norway than is generally thought. It has often been assumed that Norway of all North Sea countries needs the oil the least. Calculations such as that performed here would perhaps explain why the Norwegian Government, despite this reputation, has been very willing to encourage North Sea activities.

Beyond the theoretical/hypothetical treatment received so far, how do North Sea policies towards high-cost fields actually work in practice? To answer this a comparison of British and Danish policies in particular is extremely helpful.

There are important differences between the two nations. The resource base in the British North Sea is far greater than that in the Danish North Sea. The national attention North Sea oil and gas issues receive both politically and administratively is also vastly different. The oil industry in Great Britain is well advanced, with highly articulate pressure groups, and serves an enormous domestic market. The oil industry in Denmark serves a much smaller market, but in energy terms is much more significant than its British counterpart. Some 85 per cent of Danish energy usage is based on crude oil and oil products virtually all of which are imported (two-thirds in the form of refined products).

In policy terms the two countries represent diametric opposites. British North Sea policy is more sophisticated than Danish policy. Blocks are leased, are relinquished, and are relicensed. Economic rent is a target of policy: the British have not only a royalty charge for oil and gas, but also a Petroleum Revenue Tax to cream off the 'excess' from the North Sea. Furthermore, the British National Oil Corporation and the British Gas Corporation are highly active in the North Sea, the former 'participating' in the exploration and development of North Sea fields. In contrast, there is no competition for licences in the Danish area (as at the time of writing). Until 1976 there were no blocks.

Relinquishment provisions (post-1976) are very weak; there are no rents paid for leased territories. Apart from a 5 to 8.5 per cent royalty, there has been no rent-capture mechanism in the form of a special oil tax — and there is little chance of one appearing. The Danish state oil and gas company — *Dansk Olie og Naturgas (DONG)* — is largely a gas transportation company without any substantial North Sea interests.

The latitude the two countries allow the oil industry also makes an interesting contrast. While the British regime seeks to reconcile a socially desirable rate of activity on the British Shelf with the divergent private economic calculations of the oil industry, the Danes have no policy at all in this respect. In the Danish area, the concessionaires determine the rate of activity, but without any concept of social optimality. The only precondition to be fulfilled is that production of both oil and gas be established on the Danish North Sea Shelf (a 55,000 square kilometre area) within a certain period of time or concessionary rights lapse.

What these countries have in common are high-cost fields — and a common desire to get these fields developed. Policy-makers have sought to accomplish this objective, however, in widely diverse manners. In Great Britain attempts have been made to grant incentives for field development by exemptions or modifications to existing rent-capture legislation. In Denmark authorities have refused to even consider rent-capture legislation. The Danish Underground Consortium (DUC) has what many firms would consider an ideal investment environment. *Ceteris paribus*, one would expect greater progress in the Danish sector than in the British sector in so far as high-cost fields are concerned. Such does not prove to be the fact — as is shown in our two case studies.

Where the development of high-cost fields in the UK North Sea may have been due to discretionary economic incentives, development of Danish fields was procured through the access provisions of the Danish concession — provisions which made concessionary renewal dependent on the development of oil and gas fields. An effective alternative to discretionary economic incentive could be such changes in the North Sea licence-contract between state and oil industry. Not only could changes in access provisions be more effective, they could also be more efficient — and reward those firms most committed to the North Sea. This thesis is bolstered by evidence in the British and Danish case studies.

This policy analysis, the focus of this work, can be likened to three strands of hair woven into a plait. Two of the strands are discretionary economic incentives and changes in the access provisions of the North

Sea licence. The third strand is a comparative analysis of Danish and British policies. As in a plait, each of the strands is essential to the other two.

Given the complex nature of this analysis it would be wise to specify the approach used. The method is institutional, focusing as stated on the oil multinational as a rational (although 'bounded') actor, and the concept of a limited property rights contract to specify the interrelationship between the objectives of multinational corporations and of the national state.

1.4. The Question of Method I. The Firm and 'Bounded Rationality'

A leading manager of a major affiliate sought permission from the parent company headquarters for a multi-million dollar refinery investment. Arriving unbriefed from abroad, he was confronted with the corporation's central financial planning committee. The 'vetting' was merciless. The merits of the proposed improvement were compared with similar prospective investments in India, Brazil and Germany. Could he justify his improvement relative to these other alternatives? Overwhelmed by the wealth of other detail and fact, the manager could make only a relatively poor showing. His request was rejected. Upon discussing his failure afterwards, the manager was asked if he had talked to any of the committee members before making his presentation? He had not done so. The consequent advice was succinct: he should visit the committee members and consult with them privately before making his formal presentation. The manager, chastened, did as he was advised. His project was eventually approved.

This is a good illustration of what is meant by 'bounded rationality'. To what extent can the firm in this instance be said to have been an economically rational actor? Clearly the first 'vetting' of the manager was characterised by economic considerations of profit maximisation. Yet that the manager concerned subsequently went through a socialisation process and obtained what first had been rejected indicates that the firm was also an organisation and, hence, strict economic rationality was modified by corporate decision-making processes. In the analysis which follows, it is assumed that the oil multinational is an economically rational actor but that its economic rationality is 'bounded', influenced by non-economic factors. Chief among these are organisational procedure, oligopoly market behaviour, and political lobbying to obtain better market conditions.

The firm is an organisation. Yet the degree to which a firm can be said to follow a pattern of behaviour as specified by the neo-classical models of microeconomics or to follow a more organisationally-oriented pattern has long been a topic of debate among economists.[7] One of the primary organisational approaches, that of Cyert and March, can be cited as an example.[8] In its essentials, the Cyert and March model specified a corporate decision-making process being made by coalitions and sub-coalitions of individuals with group-satisfying goals winning out over what might be regarded as stricter economic criteria.[9] Nor need this approach be retained purely for decision-making within the firm. Virtually all fields in the North Sea are developed by consortia, groups of firms that band together to reduce risk and increase resource efficiency. Decisions regarding vital questions — block relinquishment, licence application, exploration wells, field development — are group decisions, not unlike those specified by Cyert and March. From available interview evidence, the decision-making dynamics within these groups often depend more on individuals, on rules of thumb and on bargaining processes than a simple model of profit maximisation would specify. The nature of this group decision-making is explored in some depth in Chapter 2.

That the oil multinational is an oligopoly actor engaging in oligopoly competition in an oligopoly market has been repeated so often that it is a virtual truism. Imperfections at all stages of the petroleum market have been widely analysed.[10] How does this oligopoly behaviour affect maximisation within the oil firm? John M. Blair, in *The Control of Oil*, presents a possible solution, tracing the existence of various control mechanisms, which have allowed for orderly oligopoly behaviour among the principle oligopolists in the oil industry. How this control behaviour has influenced the search for and the development of oil and gas fields is uncertain, although Blair does provocatively state: 'History provides little support for the proposition that discovery is a function of price. Indeed an argument can be made that if such a relationship exists, it is inverse.'[11] (It should be pointed out in this context that Blair is referring to the American market, and not to oil discoveries in general.) One does not need to believe all of these arguments to note that firms are interested in controlling their marketing environment. In this context, one could argue that those firms most heavily committed to the North Sea are firms with particular marketing needs. Two patterns of behaviour are possible in this regard. Companies desire to own sufficient crude for their refining and marketing needs. Similarly, companies prefer to explore and produce oil proximate to their ultimate markets. Should these two arguments hold, one would expect that the firms most heavily committed to the North Sea should either be those firms most seriously short of crude oil for their own refining and marketing purposes, or those with the most sizeable European markets. Both of these contentions are examined more fully in the next chapter.

Not only are multinational oil corporations oligopoly organisations, but they are also very powerful political actors. Much emphasis has been placed on the more overt political influence which many posit that the multinational corporations exert. The overthrow of the Mossadegh regime in Iran, complicity in the Chaco War, the Mexican Revolution of 1911, and the Nigerian civil war are but a few of the political acts which have been laid at the door of the international oil industry.[12] Whether such blame is just or unjust is not within the scope of this study. What is relevant (and indisputable) is the manner in which oil companies are capable of supplementing oligopoly control with political pressure to ensure that dominance. In the US, long before the recent fight over surplus-profits taxes, the oil industry was capable of bringing political pressure first to create advantages in the form of percentage depletion, the 'expensing' of intangible drilling costs, and the foreign tax credit, and secondly to defend these advantages after they had been won.

Most economic literature assumes that the firm works within a political context. Rationality is seen in terms of maximising profits within that framework. The firm is regarded as rather passive, adjusting to political changes within its environment rather than initiating them. The institutional approach used here argues that the situation in fact, not least in the North Sea area, is really somewhat different. Both firms and governments interact symbiotically. Rational behaviour is bounded by the ability of the firm to change the economic environment to its own advantage. The government, rather than being the staunch initiator of measures which cramp the behaviour of firms, all too often puts forward measures which, after consultation with the firm, are often considerably modified, and then implemented as policy.

The consequences of this view of bounded rationality are two-fold. To begin with, the oil industry in the North Sea constitutes a powerful political force, of fundamental import in the designing of any national North Sea policy. This statement is not as obvious as it might seem. Many in Europe, despite witnessing the long and contorted political debates over controlled and decontrolled oil, taxes, natural gas prices, and other assorted issues in the United States, feel that in their own countries the situation is somewhat different, that bureaucrats have a better hold on affairs, and that the oil industry is somehow not as potent a force as it is on Capitol Hill. The greater part of our analysis tends to disprove this notion, not only for Danish policy but also, and somewhat more surprisingly, for British policy.

In terms of organisation, 'upstream' control of resources, and political activity, 'bounded' economic rationality is significant for both the Danish and British areas are organisations, and therefore the organisational dynamic must be taken into account. They are also actors interested in preserving a high degree of control over how the resources discovered are used. In this regard the Danish and British markets are considerably different. The Danish market has long served as a target for multinational surpluses of refined products — a sort of European 'distress market'. The British market, on the other hand, is one of the largest in the world. Finally, the oil multinationals in both Great Britain and Denmark are politically powerful actors that greatly influence the ultimate shape of government North Sea policy.

1.5. The Question of Method II. The Contractual Relationship and the State

The licensing or concessionary arrangements characteristic of the North Sea are essentially limited property rights contracts. A major theme in economic literature is how 'property rights' — the existence of legal entitlements to resources which affect behavioural relations among men — modify rational economic behaviour. In the words of Furubotn and Pejovich:

> The value of any good exchanged depends, *ceteris paribus*, on the bundle of property rights that is conveyed in the transaction. For example, the value of a house will be relatively greater if the bundle of property rights acquired contains the right to exclude gasoline stations, chemical plants, etc. from the immediate vicinity of the house.[13]

A North Sea licence, not unlike a deed to a house, is a contractual property right. There are, however, some significant differences.

First, a North Sea licence is not an exclusive property right. It is limited by restrictions. Normally, the right covers the exploration, production, and sale of oil found in the licensed area. The state, however, retains a latent sovereign ownership of the oil and gas concerned. Furthermore, a licence is limited by restrictions explicitly (or in some cases implicitly) stated in the relevant statute as it is interpreted and reinterpreted from time to time. Rather than ownership of a house, a better analogy might be that of a contract between a franchiser (the state) and a franchisee (the firm). In any kind of franchise relationship there exists a contract between the franchiser and franchisee, normally conditioned by the physical removal of one party from the other. As in a franchise relationship, the state (franchiser) is not really interested in monitoring and regulating the firm's (franchisee's) behaviour. Rather, as in a franchise relationship, the state attempts to devise mechanisms which give the firm an incentive to be efficient,[14] but also an incentive to behave according to carefully specified demands. A franchiser-franchisee relationship is essentially one in which market access is granted to the franchisee by the franchiser, who retains the option of revoking this contract should the franchisee not live up to requirements posited in it.

As in the franchiser-franchisee relationship, one detects two sets of North Sea contract provisions. The first set establishes the terms of access to the resources involved — the licence award — which remain relatively fixed over the lifetime of the contract. This class of contract provisions we will term 'access provisions'. The second set of provisions is subject to change generally at the discretion of the state (the franchiser). This class of contract provisions will be termed 'discretionary provisions'.

Access provisions generally include the following contractual specifications: definition of the area awarded, generally in terms of blocks, leasing fees for the area awarded, length of time which the successful applicant may retain the awarded area, relinquishment provisions, specifications on how ownership of the area might be transferred (assigned) to other parties, and (sometimes) a specified drilling programme the applicant will undertake in order to fulfil the conditions of the award. These items are relatively fixed. From time to time, the state may add additional requirements for the applicants to be considered for the acreage — state participation, unionisation of offshore workers, and the like. But these are preconditions and have little to do with the specific provisions providing for access — the terms of the licence.

Discretionary provisions cover the levying of rent-capture legislation, the setting of field production rates, the determination of natural gas prices, the use of domestic industry in developing fields, the degree of state participation (often a precondition to access), the landing of oil and gas, state options to purchase oil produced in a period of emergency, and the like. It is important to note that while these changes are made at the discretion of the state, very rarely will the state act without consultation (and often considerable negotiation) with the groups involved. The discretionary provisions are seldom explicitly covered in the licence itself. The licence provides the framework through which discretionary provisions are implemented. Discretionary provisions are also seen as a function of time — a form of *rebus sic stantibus* applied to the North Sea context. They may be provided in the form of national legislation (as was the 1975 Oil Tax Act in the UK), they may be implicit (as in the use of domestic industry for offshore purposes) or they may be *ad hoc* (e.g. the establishment of production controls in the Norwegian 'go-slow' policy). The essential elements of these policies are illustrated in Table 1.7 for Denmark, Norway, Great Britain and the Netherlands.

These two sets of provisions — analytically separate in this study — are in fact intermingled. Many of the discretionary provisions in Table 1.7 were originally preconditions to be fulfilled prior to awarding block licences. Thus provisions as to state participation or desired onshore effects have been 'tacked on' in Great Britain and Norway in the later licensing rounds. Such tactics on the part of the state have led authors such as K. Dam to label the entire North Sea licensing system as 'discretionary'.[15] However, the fundamental provisions covering access as specified in Table 1.7 have undergone only very slight changes in the last 16 years.

The analogy of the North Sea licence to a limited property rights contract is a fruitful one. It is useful in a broader policy sense. It characterises the relationship between the oil firm, the rational economic actor (although bounded by the factors discussed in the previous section) and the nation state, an actor with conflicting objectives and diffuse interests. The approach allows judgement as to whether policies are suitable in terms of policy ends and costs. The analogy is useful in a more economic sense as well. A property rights contract approach allows for a judgement both as to a policy's efficiency and as to the efficiency of alternative policies. These arguments are further elaborated in Chapter 3, and are obviously critical to the analysis of British and Danish policies.

Not only is there some organisational and oligopolistic 'slack' in the North Sea oil industry, but the degree to which this 'slack' will influence behaviour depends on the nature of the contractual relationship the industry enjoys in the particular North Sea sector. As elsewhere in industry, the nature of the contract will influence firm behaviour. Thus

Table 1.7: Licensing Policy in Danish, Norwegian, British and Dutch Law

	Denmark	Norway	Great Britain	The Netherlands
I. Access Provisions				
Extent of licences	56,000 km² in one monopoly grant (1963). Divided into blocks in 1976. Size is 3,500 km² per block. No blocks in SW portion relinquishable before 2000	Blocks of 500 to 600 km² licensed upon application	Blocks of c. 250 km² licensed upon application	Blocks of c. 375-400 km² licensed for exploration and for development
Licensing period	Exploration period of 10-12 years for first hydrocarbon, 5 additional years for second. Production period until 2012	Exploration period of 3 years. Production period initially 6 years but extendable up to 30 years	3-year exploration period. Production period initially 6 years but extendable up to 40 years	Exploration licences granted for 15 years. Successful companies may apply for a production licence which lasts 40 years
Licensing rounds	No licensing rounds, due to original monopoly grant	Four rounds to date	Sixth round completed by end 1979	Fourth round completed 1976. Since then individual licences granted
Block relinquishment	None originally. After 1976, 50% of all but the SW sector will be relinquished after 29 years	50% relinquished after 6 years, licence by licence	50% relinquished after 6 years, licence by licence	50% relinquished after 10 years. Balance after 15 years

Table 1.7 *(contd.)*

	Denmark	Norway	Great Britain	The Netherlands
Block rents	None	Varies. Generally, 750 Nkr per km^2 for first 6 years. Thereafter yearly rentals rise to 30,000 Nkr per km^2 per annum after 10 years	Varies. Some blocks auctioned. £45/km^2 for first 6 years. Thereafter increases incrementally to £350/km^2 per annum	Exploration licences require initial bonus payment of 1,000 Dfl per km^2. 75 Dfl for next 5 years rising to between 150 and 225 Dfl for the balance. Production licences require annual rent of 450 Dfl per km^2 per annum. Payments are indexed
Drilling programme	None required	Required as part of licence application	Required as part of licence application	n.a.
II. *Discretionary Provisions*				
Royalties	Offshore 5% the first 5 years, 8.5% thereafter	Varies from 8% with a production of less than 40,000 bbls./day to 16% with production over 350,000 bbls./day	12.5% royalties may be refunded for high-cost fields	Vary with production 0-16%. If state participating, royalties are half what they would be otherwise

Table 1.7 *(contd.)*

	Denmark	Norway	Great Britain	The Netherlands
Corporate tax (CT)	37%	50.8%	52%	47%
Special oil tax	None	1975-80: 25% 1980 onwards: 35% charged with corporation tax	1975-8: 45% 1978-80: 60% 1980 onwards: 70% charged on income before corporate taxes (exemptions for 'marginal fields')	None
State 'participation'	None	Statoil up to and over 70%	BNOC up to 51%	40% optional by state
Production controls	No formal controls	Formal controls plus overall limit of 1,800,000 barrels of oil equivalent per day	Field-by-field production rate controls	No production rate controls
Legislation specifying onshore effects	None	Recent licence awards contingent on applicant's programme to stimulate domestic economy	Licence provisions specify that British suppliers, contractors be used to greatest possible extent	n.a.

the difference between the more rigorous British licence and the rather lax ineffectiveness of the Danish concessionary relationship should be manifest in the activity and development rates in the two sectors.

In the context of this book, these two general classes of provisions are important in assessing how intercorporate group behaviour responds to government policy. Of particular import is the difference in firm behaviour as conditioned by access provisions and by the discretionary economic incentives mentioned previously in this chapter.

1.6. Conclusion: High-cost Resources and Policy

The focus of this study is high-cost resources and policy. The stage is the North Sea and the British and Danish sectors in particular. The actors are the multinational corporations on one hand and the national states on the other. The time period covered is 1962-79.

Much is changing in the world of oil. Prices since 1979 have escalated. New technologies in the form of tanker-based field producing systems, 'tension leg' platforms, and 'guyed wire' platforms are making their way into the North Sea. Clearly what is defined as 'paramarginal' and 'submarginal' in Figure 1.1 will continue to change, due both to technological innovation and increased knowledge, and oil price increases.

Yet the policy element involved in high-cost fields is timeless. Despite technological progress and a doubling of crude prices, oil companies still insist that their costs have risen still further. A Mobil paper quoted in March 1980 pointedly ignored crude price increases while stressing the increased costs of developing marginal fields.[16] North Sea Governments have moved to adjust their rent-capture mechanisms to increase their shares of breaking North Sea corporate profits. The British Government raised its Petroleum Revenue Tax by 10 per cent to 70 per cent. The Norwegians raised their taxes by 10 per cent to 35 per cent — but allowed other measures to increase the profitability of high-cost fields.[17] Corporate reaction was swift. The industry quietly protested to the British Government. In Norway action was, if anything, more dramatic. Elf and Esso threatened to shelve the development of the North-east Frigg and Odin projects — two high-cost fields the companies called 'marginal'. Both firms, wryly noted by *Noroil*, were 'renowned for their hard bargaining postures with the Norwegian Government'.[18] But Esso went perhaps the furthest — threatening to delay or to abandon a scheduled three-well drilling programme. As this book goes to print, it seems likely that Esso and Elf will get their way.

It is to issues like these that this book is addressed. Whether the policy involves using a cement platform to produce 200 million barrels of (consequently) very high-cost oil or using a 'tension leg' platform to produce 100 million barrels of oil, the issues faced are the same. They are the means by which states procure the development of high-cost oil and gas resources. They remain issues of the nature of contract between state and multinational oil company, of negotiation with the oil multinational corporation, a 'bounded' rational actor.

The theme tying this study together, the development decision, generally in the North Sea and more particularly in the British and Danish sectors, will also remain. The technologies and size of reservoirs will change but the institutional dynamics will continue to plague policy-makers.

Notes

1. Expenditures in the North Sea area vary widely between oil firms. While Royal Dutch/Shell spends about 75 per cent of its non-American sums for exploration and production in the North Sea, and while BP spends about half its world-wide budget for this, other firms spend far less. Gulf, for example, allocated less than 5 per cent of its exploration and development money to the North Sea in 1977. Source: Company annual reports.

2. S.A.B. Page, 'The Value and Distribution of the Benefits of North Sea Oil and Gas', *National Institute Economic Review*, 82 (November 1977), pp. 41-58.

3. *Noroil*, V, 3 (March 1977), p. 37.

4. Personal correspondence to author from Professor P.R. Odell, Economic Geography Institute, Erasmus University, Rotterdam (8 June 1977).

5. Note that the additional reserve category, 'possible', has been omitted from the table. Such a category includes reserves from fields which are assumed to exist. This volume is concerned only with resources known with a high degree of certainty to exist.

6. A rent present due to the oligopoly nature of the OPEC cartel. Economic rent at this point is negative. The oligopoly rent is positive. The two cancel each other out at the margin.

7. Two good examples of the debate published recently are: H.A. Simon, 'Rational Decision-making in Business Organizations', *American Economic Review*, 69, 4 (September 1979), p. 493; and Fritz Machlup, 'Theories of the Firm: Marginalists, Behavioral, Managerial', *American Economic Review*, 57, 1 (March 1967), pp. 1-33.

8. R.M. Cyert and E. March, *A Behavioral Theory of the Firm* (Englewood Cliffs, N.J.: Prentice Hall, 1963).

9. Cyert and March's theory of organisational choice and control can be summarised in four points:

(1) There are multiple goals within the firm which change constantly through time. The criterion of firm choice is based on that alternative which meets most of the goals of the management committee.

(2) Alternatives are examined in only an approximate manner and seldom if ever simultaneously. Alternatives are considered sequentially and the first satisfactory alternative tends to be the policy selected. 'Where existing policy is satisfied', there is 'little search for alternatives'.

(3) The firm as an organisation avoids uncertainty generally through following regular procedures and policies reacting to short-term feedback rather than on long-term forecasting.

(4) Organisations use standard operating procedures and rules of thumb to make and implement choices. In short-run situations these procedures dominate the decisions made. Cyert and March, *Behavioral Theory*, p. 113.

10. Edith Penrose, *The Large International Firm in Developing Countries: The International Petroleum Industry* (London: George Allen and Unwin, 1968). Paul A. Frankel, *Essentials of Petroleum* (London: Frank Cass, 1969), and M.A. Adelman, *The World Petroleum Market* (Washington, D.C.: The Johns Hopkins Press, 1972) have rather thorough discussions of the issues involved in market imperfections.

11. John M. Blair, *The Control of Oil* (New York: Pantheon Books, 1976), p. 323.

12. Louis Turner, *Oil Companies in the International System* (London: George Allen and Unwin, 1978), investigates these charges.

13. E. Furubotn and S. Pejovich, 'Property Rights and Economic Theory: A Survey of Recent Literature', *The Journal of Economic Literature*, X (1972), p. 1140.

14. Paul H. Rubin, 'The Theory of the Firm and the Structure of the Franchise Contract', *The Journal of Law and Economics*, 20 (1977), pp. 223-35.

15. Kenneth Dam, *Oil Resources: Who Gets What How?* (Chicago: The University of Chicago Press, 1976), p. 4.

16. *Noroil* (March 1980), p. 25.

17. Additional measures were the acceleration of capital credits against taxes and of the option to offset all operational losses from one field against the tax liabilities of other fields. Most particularly offensive to the companies was a provision which eliminated deducting loan interest from net profits assessed for the special oil tax.

18. *Noroil* (March 1980), p. 23.

PART TWO

THE DEVELOPMENT DECISION

2 THE DEVELOPMENT DECISION — THE CORPORATE POINT OF VIEW

2.1. Introduction

The institutional approach advanced in Part One argued that pure 'economic' opportunity cost behaviour is 'bounded' by a corporate combination of organisational dynamics, oligopoly behaviour and political activity. To what extent has this argument a basis in fact?

Of these 'bounding' factors, political activity will be left to the British and Danish case studies. This chapter will explicitly examine the two other factors: oligopoly behaviour and inter-organisational dynamics. If vertical integration and control are critical to the oligopoly behaviour of the industry, then commitment to such a high-cost province as the North Sea will vary according to corporate needs for secure sources of crude and secure product markets. If organisational behaviour is a critical variable, then the dynamics of North Sea group behaviour become of interest. There is, as we will note, substantial evidence to confirm that both these points are of considerable importance to the investment decision.

2.2. The North Sea: Differing Opportunity Costs?

How does the typical oil firm, considering investing in the North Sea, measure opportunity costs among differing investment options? There appear to be many different 'rules of thumb' with regard to North Sea fields in general and 'marginal' fields in particular. Thus *Noroil* quotes CFP (Compagnie Française Petrolière) Director Louis Deny:

> Deny claims that a large field with strong production rates 'might be worth developing' on the basis of a 20 per cent return while smaller finds might be commercially viable at much higher rates, 40, 60, or or even 100 per cent.[1]

In contrast, Gulf is on record as demanding at least a 25 per cent Internal Rate of Return from its major North Sea investments. Royal Dutch-Shell requires 15 per cent. Why is there a 10 per cent difference between these two firms? Why does each differ in turn from Deny's (and the CFP's) 20 per cent rate of return?

To a degree, these differences may be overrated. 'In practice', Robinson and Morgan have correctly observed, 'discount rates will vary among companies, over time in one company, and among different people in one company'.[2] Yet there is no doubt that different firms view the opportunity costs in the North Sea in different manners. This is true not only in terms of the firm's general commitment (surveying, exploring, developing) to the North Sea *vis-a-vis* its overall commitments elsewhere; it is also true of the specific commitment by these firms to develop certain North Sea fields, particularly high-cost fields. This section will begin with the corporate view of risk and cost, especially as these are relevant to the North Sea environment. The balance of the chapter will then be devoted to explaining differing corporate preferences, and how these affect the development decision on both an individual and a group basis.

Deny's 'rules of thumb' may well seem extreme, particularly the assessment that a small field, to be developed, may have to return up to 100 per cent. Various other companies have expressed their views in a somewhat more muted fashion. One American independent claimed it would consider developing all fields with 100 million barrels (although not as a 'hard and fast rule'). An American major generated concern within the UK Department of Energy when it declared categorically that 400 million barrels of recoverable oil were the absolute minimum it would consider (although the company was undoubtedly referring to the more costly Jurassic sandstone fields of the mid-North Sea). Another American major has stated privately that it expects a field to yield 2.5 million tons of oil per year for serious consideration. Again, this judgement is not absolute. Smaller fields, the company maintained, would be considered if they were close to larger fields or could be supported by a common infrastructure and transportation system.

Two important denominators in all corporate discussions of 'marginality' are field size and rate of production. Much of this discrimination is due to a corporate perception of 'risk'. Diagrammatically (Table 2.1) this risk can be expressed as a function of field size (production rate) in conjunction with the capital costs necessary to develop the field. It can also be expressed in terms of other corporate goals: security of future supplies and the ability to assimilate or sell the crude to customers who can use it. (These can have a decided effect on corporate attitudes. One independent firm developing a small field in the British sector has been penalised heavily by the poor quality of crude produced in terms of its market selling price.)

Table 2.1: Field Size and Risk

	Large field	Small field
Unit cost	Smaller per unit (lower cap. cost per bbl.)	Higher per unit (higher cap. cost per bbl.)
Reserves	Deviation from expected reserves rather small	Higher deviation from expected reserves
Security of future supplies	High (longer field life)	Low (shorter field life)
Suitability for refinery runs	Unusual crude type easily accounted for	Unusual crude type hard to adjust to

Table 2.1 illustrates two important aspects of field development both in the North Sea and world-wide: (1) the unit cost of oil and gas from smaller fields can well be higher than that for oil and gas from larger fields, and (2) cost escalation is harder to absorb. These factors are perhaps better illustrated by Table 2.2. If one platform (out of four or five) is lost on a major project, costs will rise. (One platform, the Frigg 'DP-1' platform, has already been lost in the North Sea.) But the factor by which outlays will increase is not nearly as great as it would be for a one-platform field where the platform was delayed, lost, or damaged. Additionally, most smaller fields cannot support a submarine pipeline transport system to shore. They must therefore rely on tankers and mooring systems for delivery. For several fields, this form of delivery has proved highly insecure. In the Danish sector, the Dan has been shut down for up to six months due to mooring buoy failures. For these and other reasons, many smaller fields are prone to enormous price increases. This is certainly borne out by the high percentage increase in the capital outlays needed to develop the two smaller British fields. (Auk's rise in development costs leads the list at 260 per cent, and Argyll is second with 193 per cent.)

Increased capital costs can have a marked impact on field profitability. In Table 2.3, a crude 'sensitivity' test has been undertaken for three British fields: Auk, Forties and Heather. The last of these fields has been described by many in the industry as 'marginal' — in effect meaning that certain firms would not have undertaken the development of the field. The figures for all three fields have been computed assuming no collection of tax and royalties by the state, although all other costs have been paid. (For specification of the assumptions, see the Appendix to this chapter.)

Table 2.3 shows that even without payments to the state, capital

Table 2.2: Estimated Development Costs of Nine North Sea Fields —
British Sector

	May 1973 estimates (million $)	February 1976 estimates (million $)	Increase (%)
Argyll	15	44	193
Auk	15	54	260
Brent	500	1,160	132
Cormorant	80	198	147
Dunlin	160	395	146
Forties	360	820	127
Montrose	60	138	130
Piper	130	306	135
Thistle	160	400	150

Source: N. Trimble, *North Sea Oil Developments: Past Trends and Future Prospects*, NSSOP-10, University of Aberdeen, 1976. Data from Wood, Mackenzie and Co., *North Sea Service* (Edinburgh, February 1976).

cost increases not only significantly affect Internal Rates of Return, but also have a considerable impact on the net present values discounted by two of the 'rules of thumb' mentioned previously, 15 per cent and 20 per cent. Least affected by increase in capital expenditures is the present value (discounted at 0) for the fields concerned. Most interesting for the purpose of this chapter is the highly sensitive position of Heather.

A second source of investment insecurity is reserve estimation. Here, too, size has significant advantages. It is easier to define a large reservoir than a small one, generally speaking. First, a large reservoir will support a high number of confirmation wells. Secondly, provided it is reasonably uniform, a large reservoir allows an easier accounting of reserves. An error of 50 feet in estimating the thickness of the 'pay' strata, for example, makes considerably less difference if the reservoir is assumed to be 500 feet thick than if the 'pay' is assumed to be only 100 to 200 feet thick. This generalisation as to reservoir estimation has many exceptions. The Brae field in the North Sea comprises one or possibly several large reservoirs, which could either be a promising North Sea find, or a very high-cost field.

What is the impact of reservoir size? Table 2.4 shows the impact of a halving of reserves on the three fields. Perhaps the most interesting result of a halving of production is the effect this can have on the discounted net present value. In all three fields, there is little apparent

Table 2.3: Variations in Capital Expenditure — Auk, Forties and Heather (not including State 'Take'), Millions US Dollars (Price $12.00/bbl.)

	Auk				Forties				Heather			
	Net present value discounted at 15%	at 20%	Present value	IRR (%)	Net present value discounted at 15%	at 20%	Present value	IRR (%)	Net present value discounted at 15%	at 20%	Present value	IRR (%)
Capital expenditure	301	241	631	89.7	3,688	2,536	15,164	53.9	294	159	1,405	31.4
Double capital expenditure	217	158	541	47.5	2,910	1,692	14,264	35.7	—	—	1,005	15.01
Triple capital expenditure	133	76	451	29.6	1,343	311	12,164	22.1	—	—	605	7.0

Source: See Technical Appendix to Chapter 2.

Table 2.4: Variations in Production — Auk, Forties, Heather (not including State 'Take'), Millions US Dollars (Price $12.00/bbl.)

	Auk				Forties				Heather			
	Net present value discounted at 15%	at 20%	Present value	IRR (%)	Net present value discounted at 15%	at 20%	Present value	IRR (%)	Net present value discounted at 15%	at 20%	Present value	IRR (%)
Full production	301	241	631	89.7	3,688	2,536	15,164	53.9	294	159	1,405	31.4
Half production	111	80	274	47.3	1,333	737	7,169	33.0	–	–	505	15.03

Table 2.5: Variations in Capital Expenditures — Auk, Forties, Heather at One-half Production (not including State 'Take'), Millions US Dollars (Price $12.00/bbl.)

	Auk				Forties				Heather			
	Net present value discounted at 15%	at 20%	Present value	IRR (%)	Net present value discounted at 15%	at 20%	Present value	IRR (%)	Net present value discounted at 15%	at 20%	Present value	IRR (%)
Two times expenditure	27	–2	184	19.6	334	–	6,296	19.9	–	–	105	2.04
Triple capital expenditure	–	–	91	–	–	–	4,169	9.2	–	–	–295	–

Source: See Technical Appendix to Chapter 2.

difference between a halving of production and a two-fold increase in capital expenditures. Auk's IRR drops to 47.5 per cent with a doubling of capital expenditure and to 47.3 per cent with a halving of production. Similar figures are 35.7 per cent and 33 per cent for Forties, and 15.01 per cent and 15.03 per cent for Heather, respectively. What is significant from a development-decision point of view is that the discounted present values with a halving of production drop in all cases appreciably much more than do the other figures. Thus, for example, taking the present value discounted at 15 per cent, the return drops from $3.7 billion to 1.3 billion for the Forties. Similar figures obtain for the other fields: Auk's 15 per cent discounted value slips from 301 million to 111 million, and Heather's from $298 million to under 1 million (although the present value of Heather only drops from $1 billion to 505 million).

To sum up our discussion of field size, variation, and risk, Table 2.5 correlates the doubling and tripling of capital expenditures with halving production rates for the three fields. As this table indicates, where drastic changes are made from the original assumptions, Auk and the Forties are still good investment prospects, but Heather is 'exposed'. A combination of these factors is no doubt the reason why Heather suffers from a dubious reputation.

We have excluded taxes and royalty payments from our analysis. But even the most beneficial capital depreciation scheme, or the most efficient taxation scheme, could not have a positive effect on Heather's returns, should anticipated capital costs of field development triple and field production rates fall by 50 per cent. For Auk and Forties, the taxation/royalties problem remains the significant one if the fields are to yield acceptable returns under most circumstances. Even excluding taxes, royalties and the like, Heather could well become uneconomic.

It is high-cost fields like Heather that are of primary interest in this book. Clearly, many of the oil firms in the North Sea would never have considered Heather in the first place. Unocal and its partners did. Even accounting for the greater risk of 'marginal' resources, then, firms do have differing opportunity cost perspectives. Yet, the 15, 20, 80 or even 100 per cent 'rules of thumb' constitute only one criterion in a firm's assessment of a given project. Other less tangible factors, institutional factors, also muddle the picture. As indicated in Table 2.1, these can be the fitting of crude to a firm's refinery runs and the amount of additional security of supply a firm desires from a given field. There are others as well: proximity to markets, development of new markets and the like.

2.3. The North Sea: Differing Corporate Preferences?

Having ascertained that the oil companies in the North Sea have differing opportunity costs, we can now ask another question: how does the North Sea rank in differing corporate preferences? In other words, how do North Sea activities rate in corporate preferences world-wide? To what degree will an oil firm invest in a field in the US before investing in a North Sea prospect? The implications of opportunity costs and differing investment rules of thumb among firms in the North Sea would tend to indicate that firms rank their North Sea prospects differently. But is this really the case in fact?

There is a considerable lore on preferences among North Sea companies. Certain corporations are reputed to 'do' more than others. Three themes are common: (1) oil firms possessing large European markets will be more active in the North Sea than firms with small European markets; (2) oil companies short of crude for their refining/ marketing needs tend to invest more in the higher-cost fields in the North Sea than others; and (3) the independents – the group of 'small' firms opposed to the Seven Sisters – are more entrepreneurial, take more risks and are more satisfied with high-cost crude than the bigger Seven Sisters. Is this lore fact or fable? These rather commonsense notions could reflect a grain of truth. European oil companies, with their markets centred in Europe, could be expected to be active in the North Sea. This activity could be enhanced by European governments' promotion of 'their' oil companies. Safe, secure supplies of crude oil have always been sought by the oil industry. It is therefore logical that companies short of their own crude supplies would want to invest in a politically safe area such as the North Sea. The third contention with regard to the independents is a little harder to justify. Is it that these companies are chronically short of crude or is it that these companies are more entrepreneurial?

To what degree can these theses be tested empirically? If we had a measure of corporate commitment to the North Sea, we could tell which of these explanations was the most valid. Commitment could vary proportionately with self-sufficiency or the importance of European markets, for example. The first problem is one of defining commitment.

There are four possible manners of defining a commitment to the North Sea. The first of these is the comparison of exploration and production figures for individual companies in the North Sea with their expenditures for similar activities elsewhere in the world. Unfortunately, the information given in corporate reports seldom allows for such breakdowns and if so, only for specific companies and activities.

A second possibility is defining commitment in terms of corporate expenditures on North Sea development projects. We know what North Sea projects cost; if we assume that each corporation within a group contributes its share in proportion to its holdings, we could break down corporate development expenditures, firm by firm. Unfortunately, the results of such an exercise would be biased. It would favour those firms which have large North Sea projects at the time of this writing. It is also biased in favour of those firms which have found worthwhile prospects. Commitment is by no means a function of 'luck', at least not always.

More satisfactory perhaps is to see how many fields a firm has developed *vis-a-vis* the number of significant finds that firm has made. This is done in Table 2.6. But here too there is some unfairness; Table 2.6 discriminates against those companies which have recently made finds they are still evaluating. Similarly, it discriminates in favour of those firms which might be participating in many different North Sea groups but hold only a small share in each. Therefore a firm holding a one per cent share in several fields would get credit for all fields in which it holds shares; a firm totally responsible for three fields would only get three fields to its credit.

Probably the least biased measure of corporate commitment to the North Sea and therefore the one we will use in this context is the number of blocks awarded to a company. The reasons for this are clear: first, data are easily available, and secondly, such a measure does not discriminate against unlucky firms. And, finally, in the case of the UK, the Netherlands and Norway such block awards are given out competitively to those firms which are most willing to spend money on work programmes (and conform to governmental guidelines).[3] Generally blocks are awarded to those firms which agree to spend a maximum of resources in North Sea exploration and development.

If we define corporate commitment in terms of the number of blocks in which a corporation holds a share, the degree of corporate commitment should vary according to whether a firm has large European markets, is short of crude, or is an independent. The general pattern of block allocation after firm self-sufficiency in crude is illustrated in Table 2.7. This is a rough representation of the material with which we will work. Two things are of interest in this context, however. First, it is notable that many independents own shares in more blocks than majors many times their size. And, secondly, all the independents are crude-short, and have a low degree of self-sufficiency.

Table 2.6: Proportion of Developed Fields to Significant Finds by Company, North Sea 1977

I. Oil Fields

	Great Britain		Norway		Netherlands		Denmark[9]	
	Fields developed	Undeveloped significant finds	Fields developed	Significant discoveries	Fields developed	Significant discoveries	Fields developed	Significant discoveries
'Seven Sisters'								
Esso	5a	6a	1d	2	1	—	—	—
Mobil	1	2	1	1	—	—	—	4
Shell	5a	6a	2d	—	1	—	1	4
BP	3	6	—	1	1	1	—	—
Texaco	2b	7	—	—	—	—	1	4
Chevron	1	1	—	—	—	—	1	4
Gulf	1	5	—	—	—	—	—	—
Larger 'Independents'								
Ente Nazionale d'Idrocarburi	—	6c	8	2	—	—	—	—
Amoco	1	3	2	1	—	—	—	—
Conoco	1	5	1d	1	—	—	—	—
Phillips	—	6c	7	2	—	—	—	—
Occidental	2	—	—	—	—	—	—	—
Compagnie Française Petroliers	—	4	—	1	—	—	—	—

II. Non-associated Gas Fields

	Great Britain		Norway		Netherlands		Denmark[9]	
	Fields developed	Undeveloped significant finds	Fields developed	Significant discoveries	Fields developed	Significant discoveries	Fields developed	Significant discoveries
'Seven Sisters'								
Esso	1a	1a	—	—	3a	14a	—	—
Mobil	—	2	—	—	—	1	—	—
Shell	2	1a	—	—	3a	14a	—	—

Table 2.6 (contd.)

	Great Britain		Norway		Netherlands		Denmark[9]	
	Fields developed	Undeveloped significant finds	Fields developed	Significant discoveries	Fields developed	Significant discoveries	Fields developed	Significant discoveries
BP	1	—	—	—	—	3	—	—
Texaco	—	—	—	—	—	—	—	3
Chevron	—	—[e]	—	—	—	—	—	3
Gulf	—	—	—	—	—	1	—	—
Larger 'Independents'								
ENI	1[c]	3[c]	—	—	—	—	—	—
Amoo	4	—	—	—	—	1	—	—
Conoco	1	6	—	—	—	—	—	—
Phillips	1[c]	3[c]	—	—	—	—	—	—
Occidental	—[f]	—	—	—	—	—	—	—
CFP	1[f]	1	1[f]	3	1	3	—	—

Notes: Fields are mentioned more than once for members of the same group *if* member's holding within the group is higher than its partners (e.g. if a member's holding is say 25 per cent of a group of five — where average holding should be 20 per cent).
a. Shell/Esso fields.
b. Not including Texaco holding of Argyll.
c. Phillips and ENI are members of the same group.
d. Including a share in Statfjord.
e. Including a share in field discovered by Conoco.
f. Frigg is counted as a Norwegian and as a British field.
g. All members of one group, the Danish Underground Consortium.

Table 2.7: Crude Self-sufficiency and Block Awards — Majors and Independents

Firm	% Self-sufficient 1972	1979	Majors North Sea Block Ownership, 1979 (nos of blocks) Great Britain	Norway	Holland	Totals
Shell	83.1	104.2	75	7	37	119
Mobil	85.5	100.5	21	3	8	32
Esso	97.3	101.4	65	10	37	112
Texaco	127.9	118.4	20	2	—	22
Chevron	154.3	130.1	16	—	—	16
Gulf	165.2	105.8	31	2	7	40
BP	191.3	240.8	50	5	17	72
Independents						
Petrofina	—	23.8	29	11	11	51
ENI	39.5	41.0	32	17	11	60
Phillips	53.3	49.8	32	17	11	60
ELF/Acq.	—	51.9	34	25	7	66
Amoco	58.8	69.1	39	9	8	56
CFP	133.9	94.0	24	19	5	48
Conoco	85.0	97.0	35	7	—	42

Sources: For self-sufficiency, company annual reports; for numbers of blocks in which firms own a share, OPS, *European Continental Shelf Guide, 1979* (London: Offshore Promotional Services, 1979).

In that this universal shortage of crude among the independents could account for their interest in North Sea, we can safely reduce the possible explanations for commitment to the North Sea to two: the existence of sizeable European markets and the degree of crude self-sufficiency. How can these explanatory factors affect North Sea corporate commitment?

There are several hurdles which must be cleared before pursuing this analysis. The first is the meaning of commitment. 'Commitment' is defined for our purposes here as the number of blocks in which a firm owns a share. This is ultimately an unsatisfactory definition for three major reasons: (1) the firm concerned may only own minor shares of a great number of blocks; (2) blocks in differing sectors of the North Sea are of different sizes and therefore should not count equally; and (3) a simple block measurement does not take into account the ultimate resources of the firm — a firm with smaller assets and fewer blocks might in fact be more committed to the North Sea than a firm with larger assets and more blocks.

To allow for these factors, one should define commitment in terms of the sum of the total block fractions owned by a firm. Thus a firm with a one-twelfth interest in one block and a one-quarter interest in another block could be said to possess one-third of a block. Account should be taken of block sizes as well. Since blocks in the Norwegian sector are 2.5 times the size of British blocks (blocks in the Dutch sector are 1.5 times the size of those in the British sector), the fractions of blocks owned by firms in the Norwegian sector should be adjusted upwards by a factor of 2.5 (and 1.5 for the Dutch sector).

Firm size or capacity must additionally be taken into account. This is done by dividing the 1977 fixed assets of each firm into the adjusted number of North Sea blocks. The resulting 'index of commitment' should reflect firm commitment (preferences) fairly adequately.

The second hurdle is choosing the group of firms to be investigated. To be accurate all firms in the sampling should possess refining capacity. (This results in a bias against the wildcatting firms in the area which are not therefore included.) Additionally the firms should have been interested in the North Sea for a considerable period of time. The resulting sample includes 14 firms with the highest number of blocks and with considerable refining capacity. Seven of these firms are the majors; seven are independents. These are presented in Table 2.8 ranked according to our 'index of commitment'.

The table is a rank ordering of firms which (top to bottom) have the highest to lowest commitment in the North Sea, as we have defined the concept. How do these rankings match those of corporate self-sufficiency or those of European markets? The more closely rankings for commitment match those for self-sufficiency or those for European markets, the greater the probability that one or both of these hypotheses might be generally valid. Table 2.9 matches rankings according to self-sufficiency and proportion of European product sales to the total for each of the firms with the rankings in Table 2.7. A Kendall Rank Correlation is given for each at the base of the table along with a one-tailed probability that each hypothesis is a 'null' hypothesis. As can be seen, the scores are quite striking. There are Kendall Rank Coefficients of 0.494 and 0.516 for rankings by self-sufficiency and European markets respectively. The probability for a 'null' hypothesis in so far as self-sufficiency is concerned is 0.0069 and

Table 2.8: Sampling of Firms — Ranked According to Commitment

Firm	(1) Adjusted no of blocks	(2) Assets (fixed) $ US millions	(1)/(2) Commitment
ENI	11.7	1,160	0.0109
ELF/Acquitaine	31.5	4,375	0.0072
Phillips	24.2	3.560	0.0068
BP	50.3	7,585	0.0066
CFP/Total	16.5	1,880	0.0058
Petrofina	16.0	2,901	0.0055
Conoco	17.2	3,751	0.0046
Shell	75.0	28,685	0.0026
Esso	71.5	32,512	0.0022
Amoco	16.5	8,022	0.00214
Mobil	19.2	9,042	0.00212
Gulf	14.6	9,800	0.00149
Texaco	16.5	11,500	0.00143
Chevron	6.2	9,640	0.00064

Sources: Company Annual Reports; OPS, *European Continental Shelf Guide,
1979*.

for European markets, 0.0051. Clearly there is some statistical validity
in both explanations.

Yet there is another problem. The two explanations are interrelated.
To what degree is the 0.494 Kendall Coefficient for self-sufficiency in
fact a reflection of the European sales aspect or vice versa? To control
the third variable, one must partial it out. This can be done through use
of the Kendall Partial Rank Coefficient. The results of this use are
illustrated in Table 2.10. In this table it becomes clear that the third
variable has at best a weak negative impact on correlations between
commitment and the second variable. The Kendall Partial Rank
Coefficient for self-sufficiency is 0.507, not very different from the
uncontrolled 0.494. For the European market, the result is virtually
the same, 0.528 versus the original 0.516.

It would appear that possession of large European markets and the
vulnerability of being crude-short both independently account for a high
degree of commitment to the North Sea. Although there are no
accepted tests of significance for the Kendall Partial Rank Correlations,
it would seem that both explanations are valid.

This little diversion into statistics indicates that there are good

Table 2.9: Firms Ranked According to Commitment, Self-sufficiency, and Percentage European Sales to Overall Sales

Firms ranked by commitment		Firms ranked by self-sufficiency		Firms ranked by % European sales/total	
Name	Rank	% Self-sufficiency	Rank in group	% European sales	Rank in group
ENI	1	41	2	100	1
ELF/Acqui.	2	51.9	4	83	2
Phillips	3	49.8	3	7.7	14
BP	4	240.0	14	70.0	4
CFP/Total	5	94.0	6	80.9	3
Petrofina	6	23.8	1	52.8	5
Conoco	7	97.0	7	22.0	10
Shell	8	104.2	10	40.2	6
Esso	9	101.4	9	40.0	7
Amoco	10	69.1	5	8.4	13
Mobil	11	100.5	8	34.1	8
Gulf	12	105.8	11	20.9	11
Texaco	13	118.4	12	22.0	12
Chevron	14	130.1	13	32.9	9
Kendall Rank Coefficient		0.494		0.516	

Degree of Significance (one-tail)
H_0 (probability of 'null' hypothesis) $p = 0.0069$ $p = 0.0051$

Table 2.10: Partialling-out the Third Variable — Kendall Correlations and Partial Correlations

Explanation: Commitment a function of:	Without controlling for third variable: Kendall Rank Correlation	Controlling for third variable: Kendall Partial Rank Correlation
Self-sufficiency	0.494	0.507
European markets	0.516	0.528

grounds to suspect that corporate preferences in the North Sea do differ significantly. Additionally, there would seem to be a good case that both crude-short companies and companies with significant European markets tend to favour the North Sea province more than their crude-rich, non-European biased sisters.

2.4. The Problem of Preferences within Groups – The Investment Decision Among Firms

Not only are there differences among firms engaged in the North Sea; also, few firms own the individual blocks outright, but operate instead in consortia. (In the British sector, this is particularly true of Texaco, Chevron, Shell, and BP, but even these firms tend to hold blocks in partnerships.) Participation in a group has definite advantages: it lessens individual risk, enables the raising of capital without exposing individual firms to over-extension, and allows for the pooling of expertise and knowledge. Yet, from the point of view of the development decision, the group has a disadvantage: it can hinder consensus. What happens within a group when firms operating with differing opportunity cost perspectives are confronted with a find which will yield an IRR of 18 per cent, if some of the firms are interested in all finds yielding an IRR of 15 per cent, and if others demand an IRR of 20 or even 25 per cent? Any analysis of implicit company preferences as outlined above must recognise that even if a company places a high priority on North Sea developments, it must often contend with partners who do not.

Surprisingly, given its importance, there is very little information on company group behaviour. The number of firms involved in developing a particular North Sea find can be highly impressive. No fewer than twelve firms are co-operating in the development and operation of the Hewett Field in the British North Sea. Six of these belong to the group that discovered the field (Arpet Group). Another six belong to groups owning the adjoining blocks. How does a group of firms arrive at an investment decision? There are two categories of groups involved here: the group containing the companies that have made the relevant find, and a wider group containing two or more smaller groups that might be included if a find extends into adjacent blocks owned by other groups. Let us examine the two group types further.

(1) The Immediate Group

We can define the immediate group as comprising only those companies owning the property on which the find is made, excluding groups which might own extensions of the field concerned. (If, as in the cases of Montrose, Cormorant and Viking in the UK sector, the adjoining block is owned by the same group, the field is considered as a whole to be owned by the immediate group as defined here.)

There is little in the literature on how decisions are made by an immediate group. In the case of Hewett, for example, one authority has written that large groups are 'unwieldy with so many', but decisions are 'agreed to by a minimum percentage of say 60 per cent'.[4] What, though, does this mean specifically? Is the '60 per cent' based on group ownership, or is it based on the number of members within the group? Is it '60 per cent' for some decisions and another percentage for other decisions? Sources are generally unclear.

Certain points can be ascertained, however. Through interview data collected by the author, the following conclusions appear valid:

(a) The dynamics of group interaction can be vital. Some authorities in the industry even talk of a group 'fetish', a conviction that the make-up of a group determines absolutely its behaviour. Certain companies have 'gamed' for mathematical answers as to what constitutes an effective group. The trend in other companies is to sort through the piles of group agreements which have been contracted in the past. 'There is a certain tendency to repeat the form of previous agreements which have been successes', a Petroland manager declared, 'irrespective of the fact that "success" might have little to do with the terms of the agreement'. Much time and effort is spent by companies operating in the UK North Sea in meeting their partners, convincing them of the correctness of this or that course, and attempting to get group approval with or without a 'show of hands'.

(b) Voting procedures are different for different issues. While a conditional majority may suffice for a development decision in one type of group (generally 60-66 per cent is most often mentioned, based on percentage holdings), for other types of groups, such decisions must be unanimous. This is particularly true of a group containing no more than two members (Shell-Esso, for example). For other issues, percentages must differ. The decision to relinquish a block is not unusually unanimous. The same can hold for a 'farm-in', when one of the partners in the group sells its holdings to an outside company that assumes an active (or inactive) role within the newly reconstituted group.

(c) Small groups are not necessarily the most effective. One might expect that small groups would have a definite advantage over large groups, that a consensus would be easier to achieve among a few than among many. No doubt this is often the case (as with Hewett). But group effectiveness is frequently less a function of size than of the expertise or preferences of the members concerned. Two extreme cases can be cited in this regard. One large group in the British North Sea is still (as of this date) assessing a find which could either be one of the most significant in the sector, or a very expensive business. They have drilled almost a dozen holes with varying results. The meetings of this group have been described as 'almost a convention', with formal presentations and a show of hands. Yet progress has been possible because one firm, the operator, possesses the bulk of the expertise. Most of its partners are 'into oil' as a secondary activity. On the other hand, a group of three companies very active in North Sea exploration — consisting of a British government corporation, a 'crude-rich' major and an active 'independent' — has been able to accomplish very little. While the respective petroleum engineers deadlock over development prospects of several finds, rumours are rife that one of the three firms involved 'does not want to get involved because its North Sea crude types do not fit into its refinery "runs"'.

Troubles within the group are often predicated on questions of finance. Smaller firms may be incapable of raising the kind of financing necessary to develop a fund profitably. There are two specific examples of this 'exposure': the development decisions behind the Piper and Ninian fields.

The controversy surrounding the Piper field had to do with the financing of a one- or a two-platform system. A two-platform system would have cost more, but it would have also earned considerably more over the lifetime of the field. Yet a one-platform system was adopted. Why? Professor Odell notes a plausible explanation for this irrational behaviour:

> This suggests that the decision should perhaps be measured against other economic variables: notably possible limits on the peak borrowing powers available for the development of any single oil field by the companies (Occidental, Thompson Newspapers, Getty Oil and Allied Chemicals) concerned. Though they are large companies by non-oil industry standards, their 'exposure' to their respective shares of the more than $420 million (later $650 million) was great. Indeed, they had to arrange somewhat convoluted financing deals in order to raise the money required.[5]

A not too dissimilar situation arose in the group developing the Ninian field. The issue here was disagreement among the partners as to the number of barrels of oil ultimately recoverable from the structure. Chevron and BP were cautious, estimating this amount at between 840 to 920 million barrels. Burmah disagreed, arguing that the recoverable reserves could be as high as 1.2-1.35 billion barrels (280-510 million barrels more than its partners). DeGolyer and MacNaughton, the

Texas consultant firm, estimated 1.11 billion barrels.

The cause of the disagreement was the percentage of oil which could be exploited from the formation. DeGolyer and MacNaughton derived its figures from a recovery rate of 37.1 per cent. Burmah's figure was based on recovery rates from similar formations elsewhere in the North Sea of between 40 and 45 per cent. The differences between Burmah and its partners were significant, both in terms of the ultimate production plans and of project cash flows. Nevertheless, in the press, the difference was ascribed to a political desire on the part of Burmah 'in light of negotiations taking place with the Government over the disposal of some of its assets to British National Oil Company'.[6]

What these accounts miss is perhaps the most critical factor: that differences over reserves and investments are highly important. Whether the reserves of Ninian vary by about 500 million barrels upwards or downwards is not merely an argument as to the financial validity of this or that company; it can be the difference between earning a substantial return or 'losing one's shirt'. Given that oil companies have expressed different preferences about the cost of resources which are 'worthwhile', it is absolutely vital that a common denominator acceptable to all is achieved. Given that members in a given group do not have a common opportunity cost perspective (even if they had in the beginning, it could change radically with time) how do they arrive at a development decision? The answer to this question is vital to the development of higher-cost fields, the focus of our analysis.

Generally speaking, two measures are utilised in most groups: conditional voting and the inclusion of a 'self-risk' clause. The first of these measures enables a group to get around the prickly question of unanimity. If 60 per cent of a group are interested in developing a field, the remaining 40 per cent are forced to support the decision, sell their shares to others who are willing to invest in the prospect, or opt out of the development prospect.

The use of conditional voting must be seen in context with the 'self-risk' clause. Conditional voting and self-risk are frequently the minimum demanded by oil companies. While conditional voting enables a project which might otherwise be starved for lack of support to go ahead, the 'self-risk' clause is a sort of insurance possessed by the minority. 'Self-risk' allows a member of the group to act on its own in exploring for, confirming or developing a project either alone or in company with like-minded partners. This is done at the company's 'own risk'. Conversely, 'self-risk' enables dissenters to stand on the sidelines and let their partners develop a project. Most agreements

contain formulae which provide for flexibility around self-risk clauses.
Therefore, should one member insist on a well which is successful, it
is often possible for other members, upon payment of a certain penalty,
to reap the benefits of the find.[7] Depending on the circumstances
envisaged, there is a wide variety of provisions under the rubric 'self-risk'
covering various contingencies which might arise.

(2) The Extended Group

How are decisions made for a find which extends over several North
Sea blocks and is owned by a dozen firms in as many as three groups?
British and Norwegian law state clearly that each field is to be developed
as a unit. Such a requirement is written into the licence to explore and
exploit hydrocarbon reserves. In the UK when a development plan is
hindered by disagreements among the extended group, a new plan may
be worked out by the Minister of Energy 'which shall be fair and
equitable' to all concerned. If there is disagreement as to the fairness
of such a scheme, there is room for arbitration.[8]

Yet is the law effective in all cases? A good example of how it may
not work can be seen in the development of the British Forties field
by BP. Seven per cent of the area of the field (although not that
amount of recoverable reserves) is within an adjoining block held by
Shell/Esso. This fact has played a critical role in Professor Odell's
criticism of platform location on the Forties field:

> There is however, one other important factor [other than unstable
> sea bottom] which affects the chosen B.P. location for its platforms
> in a west/east direction. This is the incidence of the North Sea block
> boundary at the point where the field 'tails out' towards the east.
> This adjacent block is under concession to Shell/Esso with which
> B.P. was not able to reach a unitisation decision on the development
> of the field. B.P. thus had no opportunity to locate one of its
> platforms at a point so far to the east that it could deplete the oil
> under the Shell/Esso block.[9]

The Odell and Rosing study states that a fifth platform for draining
the area had been planned, but that a feeling developed that such a
platform would not be economic even given a unitisation agreement
with Shell/Esso.[10] (Unitisation is an agreement by the owners as to the
single most efficient way of exploiting a field.)

Maps 2.1 and 2.2 illustrate the problems of fields crossing two or
more blocks. Ideally, unitisation should solve the problems of all the

Map 2.1: Viking Graben — Map Showing the Problems of Delineation and Block Allocation as of October 1976

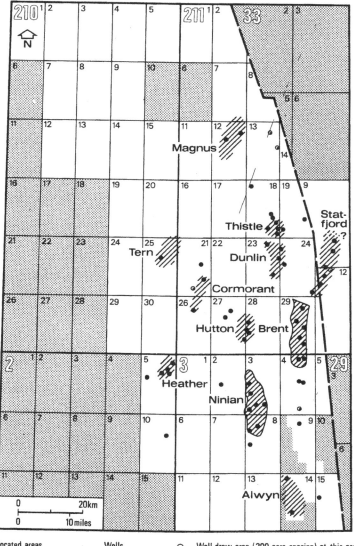

Source: P.R. Odell and K.E. Rosing, *Optimal Development of the North Sea's Oil Fields: A Study in Divergent Government and Company Interests and their Reconciliation* (London: Kogan Page, 1977), p. 32.

Map 2.2: South of the Viking Graben — Map Showing Problems of Delineation in this Region

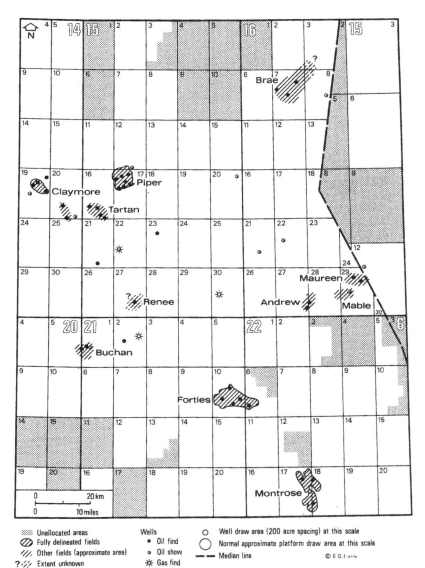

Source: Odell and Rosing, *Optimal Development*, p. 33.

fields which, unlike Montrose, lie astride two blocks. The nagging question which remains, however, is how easily unitisation agreements can be reached for smaller high-cost fields if this has been so difficult with regard to the Forties field. Consider, for example, a scenario where a single field stretches over two blocks. Groups in each block would have differing preferences, differing assessments of how much oil (or gas) there is, and differing opinions as to how much belongs to whom. Even if one group wished to develop the field, it could not do so without draining a portion of the structure in the adjoining block.

The room for corporate manoeuvre in this game could be significant. A company might, for example, try to interpret the field so as to allocate itself (or its group) the greatest proportion of exploited oil or gas, while simultaneously reducing its investment to a minimum. Given the desire of the other firms (group) to develop, how much can it demand to achieve a maximum for itself and keep the others interested? The concrete negotiation points are numerous: size of investment, placement of platforms, estimation of reserves, calculation of differing IRRs and the like. These can all become pieces on the corporate chessboard in a game in which the stakes are worth millions.

To untangle these complex and difficult problems, consultant firms such as DeGolyer and MacNaughton appear to have won themselves a specialty in delineation of some of the major fields in the North Sea: Ninian, Statfjord, Frigg, Murchison. To date, delineation and unitisation have been primarily accomplished for major fields (Ninian) and for medium fields (Murchison) and major fields which cross national boundaries (Frigg, Statfjord). The issues involved are extremely technical. Even with consultant firms, the work Norwegian authorities had to do with regard to Frigg was immense.

2.5. The Development Decision — The Problem of Access

If for one reason or another group preferences differ, what are the chances that other firms can enter into the group or obtain the field in question and develop it? In Chapter 1 it was noted that for high-cost fields to be automatically developed in accordance with a 'pure' opportunity cost perspective, there should be free access to those fields. The institutional perspective developed in this chapter points to a 'stickiness' in the development-decision process. Only when fields extend across several blocks and the 'extended group' is split, can the government intervene and provide impetus for field development.

Table 2.11: Rate of Activity on Retained Licensed Blocks of Various Groups Comprising Shell (Shell/Esso), Amoco, BP — British Sector Only, 1964-72

	Drilled blocks	Undrilled blocks	Undrilled blocks (relinquished portion drilled)
Shell/Esso			
Round One (1964)	12	11	1
Round Two (1965)	3	3	1
Round Three (1970)	3	4	3
Round Four (1972)	10	4	0
Totals	28	22	5
BP			
Round One (1964)	3	1	0
Round Two (1965)	3	0	2
Round Three (1970)	1	5	2
Round Four (1972)	13	4	1
Totals	20	10	5
Amoco Group			
Round One (1964)	8	3	0
Round Two (1965)	3	4	1
Round Three (1970)	2	0	1
Round Four (1972)	5	6	1
Totals	18	13	3
Totals by round			
Round One (1964)	23	15	1
Round Two (1965)	9	7	4
Round Three (1970)	6	9	6
Round Four (1972)	28	14	2
Grand totals	66	45	13

Source: OPS, *European Continental Shelf Guide, 1979.*

Governments do not enjoy this power where fields are wholly contained within one block or within several blocks all of which are owned by the same group.

This 'stickiness' is reinforced by the extreme reluctance with which oil firms give up the blocks they have been awarded. Table 2.11 indicates the degree to which three groups, Shell/Esso, BP and Amoco, have acted on undeveloped blocks they still held as of 1979. Many of these blocks are undrilled, despite the fact that they were awarded up to 14 years ago. Many of the blocks are drilled but are kept around for one reason or another — either after relinquishment of undesirable acreage (column 3) or in their entirety (column 1) — presumably because of their future value. The three groups taken as examples are notable because of their activity in the North Sea. They are committed firms. What the figures would be for more uncommitted firms will be discussed at a later point.

In Table 2.11, one might expect that many of the more recent blocks are yet undrilled. After all, considerable investigation must be made before exploratory drilling takes place. But remarkably, many of the blocks received in earlier rounds have not yet even been explored. What do the 23 blocks drilled upon and held by these companies since 1964 contain in the way of oil or gas reserves? What are the potential reserves of the 15 blocks received in 1964, but which have yet to be drilled upon? The answers are purely speculative — for all except those in the groups retaining the blocks. Access can be obtained by 'farming-in', but such access is on the terms of the groups concerned. There is little to indicate that the Shell/Esso group would enjoy outsiders meddling in the 11 undrilled blocks retained since 1964.

There is little the British state can do presently to encourage a higher degree of access. Whom the groups wish to have as partners despite the role of the BNOC remains a matter of their preference, not that of the British state. Despite the general furore over licensing policy, with the companies complaining that recent licensing rounds have been too small, there has been little recognition of the problems involving already licensed blocks which companies have yet to investigate.

2.6. Conclusion — The Development Decision in an Institutional Perspective

At first sight it would seem that the corporate development decision is relatively simple. If one applies a 'pure' opportunity cost perspective to North Sea fields the issues remain clear-cut: those fields which promise good returns are developed. Fields which are more costly are reserved for future decision. Risk enters corporate calculations. 'Marginal' fields are defined by firms in terms of sensitivity to environment, higher discount rates being used as a 'rule of thumb' for field development where the risk is higher.

In the introductory chapter, we argued that an institutional perspective complicates this view considerably. Opportunity costs vary among corporations. Preferences can differ widely as well. Different North Sea groups will have different internal dynamics. Access to known reserves is somewhat less than perfect. This institutional approach views the development decision as an obstacle race by the corporate partners in a group, as well as a function of opportunity cost. We have sought in the foregoing to substantiate this institutional interpretation. Yet there are a few points yet to be made.

The group is of particular importance to the institutional interpretation both in terms of the initial development decision and in the manner in which the field is exploited.

(a) The Development Decision

The number of high-cost fields that remain undeveloped in the North Sea because the discovering group cannot arrive at such a decision can never be known. What is certain is that many firms will insist on a majority decision/self-risk provision in the group agreement as insurance against being placed in a 'locked in' position. For those governments (particularly the Danish Government), which desire the development of 'marginal' reserves, the nature of group agreement must therefore be of considerable importance. If we assume that the typical North Sea group agreement consists of both a 66 per cent majority decision clause and a self-risk clause, there are four possible decision outcomes (illustrated in Figure 2.1). The diagram of decision outcomes emphasises the distinction between the legal provisions and financial/managerial/ technical capacity to carry out the intention of the minority group (with self-risk) and the majority group. It does not necessarily lead to a development decision. Many in the majority might condition their support on gaining the approval of a partner in opposition to the project. Further, it is not inconceivable, given the minimum majority, that the partners who have opted in favour of a development scheme may lack the means to carry it out. This is particularly true of smaller partners with fewer financial resources.

It is of paramount importance, given group interaction with regard to the more costly resources in the North Sea, that governments allow a maximum degree of flexibility to reach a positive decision. Old partners must be permitted to sell out, and new partners to 'farm-in', or enter, the agreement. Similarly, sales of shares in the partnership might be encouraged. Under no conditions should a large group be allowed which requires unanimity on development decisions. Oddly enough, the mere possibility of government participation can also have a positive effect on development decisions. If a minority attempts to develope a field in the face of opposition from its partners, it could well find financial support and expertise from a state company even if the state company is in effect only a 'sleeping partner' within the group.

Figure 2.1: Decision Tree — North Sea Group Working with 66 Per Cent
Development Decision Provision and Self-risk

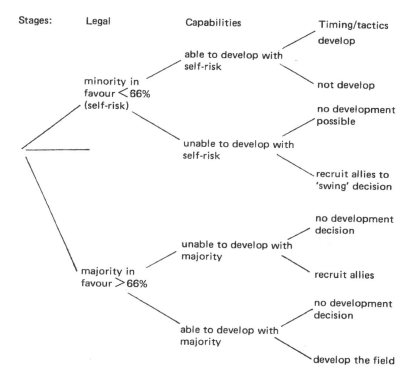

(b) The Manner of Field Development

This is of equal importance to a positive decision to develop a 'marginal'
field. A development decision is not just a decision *to develop* a field. In
many groups, the operator's plans for field development can circulate
for months for comments from its partners, including inevitable
amendments as to what each partner would like to see. In this process,
it is not unlikely that partners expecting a higher return on capital
investment might want to amend development plans towards this end.

Evidence of this is scanty. Odell mentions the two platform plans
for Piper and the problems of capital exposure of some of Occidental's
smaller partners. It is not impossible that, in order to reach the lowest
common denominator, significant portions of an original development
plan may be given away to gain the support and assent of the majority
of the partners concerned. However, in seeking to please all the partners,

a group could well wind up displeasing a North Sea government through insistence on flaring a gas, on the use of floating production platforms, on a high rate of production, and the like.

Government policy towards these problems has been to allow corporations to retain the initiative. Such a policy might make sense given a large number of attractive prospects, and a development decision process which works smoothly. Problems arise when the number of attractive prospects declines, when the development decision process does not work optimally, and when the government concerned is desperate for crude oil for self-sufficiency purposes.

Notes

1. *Noroil*, IV (October 1976), p. 29.
2. C. Robinson and J.R. Morgan, 'The Comparative Effects of the UK and Norwegian Oil Taxation Systems on Profitability and Government Revenue', *Accounting and Business Research*, 25 (Winter 1976), p. 6.
3. Such a measure must exclude the Danish and German shelves. Block awards have never been made in the first and no work programme criteria are used in either. Neither has leasing systems.
4. *North Sea Oil and Gas* (London: Scrimagour & Co., 1974), p. 15.
5. P.R. Odell and K.E. Rosing, *Optimal Development of the North Sea's Oil Fields: A Study in Divergent Government and Company Interests and their Reconciliation* (London: Kogan Page, 1977), p. 139.
6. Ray Dafter, 'Chevron Confirms Ninian Oil Field Reserves', *The Financial Times* (19 February 1976), p. 8.
7. This sort of action can be used to provoke a majority firm to action. The threat of a step-out well (confirmation) performed at its own risk was being used in 1977 by a minority partner in a Dutch group, to provoke its larger partner to support a development scheme. If the step-out well were to be successful, the minority partner would possess hydrocarbon rights for an area around the successful well. The circumference of such an area was not disclosed, but it was considerably larger than the drawing area of the well concerned.
8. K. Dam, *Oil Resources: Who Gets What How?* (Chicago: The University of Chicago Press, 1976), p. 45.
9. Odell & Rosing, *Optimal Development*, p. 79.
10. Ibid., p. 79.

3 GOVERNMENTAL REGIMES AND THE DEVELOPMENT DECISION

3.1. Introduction: The Contract

What should be the purpose of the North Sea licence as a contract? There are many answers to this question. But in the context of this analysis, several aspects are particularly notable.

First, the contract should promote efficiency in corporate behaviour. To procure the development of as many high-cost resources as possible, the North Sea contract should require North Sea consortia to develop all fields to the point where the marginal revenue of the incremental field is equivalent to the marginal cost of developing the incremental field. There can be little doubt that this is the ultimate aim of firms' behaviour as well, but, as noted in Chapter 2, oil multinational rationality is 'bounded' by other factors. A major purpose of a North Sea licensing policy should therefore be to eliminate as much slack as possible in multinational corporate behaviour.

Secondly, the contract — licensing policy — should aim to reduce the contractual costs for the government to as low a level as possible. Bureaucratic mechanisms for administering oil multinational behaviour should also be efficient. Regulations should be easy to administer and hard to evade. Here, too, there is considerable evidence that this is not the case in the North Sea.

Part One spelled out two classes of contract provisions: the relatively immutable access provisions, and those provisions which have been altered at state discretion. Generally speaking, the access provisions are the more efficient of the two. To support this contention, this chapter will contrast the impact of the two sorts of provisions on behaviour of the firm.

3.2. Access Provisions: I. The Exploration Stage

Although all North Sea regimes but the Danish have initial periods of geological and geophysical reconnaissance called 'exploration periods', there can be little doubt that the most significant period of exploration comes later upon the awarding of licences and the commencement of exploration drilling. This is the facet of exploration of interest in this context.

Access provisions to improve the speed and efficiency of offshore exploration are of two kinds. The first is the set of provisions establishing a system of interim rental payments geared to the amount of acreage licensed. A lump sum is advanced upon the awarding of a licence — generally a fixed per block sum — which covers a period of years (six in the UK). For the group wishing to retain acreage beyond this period, periodic payments begin and escalate sharply on a *per annum* basis. A second incentive involves the 'relinquishment' of licensed acreage to the state after a specified number of years. Relinquishment rates and methods vary from country to country.

Assuming that the North Sea groups concerned are economically rational, drilling activity should progress to the point where the anticipated marginal benefit in terms of future revenues of the additional exploration well equals the marginal cost of drilling that well. Beyond this point, any further drilling will decrease the present value of the real estate concerned.

Periodic *rental payments* increase exploration costs, and unless minimised reduce the present value of the real estate. In other words,

$$(3.1) \quad PV_L = \sum_{t=o}^{T} \frac{O_a}{(1+i)^t} - \sum_{t=o}^{T} \frac{D_a}{(1+i)^t} - \sum_{t=o}^{T} \frac{R}{(1+i)^t}$$

in which O_a represents the anticipated positive and negative project cash flows (net of taxes and royalties), D_a represents the anticipated survey and drilling costs, and R the additional costs of area rentals after the sixth year. (These values are discounted to a present value at the discount rate i.) Given this situation, the maximising course for the group would be to explore as quickly as possible to minimise the retained acreage for licence L, thereby maximising its present value (PV_L). All acreage where the marginal benefits per exploration well outweigh the well's marginal costs will be explored and, where justified, relinquished.

Relinquishment works in much the same way. Here:

$$(3.2) \quad PV_L = \sum_{t=o}^{T} \frac{O_a}{(1+i)^t} - \sum_{t=o}^{T} \frac{D_a}{(1+i)^t} - \sum_{t=o}^{T} \frac{O_f}{(1+i)^t}$$

in which O_f represents foregone real cash flows, those potential revenues from undiscovered/undeveloped finds which the group was forced to relinquish.

So far there have been two ideal systems, one in which there are periodic rental payments and one in which 100 per cent of the licence not containing exploitable resources is relinquished. Given the present area rental rates and the escalating price of oil, it is easy to prove that, generally speaking, for all but the most high-cost prospects:

$$(3.3) \quad \sum_{t=o}^{T} \frac{O_f}{(1+i)^t} > \sum_{t=o}^{T} \frac{R}{(1+i)^t}$$

This is due to several factors: first, rental rates are very low *vis-a-vis* the present value of oil and natural gas resources; secondly, appreciation of oil and gas prices in recent years for all but the smallest reservoirs has far outstripped rental-rate penalties; and thirdly, rental rates are treated as exploration expenses and are thus deductible from royalties and taxes, which reduces their effectiveness as incentives to exploration.

Yet the systems in the North Sea are not ideal. In both the British and the Norwegian sectors only one-half of a licensed area is relinquished after six and nine years, respectively. This situation can be expressed in the following manner:

$$(3.4) \quad PV_L = \sum_{t=o}^{T} \frac{O_a}{(1+i)^t} - \sum_{t=o}^{T} \frac{O_{fr}}{(1+i)^t} - \sum_{t=o}^{T} \frac{R(1-r)}{(1+i)^t}$$

in which O_{fr} stands for foregone cash flows from the resources in the relinquished portions of the licence alone, and $R_{(1-r)}$ for the periodic payments for the retained acreage. In such a situation, there are two critical points. The first is an economic equilibrium point. The periodic rental payments should influence the firm to retain all acreage the prospective value of which exceeds the value of the periodic area rental payments. The second point is imposed by time, when the firm determines which of its licensed acres should be relinquished and which retained. Prior to that point the group may drill at a high rate, but a rate only necessary to determine which portion of a licence should be relinquished. Thereafter the rate of exploration will be determined not necessarily by the need to explore to the point where the anticipated marginal benefit per well is equal to the well's marginal cost, but by commitments elsewhere in the world of oil. Ultimately, group behaviour will be determined by marginal cost and marginal revenue considerations, but the need to drill to this point within a short period is no longer as pressing. If other prospects are more attractive and involve lower costs, it is economically rational to sit on retained acreage. In other words, there is a 'jointness' in rational North Sea group behaviour when it comes to exploration.

In a sense, 'jointness' is encouraged by licensing systems. Since only one-half of the licensed area is relinquished, and not one-half of each licensed block, it is rational to apply for as much 'whale pasture' (worthless blocks) as possible in conjunction with applying for worthwhile blocks. The more the 'whale pasture', the more the acreage which can be automatically relinquished as soon as possible, and the less necessary activity on promising blocks — all within the limits of the approved drilling programmes (which were rather lax in the early period of the North Sea).

The pattern of activity in the British area confirms this 'jointness'. Table 3.1 gives the rates of relinquishment of full blocks. Of the blocks licensed in the First Round (1964), fully 192 were relinquished without any exploration wells drilled. A further 78 blocks (or the fragments of 78 blocks) were still held in 1979, undeveloped. Similar figures obtain for Rounds Two (1965) and Three (1970). The proportion of full blocks relinquished attained record heights in the aftermath of the Fourth Round (1972), although a considerable number of blocks from that round are still being held.

A further condition of this 'jointness' is that there should be a relatively high number of undrilled blocks held by the more active North Sea groups. It is precisely these groups which have the largest licence allocations. Table 2.11 in Chapter 2 gave the numbers of these blocks for some of the more active companies in the British area. Particularly spectacular in this regard is the record of the Shell/Esso group.

Yet how do relinquishment/area payments and area rental schemes affect industry drilling activity? Does the British system of relinquishment actually affect the rate of activity in the British area? Evidence suggests that it does. As stated earlier, periodic rental payments have a low incentive on drilling activity. In countries with longer exploration periods (and more lenient relinquishment terms), the pattern of drilling should be spread out. Companies would stick to a prearranged drilling plan — so many wells per year and no more. In contrast, in those countries with tougher relinquishment provisions and shorter periods before relinquishment, it would be reasonable to

Table 3.1: Rates of Activity — Fate of Licensed Blocks Rounds 1 to 4, UK Continental Shelf

Operators	Round One			Round Two			Round Three			Round Four		
	Full blocks relinquished		Blocks held*	Full blocks relinquished		Blocks held*	Full blocks relinquished		Blocks held*	Full blocks relinquished		Blocks held*
	with drill	without drill		with drill	without drill		with drill	without drill		with drill	without drill	
Shell	3	30	31	1	7	4	1	0	4	6	23	21
BP	4	12	4	0	4	3	0	6	9	3	7	7
Mobil	3	4	6	0	0	2	0	0	2	2	1	6
Texaco	1	4	4	1	0	3	1	3	1	0	2	5
Chevron	2	11	0	0	0	0	0	0	0	0	0	5
Amoco	9	21	6	0	5	10	0	7	2	6	3	10
Conoco	1	0	6	0	1	5	0	3	4	3	9	14
Phillips	2	13	9	0	0	3	0	1	10	3	1	9
Total	4	4	2	4	1	12	0	0	3	1	2	5
Gulf	4	15	0	1	3	1	0	2	0	0	0	0
Other	23	79	10	7	13	0	1	27	8	3	49	16
Totals	56	192	78	14	34	43	3	49	43	27	97	98

*Blocks held is defined as blocks still under licence whether they are 'full blocks' or the last remains of a 'full block', the majority of which has been relinquished. The relinquished figures do not include these fragmentary blocks which are given up although these fragments are often listed as being blocks in themselves.

Source: OPS, *European Continental Shelf Guide, 1979* (London: OPS, 1979).

see a high rate of activity on leased blocks during the first six years perhaps culminating in years four to six. This period of activity would be followed by a lower, more constant rate of drilling as systematic drilling continued on retain acreage. In this latter period of activity, area rental payment would have little or no effect on drilling rates.

Substantial confirmation of these hypotheses can be found in a comparison of the British (six years before relinquishment) and the Dutch (ten years before relinquishment) provisions. Table 3.2 compares the distribution of exploration wells in the first four British rounds with the Dutch licensing rounds of 1968 and 1970. (The approximate deadlines for relinquishment are underlined in the table.) In all four British rounds, the general pattern of drilling tends to confirm our hypothesis — although there is probably insufficient evidence to draw much of a conclusion from the Third and Fourth Rounds. The drilling rate on the Dutch acreage is of the two much more constant, peaking in 1977 and 1978, the two years in which relinquishment of blocks leased in 1968 fell due.

Table 3.2: Total Drilling Rates by Year for the Different British and Dutch Licensing Rounds — Exploration Wells

Year	British licensing rounds				Dutch licensing rounds	
	1st Round 1964	2nd Round 1965	3rd Round 1970-1	4th Round 1972	1st Round 1968	2nd Round 1970
0	—	—	3	1	7	2
1	9	—	5	13	16	2
2	26	6	6	30	15	1
3	40	2	2	46	14	2
4	32	5	6	74	15	4
5	44	8	9	53	16	4
6	<u>16</u>	<u>13</u>	<u>4</u>	<u>71</u>	12	2
7	5	3	4	25*	12	3
8	9	2	1*		17	3*
9	14	3			22	
10	5	2			<u>11</u>*	
11	1	2				
12	3	1*				
13	1					
14	3*					

*First eight months, 1978 only.

Source: OPS, *European Continental Shelf Guide, 1979.*

Table 3.3: Drilling Rates (UK and Norway) versus Drilling Rates (Netherlands) for Three Oil Multinationals (All Rounds) — Exploration Wells

Year	Shell/Esso		Amoco		Total	
	UK/Norway	Netherlands	UK/Norway	Netherlands	UK/Norway	Netherlands
1964	—	nl*	—	nl*	—	nl*
1965	3	nl	4	nl	1	nl
1966	1	nl	4	nl	—	nl
1967	5	nl	4	nl	2	nl
1968	7	4	7	—	2	1
1969	7	2	2	1	7	1
1970	4	8	3	—	1	—
1971	9	6	4	—	5	1
1972	8	4	8	—	4	1
1973	5	5	7	—	5	3
1974	7	4	5	1	7	4
1975	10	4	4	—	11	2
1976	6	9	6	—	10	—
1977	8	7	—	2	5	—
1978	2	4	—	2	3	1

*nl = no licensing rounds.

Source: OPS, *European Continental Shelf Guide, 1979.*

Thus far we have only looked at 'jointness' — intensive drilling on the most promising blocks and automatic relinquishment/no drilling at all on other blocks — in the context of one nation's particular sector. But what of 'jointness' internationally? To what extent can drilling rates in an area with a six-year relinquishment provision affect rates in an area with a ten-year provision: for example, the UK versus Holland? Here the evidence is not as clear. It is useful to look at three corporations in particular in this context. Using the Dutch ten-year system for comparison and combining drilling rates for all rounds for the Norwegian and British areas (both with a six-year relinquishment), we obtain the results shown in Table 3.3 for the Total, Shell/Esso and Amoco groups.

Any alleged 'jointness' in international exploration efforts must be carefully qualified. Clearly the geological and economic prospects in the areas differ considerably. The geological promise of licensed acreage

in the same sector can also vary among corporate groups (Shell/Esso –
NAM – is generally thought to have the most promising Dutch acreage).
Still, in about 60 per cent of all cases after 1968, for these three
corporations, a fall in the drilling rate in the Dutch area is accompanied
by a rise in the number of wells in the British/Norwegian areas, and *vice
versa*. This average varies among the groups, being virtually insignificant
for one group and over 70 per cent for another. The evidence is highly
speculative and sketchy, but one can tentatively state that the form of
licence contract – and whether the licence includes relinquishment –
may in certain cases affect drilling activities outside national boundaries.

Thus in the exploration stage there are provisions in the North Sea
licence contract which promote speed and efficiency in exploration.
The most effective of these is relinquishment. The use of periodic
payment systems is a far more latent incentive. Yet, how does the
licence contract affect the development decision, itself? To date North
Sea licences have promoted an emphasis on development through setting
the terms for exchanges of ownership interests among firms with
differing priorities – the establishment of a market in offshore real
estate. Thus before proceeding to the 'discretionary economic
incentives', let us glance briefly at North Sea 'assignment policies'.

3.3. Access Provisions: II. Assignments and the Development Decision

Of all the provisions of the licensing contract, those concerning
'farm-ins' and 'farm-outs' come the closest to dealing with the problems
of 'bounded rationality' – the problems discussed briefly in Chapter 1
and elaborated further in Chapter 2. In the latter chapter, emphasis was
placed on farm-ins and farm-outs. These sales or shifts in block
ownership are in reality changes in ownership of licences pertaining to
the blocks concerned. Such a change of ownership is also known as an
assignment or reassignment of interests. Moves of this sort generally
require government approval.

Within the North Sea, group assignments or farm-ins are relatively
common and may take diverse forms. Firms buying into a block may
do so through cash payment; more commonly the drilling of an
exploration or delineation well is the form of payment. Alternatively
farming-in may be contingent on the financing of a development project.
Assignments can be relatively unplanned, occurring at short notice.
They may also be the result of contractual rights previously agreed to
among the partners of the group owning the licence. Normally, however,

despite the many forms and shapes assignments can take, the practice of farming-in or -out is rigidly controlled within the group, often requiring unanimity — in practice if not in legal fact.

British and Norwegian authorities tend to impose stricter criteria on changes within groups than do the Danish or the Dutch. Since the passing of the British Petroleum and Submarine Pipelines Act, the UK Government has extended its power. Previously, the Energy Ministry had control over the transfer of licences; with the implementation of the Act it controlled not only the transfer of the licence but also transfers of control in the licensees. Ministerial approval of assignments is rarely public. Its approval criteria are thought to be the same as those it uses issuing licences in the first place. Up to 1979, this meant a spate of transfers of interest which have been contingent on BNOC's acquiring a potential interest in a discovery.[1]

Although more and more stringent criteria might conceivably make the British assignment system less flexible and thus deter group formations positive to a development decision, corporate sources have assured the author that the system is really quite free in practice. Whether they will continue to share this belief in the future is quite another matter.

While less is known of Norwegian assignment policy, it is as interesting as the British policy. In 1969 there was a major redistribution of interests between the Phillips Group and the Petronord Group when these two exchanged interests from licences 16 and 9, respectively. Although this exchange occurred before the discovery of Ekofisk, the addition of Elf-Acquitaine, Total and Norsk Hydro to the Phillips Group undoubtedly gave the latter increased resources on which to draw. Today these two groups hold 15 of the original blocks in common — a total of about 3,000 square kilometres. Another interesting assignment occurred over the Valhall field. Here the Norwegian Oil Consortium, a minority member in the Amoco discovery group, received credits of up to $100 million from Svenska Petroleum in return for rights to buy 43.8 million barrels of NOCO's oil from Valhall and its undeveloped sister field Hod, and the right to a ten per cent share in block 2/9. 'Farming-in' arrangements conditional on the drilling of an exploration well are not uncommon. Recently, both Union Oil of California and Norsk Gulf have begun this practice, the former picking up 54 per cent of the blocks from the Amoco Group and assuming operator privileges.

Assignments are most free in the Netherlands. Here the advent of small firms with names not usually recognised in public — Deep Sea

Venture, Tesoro, Van Dyck Oil, Scurry Rainbow, and the like — has been striking. It is not unusual to see up to four or five changes in partnership on a block without any wells at all being drilled. Block interests are exchanged in such a welter of activity that it is not uncommon for histories of block ownership to include such phrases as 'interests subsequently changed at various times' and 'these interests subsequently revised to those shown above'.[2] While perhaps liable to charges of allowing speculation in offshore real estate, there can be little doubt that this policy has enhanced development. The Placid Group, for example, has been both one of the most active in exchanges of interests, and one of the most development-oriented of the Dutch North Sea groups.

The situation is entirely different in the Danish offshore. Here, the single concessionaire has twice allowed a major redistribution of interests in the Danish Underground Consortium. Once in 1967, Chevron and Texaco were permitted to join the DUC. Again in 1975, interests to various parts of the extensive monopoly concession were redistributed among the partners when Gulf, the operator, left the area. All attempts to 'loosen' the situation from the state's side have run into legal or political difficulties.

Government control of assignment policy goes to the heart of one of the institutional aspects of the development decision — that of access. Through controlling the conditions under which assignments are made, governments can hope to inject drive into groups hopelessly split over various development projects. A narrow assignment policy with rigid controls could have an opposite effect. It is curious, but one could well argue that the BNOC's 'right of first refusal' to farm-in deals might actually have retarded the progress of attractive prospects. Here, companies locked in disagreement over whether to proceed with an exploration well, an appraisal well, a development of a prospect, would not consider a farm-in or farm-out for fear that they might get the BNOC in the group as a full partner with considerable rights of decision.

3.4. Discretionary Economic Incentives and the Development Decision

If assignment policy only indirectly provides a spur to development of high-cost resources, the use of discretionary economic incentives attempts to tackle the problem more directly. By granting and/or royalty exemptions, the state can attempt to affect corporate opportunity cost perspectives. Preferences for high-cost fields are of

many types (Table 3.4). The most explicit are the British exemptions
of high-cost fields from the Petroleum Revenue Tax (PRT) — the impact
of the 500,000 metric ton/annual exemption (before 1979 this was a
one million ton exemption), the 30 per cent 'tapering' provision, and a
discretionary remittance of royalties (these provisions are all described
in more detail in Chapter 5). Both the Netherlands and Norway have
sliding royalty scales (adjusted in accordance with production) which
should encourage development of smaller, lower-producing structures.
The Dutch allow ten per cent of operating costs to be deducted from
corporate taxes. This measure again allows for smaller, more expensive
fields to be developed since operating costs can be correspondingly high
on such fields. Other provisions have existed from time to time, but have
been abandoned. The Dutch exemption of small fields from a general
requirement of state participation in field development and production
has been abandoned with the general increase in oil and gas prices, for
example.

There is nevertheless a more or less constant discussion about
discretionary economic incentives in the North Sea. Virtually every
government in the North Sea has toyed with the possibility of granting
such incentives and on more than one occasion. There are three factors
which count against such discretionary economic incentives: first, it is
questionable how effective they are; secondly, it is difficult to exempt
certain high-cost fields from the general run of high-cost North Sea
fields (discriminatory rules favouring one sort of field over another are
hard to enforce); and thirdly, such rules as those illustrated in Table 3.4
are costly both in terms of enforcement and in terms of lost government
revenues.

Of these three factors, the first two will be the focus of the analysis
of British and Danish policies. The third, the cost of enforcing
discretionary economic incentives, will form the balance of this chapter.

3.5. The Cost of the North Sea Contract and Discretionary Economic Incentives

The cost and relative efficiency of various contract forms is a not
uncommon theme in property rights literature. In this context, when
the North Sea licence or concession is seen in terms of cost or
efficiency, it is clear that generally there are more efficient forms of
contract.

S. Cheung's classic paper on share-cropping in China distinguished

Table 3.4: Discretionary Rental Legislation

	United Kingdom	Norway	Denmark	The Netherlands
a. Taxes	500,000 mts. crude 40 bcf gas exempt from PRT per annum for 10-year period	No exceptional provisions for high-cost fields	No exceptional provisions for high-cost fields	No exceptional provisions
	If pretax profits less than 30% of total capital expenditures, PRT is refunded			
	All profits above 30% not taxed if government cut above that mark is more than 80%			
b. Other (not specifically aimed at high-cost fields)				
(i) Capital depreciation	135% of capital costs free before PRT. 100% depreciation on virtually free terms before corporate taxes	100% capital depreciation over 6 years (straight line) including exploration costs	30% declining balance depreciation. Does not include exploration costs	10% straight line for platforms, 5% for pipelines
		Credits per annum of 10% historical capital expenditure first 15 years (after 1980: first 10 years)		

Table 3.4 *(contd.)*

	United Kingdom	Norway	Denmark	The Netherlands
(ii) Royalties	12.5% royalties remitted if required for field profitability	Royalties never remitted but on sliding scale depending on production rates	No special royalty provisions. Royalties 5% first 5 years. 8.5% thereafter	0-16% royalties depending on production rates
(iii) Other	—	Operating bases from one field fully and immediately deductible from revenues of other fields	—	10% deduction for operating costs allowed from taxes

between differing kinds of contracts in terms of the interaction of risk and transaction costs — the costs to tenant and to landowner of a contractual arrangement.[3] Kenneth Dam has written a similarly well-known treatise on rent capture and North Sea licensing policies, comparing these unfavourably to American systems of bonus payments auctions. His criticism is based on two grounds: inefficiency and an ultimate distrust of state discretionary powers. Curiously, Dam concentrates his arguments regarding inefficiency on the price mechanism — ignoring the other aspects of inefficiency, aspects which are central in this context.

What are the transaction costs to the state of the North Sea contract? To begin with, there is a cost implicit in any form of discretionary licensing form over and above the price mechanism, the cost of enforcement and administration. Generally speaking, the easiest manner for the state to enlarge its 'cut' is directly out of gross project revenues — enlarging its royalty rates. More difficult is enforcing a percentage due to the state from oil industry profits. Finally, contract costs are perhaps highest in state participation schemes.[4]

(i) The Problem of Royalties

Royalties are widely contended to be the most sure form of state income in that they are calculated on gross project revenues, not on profits after expenses. What this contention ignores is the difficulties of determining gross revenues. Crude oil (and gas as well) can have significantly different prices. That differing grades of crude sell at different prices is perhaps well-known. Less well-known is that prices for the same grade of crude can vary, depending on the amounts sold and to whom. State income from royalties can therefore vary widely for the same grade of oil, making the question of price and hence of gross revenue highly relative. The best available example of this can be found in the seventh and eighth tanker loads of oil from the Danish Dan field and the value of this oil as reported by the DUC. Due to a breakdown in the production system at the Dan field, a tanker load of crude produced during the period November-December 1973, was not landed in Denmark until 3 February 1974. What was the value of the Danish oil? The values declared for royalty purposes at the time for the partners in the field, Dansk Boreselskab (DBS), Gulf, Shell, Chevron, and Texaco, are shown in Table 3.5.

The contrasts in value for tanker load 7, the tanker load preceding the 1973 crisis, vary from a low of $3.47 per barrel to a high of $4.15. But this difference pales in comparison to that for load number 8,

Table 3.5: Declared Value of Dan Oil per Barrel for Royalty Purposes, 16 October 1973 and 3 February 1974

Load No	Unloading date	Price: DBS, Gulf, Shell	Chevron's price	Texaco's price
7	16/10/73	$ 3.4685	$3.48	$ 4.15
8	3/02/74	$11.8570	$4.75	$13.00

Source: Letter to H. Jørgensen and L.B. Rasmussen from Revisionsfirmaet Seier Pedersen, 2 February 1975.

where the declared crude value varied from a low of $4.75 reported by Chevron to a high of $13.00 reported by Texaco! The Danish state, even allowing for the deduction of transportation costs, collected anything from 33 cents per barrel to over $1 per barrel in royalty charges, a considerable variation in royalty charges and in royalty revenue to the state, if not a variation in taxation revenues. Clearly, the degree to which the oil companies engage in such practices can reduce the revenues of North Sea states and considerably increase the companies' gains.

This Danish case is but one example of a major problem currently facing bureaucrats: that of assessing the value of the oil and gas sold. Different bureaucracies have adopted differing methods to this end. The British Inland Revenue Service, for example, has an office which determines the quality and the marketing connections for each variety of crude produced in the North Sea and assesses each at a different value for royalty and taxation purposes. The Norwegians take the price of a 'standard crude' and base their assessment of value on this. The Danes appear to be alone in letting the companies operating on the Danish Shelf determine what the proper value of the crude sold is, and pay accordingly. In this context it should also be pointed out that national tax authorities can occasionally decide on a value for crude oil which is too high, and thereby penalise companies which are producing low-grade oil or producing oil in amounts too small to demand the proper premiums on the refinery market.[5]

The determination of gross revenues and, hence, the royalty due to the state does involve considerable expense. This expense is of two kinds: the costs of creating the bureaucratic expertise to check prices received for oil, gross revenues and royalties due; and the occasional error which either unnecessarily penalises the state or inflicts unreasonable loss on the companies concerned.

(ii) The Problem of Taxes

There is a host of measures which affect the true incidence of North
Sea oil taxation legislation. A large part of the corporate taxes collected
can be offset against taxes elsewhere in the world. Thus a double
taxation treaty between Great Britain and the United States allows
American companies not only to offset the 52 per cent British
corporation tax against taxes payable in the United States, but also to
offset the 70 per cent PRT. To evaluate the true and full impact of
these taxes on American corporations, it would be necessary to
reconstruct their global financial records.

Nor is this the only benefit American oil legislation confers on US
companies. Through constructing an 'X company', note R.F. Hayllar
and R.T. Pleasance, 'a situation [occurs] in which the British company
exploring and producing in the North Sea is associated with and
controlled by its American parents'. That this has advantages is clear;
'The "X company" is treated as the British legal entity, and incurs all
the rights and responsibilities nominally undertaken by its British
affiliate'. Yet, 'it is simultaneously eligible for US tax incentives and
can set off [North Sea] tax losses during the exploration and
development periods against US taxable profits arising elsewhere in the
same US group of companies'.[6]

Yet another benefit affecting the corporate taxation of virtually
every North Sea regime is that firms can subtract interest payments
from their tax liabilities. There are two fundamental sorts of finance:
bank or project finance, and finance from the parent corporations in
the group. Particularly worrisome to governments are intercorporate
loans. In the British case, write Hayllar and Pleasance, concern has
focused on the 'possible loss of UK tax through the adoption by
overseas domiciled groups of thinly capitalised corporate structures
in which the subsidiary company operation in the UK has a
disproportionately high amount of loan capital'.[7] In such a case, a
group of companies minimise the incidence of corporate taxes on their
British affiliate while simultaneously earning a return on their
'investment' in the form of tax deductible 'interest'. The result is a
'siphoning' of profits from the UK affiliate and from British
jurisdiction. While the British have acted to close off abuse of this
option, it is clear that possibilities remain. Elsewhere in the North Sea
it is doubtful whether practices as strict as the British have been
adopted.

Timing of corporate tax, petroleum tax, and royalty payments can also affect corporate profitability. Thus in the Danish case, a full year is allowed before royalty payments are made, and two years for corporate taxes. Delayed payment improves cash flows directly and indirectly. The two-year delay in tax payments improves the IRR values of Danish projects by about two to three per cent, for example. Furthermore, indirectly, the sums of money during the 24-month period between incurrence and payment can be invested in short-term alternatives, thereby earning interest which the state never takes into account. Regulations in this respect are considerably tighter outside the Danish North Sea.

Generally speaking, the complications of enforcing North Sea taxation rules lie in the conflict between equity and the particular requirements of taxing a natural resource industry. The maintenance of corporate taxes is a concession to taxation equity. The oil industry should be equally placed before the law with other industries. Yet at the same time, because of the nature of the oil industry, to base tax regulations fully on equity would lead to an inefficient capture of rent. There are too many opportunities for diversion of capital. Taxation directed at rent capture, while inequitable on the other hand, is ideally suited to this particular goal. Thus the provisions of the PRT in the United Kingdom are defined so as to avert the problems which occur given the normal corporate tax regime. There should be little cause for wonder, therefore, that more recent British endeavours to capture the 'windfall' profits characteristic of North Sea activities should focus on increasing the PRT to 60 per cent, then 70 per cent, and decreasing the 'uplift' to 35 per cent. Corporate taxes alone are simply inadequate for states to collect the revenue they feel they deserve.

(iii) The Problems of Participation

There is a good case for arguing that of all the various facets of the North Sea licence, the enforcement of participation involves the heaviest costs. Here, unfortunately, evidence is sketchy. Dam, for example, likens the involvement of the BNOC and Statoil in North Sea group activity to that of a bank — the state firm supplying money and sharing profits, but exerting little real influence. Dam emphasises two aspects of such participation: first, the degree to which state participation actually increases development profits — the companies being able to get better leverage and better interest rates with the state underwriting the project — and secondly, the degree to which the state firm is liable for exploration expenditures or not, the so-called 'carried interest' scheme.[8]

Government negotiators are well aware of the problems involved in participation. Therefore, the various participation programmes should allow for the better leverage and interest rates which the oil companies obtain. This must be a difficult procedure to follow. With regard to government sharing of exploration expenditures incurred before development, the questions are no less difficult. Which seismic surveys, and which exploration or confirmation wells, is a government company liable for? Do such reimbursements concern only the most narrow exploration expenditures — the discovery hole and the subsequent confirmation drillings? Do state firms pay for all the exploration wells in the block — although there may be more than one field in the relevant block? Or are state firms liable for all exploration expenses concerned with the particular 'geologic play' in the area involved?

Additionally, government firms enter into these agreements as more or less 'equal' partners — without, however, any decisive say in many of the issues which concern the group. What expenses are involved in this admission to the group? Are the BNOC and Statoil liable for payments for group management, for the technology used in the development plan, for services in producing and/or marketing the oil, or for the salaries of key management personal? If they are liable, is it on the same terms as the other members of the group concerning payments to the operator?[9]

Even if there are no 'hidden costs' such as those described, there remain enormous difficulties in finding qualified persons to manage the state company. Managers of a state company have two functions: they must interact with the managers of the various operating groups in the North Sea in a co-operative manner, and they must also function as a means of state control. This is a lot to ask of management even if it is staffed by highly qualified personnel. Normally, one function is sacrificed to the other. There is no mechanism guaranteeing government or state control in such an arrangement. Indeed, if control is the envisaged aim of participation, it might be cheaper (or more effective) 'to exercise control through legislation than through acquisition of a majority of equity'.[10]

If enforcement of the North Sea licence contract is a costly business in terms of royalty and tax collection, and state participation, what is the impact of special economic incentives? The answer would seem to be that such incentives increase the costs considerably.

Norway and Holland have special royalty rates geared to production. The so-called 'sliding scale' royalties are based on the premise that small fields (with low production rates) are less economic than larger fields.

The companies argue that this premise is false. Large fields can also be very costly. Even granting this argument, the question arises as to whether royalty rates should be geared to a given rate of profitability regardless of whether the field concerned is large or small. (As we will see in our analysis of British legislation, this is close to some of the arguments advanced by the industry with regard to eventual remission of royalties for high-cost fields.) Additionally, sliding scale royalties are complex to administer. Here their progressive character can create a disincentive to what might be regarded as an optimum rate of production.[11]

A look at the impact of tax legislation on North Sea profits raises the question of whether special economic incentives are needed at all. Let us take an example. It is not uncommon for one group to use the positive income flows from a field to invest in yet another field (with appropriate deductions for corporate taxation purposes). This practice has two consequences: (1) it increases the short-term corporate 'take' from producing fields very considerably; (2) it renders the common practice of assigning Internal Rates of Return for individual fields questionable. The degree to which cash flows from field X fuel investments on field Y, and are hence not subject to corporate taxes, and the degree to which profits on these two fields are thus interdependent, make it difficult to claim that field Y is 'marginal' because it alone returns only 15 per cent. In reality it is therefore impossible to declare a field 'high-cost' or 'marginal' simply because it by itself has a low Internal Rate of Return. Investment in the field must be seen in terms of all the activities of the group within the national sector. If investment in field Y, our 15 per cent example, increases the profitability of field X, the well-paying field, this investment may no longer become questionable. Depending on the circumstances, it could even be a very good investment. In a North Sea sector, it is the combination of fields which allows a group to maximise its profits. This combination renders assessing individual fields in isolation, as if the others did not exist, somewhat unreal.

Furthermore, special economic incentives conflict with the notions of tax equity. Tax law should ideally be formulated so that rules apply to all fields — whether high- or low-cost. In granting incentives for the development of high-cost fields, one is confronted with whether the same incentives apply to all resources. There are two choices in this context: some sort of definition can be made enabling discrimination in favour of high-cost fields; or rules can be designed which apply to all resources — high- and low-cost — with the expectation that while all fields benefit, high-cost fields benefit more than the lower-cost fields. Whichever course is chosen, it will be expensive for the state. If one attempts to define a high-cost field for the purpose of preferential treatment, one must use a very precise definition. In that it is ultimately the North Sea group which claims the field is high-cost, there must be considerable checking and enforcing prior to the granting of preferences. If on the other hand, one designs a rule which benefits all fields, it is at the cost of foregone tax revenues from fields which did not need the benefits.

Additionally, special economic incentives complicate problems of checking and enforcing corporate tax returns. This is complex enough with interest payments, transfer prices, X-company provisions, expensing allowances, and the like. The problem of adapting a policy of special incentives to such procedures will complicate administrative procedures enormously.

Special economic incentives interact with participation as well. The most obvious case of this interaction is in the Netherlands, where the government for a period of time 'waived' its right to a participation agreement in cases where fields were small and/or high-cost. Clearly what is 'small' or 'high-cost' in this instance is in the eye of the beholder. Depending on the circumstances, it could well pay a group thinking of investing in a field to claim that it was 'small' or 'marginal' and thereby avoid the necessity of a participation agreement. It is perhaps significant that this provision is no longer regarded as applicable, due, this author was assured, to 'higher post-1973 prices'.[12] Degree of government participation in Norwegian licences is often specified in terms of field size/daily production. Here too, problems could conceivably arise, particularly in the decision of how extensive government participation should be. A company could minimise participation through arguing for a small field/low production rate. Conversely, it could increase government participation through arguing for a large field/high production rate — depending on the circumstances. Similarly, in making 'participation' a topic for negotiation explicitly, it is possible for companies to make a special case for underwriting some of the risk elements in an envisaged project — either in the form of greater government ownership or through other measures (preferential terms for 'buy-back' crude, special financing terms, special licence arrangements, and the like).

3.6. Conclusion: The Development Decision, the North Sea Contract, and Discretionary Economic Incentives

After discussing the development decision from the industry's vantage point in Chapter 2, this chapter has reviewed the contractual context within which the government exercises influence on the development decision. With regard to licensing policy, there would appear to be a lacuna here. Norway, Great Britain, and Holland have relinquishment policies designed to prompt efficient, rapid exploratory efforts. The impact of these policies is different, the forced relinquishment of one-half a licensed area being by far the most effective incentive. Still, the aim is the same in all these nations.

When it comes to field development, licensing policy does little except to establish the 'rules of the market' in which shares in licences are bought and sold — assigned and reassigned. Unlike licensing for the exploration stage, there are no contractual 'spurts' to encourage rapid development. Rather than utilise block rentals or block relinquishment, governments are inclined to encourage production from higher-cost prospects through discretionary economic incentives. These can take many forms, but are thus far only prominent in the British regime.

Such incentives involve the loss of government revenues. They also involve an increasing degree of complication and cost in licensing systems already characterised by a high degree of administrative cost and complexity. Royalties, taxes — both general and those aimed at rent capture — and participation were reviewed in terms of administrative effort and expense. It is difficult to perceive that such measures as the British discretionary refund of royalties notably improve the situation.

Furthermore, North Sea licensing systems have been labelled 'discretionary' by no less an authority than Kenneth Dam. Dam's critique of the system focuses on the allocation — and the use of allocative criteria to favour specific governmental objectives: a rapid rate of exploration, the favouring of Norwegian or British interests, the use of British or Norwegian supplies, materials, labour, and the like. What Dam omits in his critique is that such discretionary allocation systems have a built-in tendency to create special provisions, exemptions, waivers, and refunds which can ultimately not only cost the state dear, but could if unrestrained vitiate the entire purpose of the licensing system. Nowhere is this more clear than with regard to discretionary economic incentives, as has been done in the context of this chapter.

What could such discretionary economic incentives have to recommend them? Could not such incentives be justified if they are linked to a positive effect on the North Sea decision-making environment? For the answers to these more specific questions it is necessary to turn to the two case studies: the British licensing system and the Danish concession.

Notes

1. K. Dam, *Oil Resources: Who Gets What How?* (Chicago: The University of Chicago Press, 1976), p. 48. Such cases include the United Canso sale of interests in Thistle to Deminex, Berry Wiggins' sale to United Gold Fields, and the widely publicised Burmah Oil case.

2. *European Continental Shelf Guide 1979* (London: Offshore Promotional Services, 1979), p. 331.

3. Steven N.S. Cheung, 'Transaction Costs, Risk Aversion, and the Choice of Contractual Arrangements', *The Journal of Law and Economics*, II, 1 (April 1969), pp. 23-42.

4. In addition to Cheung, 'Transaction Costs', and Dam, *Oil Resources*, see Paul H. Rubin, 'The Theory of the Firm and the Structure of the Franchise Contract', *The Journal of Law and Economics*, 20 (1977), pp. 223-35, and John Umbeck, 'A Theory of Contract Choice and the California Gold Rush', *Journal of Law and Economics*, 20 (October 1977), pp. 421-37.

5. The author knows of one such example in the British sector. Here an American independent is producing small quantities of a poor grade oil and has had difficulties with the British Inland Revenue Service as to the oil's proper 'value'.

6. R.F. Hayllar and R.T. Pleasance, *UK Taxation of Offshore Oil and Gas* (London: Butterworths, 1977), pp. 103-5.

7. Ibid., pp. 153-4. See p. 153 for definition of guidelines for such corporate loans.

8. See Dam, *Oil Resources*, pp. 137-41.

9. The use of participation as a means of control is a much overlooked topic. An excellent general treatment is that of Edith T. Penrose, 'Ownership and Control: Multinational Firms in Less Developed Countries' in G.K. Helleiner (ed.), *A World Divided* (Cambridge: Cambridge University Press, 1976), pp. 147-77.

10. Ibid., p. 170.

11. This point is made in a very telling manner by Dam, *Oil Resources*, pp. 134-5.

12. Interview, Department of Economic Planning, The Hague, August 1977.

PART THREE

THE UK OFFSHORE

4 'MARGINAL' FIELDS — HIGH-COST FIELDS IN A BRITISH POLICY CONTEXT

4.1. Introduction

The industry policy statement was unequivocal: 'Most new fields in the small and medium categories will not be developed', it stated, 'if the Petroleum Revenue Tax is levied. The industry can foresee no likelihood of a reduction in exploration and development costs in the near future nor a rise in crude oil prices in real terms. There will be less and less incentive to explore for smaller fields'.[1]

How does the oil industry view high-cost fields in practice? Thus far, discussion of industry preferences and government policies has been somewhat theoretical. Evidence is needed to support the contentions of Chapters 2 and 3.

High-cost — or in British offshore parlance 'marginal' — fields have been the topic of negotiations more than once. The United Kingdom Offshore Operators Association, the source of the industry policy statement above, has both discussed the problem of 'marginal' fields repeatedly with the British Government and utilised the topic in public debate. The issue to which the statement was addressed was the introduction of the Petroleum Revenue Tax (PRT) in 1975. Yet, again and again the theme recurs. If Britain is to have self-sufficiency, policies on high-cost fields must be changed. The theme is only slightly different with regard to British gas fields. The 'Northern Lobe' of the West Sole Field, Dudgeon Field and so forth will not be developed until the industry receives a better (higher) price for natural gas. (Implied in the statement is that the price of gas from fields already in production should be higher as well.)

Government circles give one a very different impression. Here opinion is that there is no such thing as a 'marginal' field, that all fields called 'marginal' by the industry are quite profitable, and that the industry is really desirous of getting something for nothing.

How do these divergent opinions occur? Is the industry really interested in developing high-cost fields; or are the oil companies attempting to get 'something for nothing'? In Chapter 3 the nature of the North Sea licence was discussed — both in terms of the contract regarding conditions of access and in terms of the inclusion of discretionary economic incentives. In contrast to the Danish case where the focus is on the access provisions, what is of interest here is the British system of discretionary economic incentives. How have these incentives originated? To what degree are they needed to procure the development of oil and natural gas? These are the questions asked in this and the next two chapters.

4.2. The Fields

Alwin, Andrew, Argyll, Auk, Beryl, Claymore, Cormorant, Dunlin, Heather, Hutton, Maureen, Montrose, and Thistle; Amethyst, Ann, Big and Little Dotty, Dudgeon, the 'North Lobe' of West Sole, Rough, Scram, and Shawn: those familiar with the North Sea will recognise this as a list of oil and gas fields (respectively) within the United Kingdom sector. These fields have something else in common: they have all at one time or another been designated 'marginal' fields.

The first list is of the oil fields that were called 'marginal' by the oil industry when it entered negotiations with the British Government regarding the Oil Tax Act of 1975. Some of these fields are quite small; Argyll, for example, has estimated reserves of 30 million barrels. Some of them are quite sizeable; Dunlin, Thistle, and Claymore have estimated reserves of over 500 million barrels apiece, and Beryl A's reserves alone amount to around 400 million barrels.[2]

The combined reserves of these fields, large and small, accounted for about 37 per cent of British oil under development as of late 1978. The gas fields listed are a series of smaller structures in the southern British North Sea. Some of them, not unlike the oil fields mentioned, are currently (or were previously) under commercial development: Big Dotty, Little Dotty and Rough. Many more have not been touched. Still others are extensions of fields which have not yet been developed, the 'North Lobe' of the West Sole field for example. (There are also extensions of the Hewett and Indefatigable fields which could be developed.) The Riggs National Bank Study of August 1977 listed no fewer than 30 separate discoveries, fields which may be developed in the shorter or longer term. The significance of these reserves is difficult to judge. Many have not been delineated so that guesses in this regard could well be off the mark. Still, if we define these fields as comprising the 'probable' and 'possible' reserve categories in the figures provided by the British Government for fields under contract to the British Gas Corporation plus all the other reserves in the southern North Sea, they contain a very hefty 226 billion cubic metres. This amount is 51 per cent of the reserves contained in proven fields under contract within the southern British North Sea area and about 35 per cent of all the resources in the southern area,[3] and these may be conservative estimates.

Although these fields have all been described as 'marginal', the political policy contexts within which they have been designated 'marginal' are significantly different. In the case of oil, the context was the discussion of rent capture, the Petroleum Revenue Tax introduced by the Oil Tax Act of 1975. For natural gas, the context was selling the gas reserves to a *de facto* if not *de jure* monopsonistic purchaser, the British Gas Council (later the British Gas Corporation). That the exploitation of oil should involve the question of rent 'capture' and that of natural gas, monopsony powers is not surprising. The different political economic issues involved in oil and gas exploitation are tied to the respective characteristics of the two fuels.

4.3. High-cost Oil and Gas Resources: The Different Issues

High-cost oil resources have been covered in general terms in Chapter 3. What is notable about oil is the ease of its transportation, refining, and distribution. The degree of multinational corporate control over each stage in this process has been widely discussed outside the confines of this book. Indeed, it has been argued in other contexts that it is not only necessary, but also desirable for oil firms to have a high degree of vertical integration.[4] Whether an oil field is judged 'marginal' or not is therefore very much a function of company preferences as well as the cost of developing the resource. This is true of natural gas as well, but when the natural gas is sold further to a monopsonistic purchaser, oil companies lose control of the fuel. How natural gas is marketed and where becomes the concern of the Gas Council, not of the companies. It is this loss of control which many companies found disturbing, particularly in the case of the southern British gas fields.

Furthermore, any discussion of natural gas quickly focuses on the issue of price. Although the price structure of crude oil is incredibly complex, there is arguably a 'world oil price', in reality a world oil price structure. No such structure exists for natural gas. The political economy of natural gas revolves around local markets at the end of the natural gas pipeline. To date there is no internationally recognised set of prices such as those of OPEC for crude oil. Nor is there a 'spot market' for natural gas. Throughout the history of a producing gas field, the buyer and the seller, if they are different entities, are tied to each other in a symbiotic relationship.

Such a symbiotic relationship in the case of the southern British Basin gas field consists of the various producing groups on the one hand and the British Gas Corporation on the other. Whether a gas field is judged 'marginal' or not can be dependent on this relationship. Neither the prevailing level of 'world' prices nor the existence of taxes really has much to do with the arguments of the oil companies that the gas fields mentioned in this context are 'marginal'. Rather, production from these fields depends on the BGC offering substantially better contract prices than has been the case to date.

Contract prices, particularly those offered in 1968-72, are therefore the focus of any study of British gas fields. Here the determinants of contract prices are highly unclear. It is often contended by commentators that the Gas Council in 1968-9 was interested in 'cost' prices and that the oil companies were more interested in 'market prices'. The definition of these terms has never been made precise to the author's knowledge.[5]

Spokesmen for the British Gas Corporation for example have denied any cost-price strategy, a contention which is inevitable given the widely different cost perspective of the companies involved and the difficulties of implementing such a tactic.

A focus on natural gas prices alone is highly unfortunate for two interconnected reasons. First, such a focus obscures the role of other vital issues such as 'load factor', 'production profile', price renegotiation clauses and contract length. This is perhaps natural in that so little has been written on natural gas negotiations and marketing for the general public. Secondly, such a focus ignores or plays down the enormous influence which the commercial considerations of the Gas Council had on the pricesetting. These two facets are interlinked in that the commercial considerations of the Gas Council were hardly expressed in terms of price alone, but in the general terms of field development. Indeed, one can argue that it was not price alone but the overall general terms on which Southern Basin gas could be produced which led to tension between the oil companies and the BGC. A focus on the 'rent' capture aspect of natural gas prices to the detriment of other factors completely ignores the fundamental nature of the Gas Council-oil company conflict.

4.4. 'Marginal' Fields: The Political Nature of the Problem

On the face of it, the issues behind the British discussions of 'marginal' fields are completely different for oil and gas fields. For oil the issues were (and are) fundamentally simple. The British Government, following the OPEC price increases of 1971-4, desired to implement a 'windfall' tax, a Petroleum Revenue Tax to assure the collection of the additional rent involved in North Sea oil production. The companies, for their part, were highly reluctant to acquiesce to such a tax. Largely through the United Kingdom Offshore Operators Association, they argued cogently that there were many marginal fields in the British North Sea necessary to fulfil British aims of self-sufficiency which would be made 'uneconomic' by the imposition of such a tax. Even today the issues of 'marginal' oil fields are largely those of the impact of rent collecting mechanisms on future production possibilities.

For southern British North Sea gas the issues are infinitely more complicated. Here it can be argued that the commercial considerations of natural gas marketing combined with a certain degree of British nationalism to render the cost of developing the gas fields discovered after 1964 high. The subsequent developments in oil prices, which soared in contrast to contractual gas prices for fields such as West Sole, Hewett, Leman, and Viking, has rendered further development of smaller fields in the area almost unacceptably high. The particular circumstances under which the Gas Council and the oil companies negotiated the gas contracts of 1968-72 are fundamental to an understanding of the marginality both of those fields as yet undeveloped and of undeveloped extensions of already developed gas fields.

These technical differences are very important. Yet even more crucial are the similarities. For both the Southern Basin gas fields and the North Sea oil fields, the argument that 'marginal' fields will not be developed unless some form of relief is granted constitutes a fulcrum from which the oil industry has persistently attempted to lever the government of the day to its point of view. The use of this fulcrum is the topic of this section. It is the fundamental characteristic of the British discussions over the fate of 'marginal' fields.

Notes

1. United Kingdom Offshore Operators Association, paper as quoted in *Noroil*, III (February 1975), pp. 17-18.
2. That is excluding an estimated 200-300 million barrels in Beryl North.

3. It should be noted that in terms of the resources of the entire British North Sea – including noticeably the reserves of the Frigg and Brent fields, the amount is considerably smaller – about 14.7 per cent of all the anticipated resources available to the United Kingdom. See Kevin Done, 'British Gas Wins Room to Manoeuvre', *The Financial Times* (1 December 1978), p. 8.

4. The most extreme proponent of this point of view is Paul Frankel. See his classic, *Essentials of Petroleum* (London: Chapman and Hall, 1949, 1969). For a contrasting point of view see M.A. Adelman, *The World Petroleum Market* (Washington, D.C.: The Johns Hopkins Press for Resources of the Future, 1972).

5. See Kenneth Dam, *Oil Resources: Who Gets What How?* (Chicago: The University of Chicago Press, 1976), pp. 83-6; Keith Chapman, *North Sea and Gas* (Newton Abbot: David & Charles, 1976), pp. 130-1. What is 'cost' price? Is it determined by average costs or by marginal costs – and how? What is 'market price'? Such a price can hardly be based on the price of liquefied natural gas. Neither could a 'market price' be based on prices elsewhere on the European continent, particularly in that the Gas Council was facing an enormous investment in distribution and transmission lines, in gas appliances, and in storage facilities. Generally, a case might be made that the price of natural gas should be equivalent therm for therm of the price of the oil product which it replaces. But even this argument has flaws in that oil products have widely varying price levels and serve widely differing markets.

5 BRITISH POLICY AND 'MARGINAL' FIELDS: THE CASE OF OIL

5.1. Introduction

It is perhaps significant that 'marginal' fields became an issue in the British political arena with the introduction of the Oil Tax Bill in the British House of Commons in November 1974. UKOOA (the United Kingdom Offshore Operators Association), the inter-industry group most concerned with offshore exploration and development policy, did not react at first. The bill was instead considered by the United Kingdom, Oil Industry Taxation Committee, an inter-industry group specially designed to analyse British taxation measures. This group, largely consisting of lawyers, studied the matter for a considerable period, finally reporting what the proposed bill would do to the oil companies' exploration and producing activities. 'When I found out what the proposals meant', declared one senior oil economist working with a large American Independent, 'I went to the director and explained it to him. His reaction was "we can't do business in this country under these conditions".'[1] This was the beginning of long and complicated negotiations.

Shortly after the introduction of the Oil Tax Bill, governmental bureaucrats were requested to define 'marginal' fields and to devise methods by which these fields might be taxed. The bureaucrats went to work. The exercise resulted in reams of computer 'print-out', all sorts of variations and sensitivity tests — but no satisfactory definition of the term 'marginal' field.

The British discussion of 'marginal' fields is closely tied to the discussion of the capture of the economic rent involved in oil field exploitation. Such a focus involved a bewildering sequence of events beginning in 1972 with the sensational revelations of the House of Commons Public Accounts Committee that British taxes were ill-designed for the purpose of capturing 'windfall' profits made on British fields, to a reconfirmation of a 60 per cent Petroleum Revenue Tax by the Conservative Government in the summer of '79. The major events in this period, culminating in the summer of 1979, are highlighted in Table 5.1.

The shifts in policy are remarkable. As early as 1972 there was talk of special oil taxes, yet it was not until after the OPEC price increases

Table 5.1: Chronology of Rent-capture Legislation — Oil Tax Act of 1975

Date	Institutions involved	Topic
Summer 1972	House of Commons Public Accounts Committee	Review of UK licensing policy leads to the revealing of omissions in oil tax policy
September 1972	Under-secretary Tuck, Department of Trade and Industry	Circular letter to oil companies ('Tuck letter') containing 12 policy points — including special taxes on oil profits
1973-4	OPEC price increases	
July 1974	White Paper of Labour Government	Declares government policy aim of increasing revenue from Continental Shelf
November 1974	Department of Energy	Introduction of Oil Tax Bill
December-March 1975	Department of Energy, government, UKOOA	Negotiations over the form of the forthcoming Oil Tax Act (OTA)
May 1975		Oil Tax Act of 1975 receives Royal Assent
Summer 1978	Department of Energy	In review of Oil Tax Act, the PRT is increased to 60% (from 45%), allowances and 'uplift' decreased. To take effect 1 January 1979
	UKOOA and companies	Protest against change in OTA and against licensing policy in general. Conservative Party sympathetic to these points of view
Winter 1978-Spring 1979	OPEC price increases (informal use of surcharges)	
May 1979	PC victory	Sweeping reforms of the BNOC, OTA, licensing policy promised
June 1979	OPEC price increases	Light North African crude reaches $23.00/bbl.
Summer 1979	Conservative Government	Reaffirm PRT at new 1979 levels

of 1973-4 that any bill was presented to the House of Commons. The terms of this bill were debated, then amended and finally enacted. Yet three years later, the Labour Government increased the Petroleum Revenue Tax levels to 60 per cent. This was repudiated by the Conservative Party then in opposition. When the Conservatives came to power in 1979 however, oil prices once again had been increased. It was a Conservative Government which reaffirmed the increases of the PRT.

If this seems all a bit confusing to the reader, he is not alone in his confusion.

For our analysis the events in Table 5.1 fall into three periods. The first period lasts from 1972 to the adoption of the Oil Tax Act in 1975; the second, largely an analysis of how the Oil Tax Act affected 'marginal' fields, covers the period until summer 1978; finally some of the issues which have arisen since summer 1978 are briefly analysed.

The analysis of high-cost fields in this context involves the answering of several questions. To what extent have high-cost resource considerations influenced British policy? Has this influence been beneficial? Have the oil companies really been interested in these high-cost fields? Finally, and perhaps most controversially, was the motivation behind the oil company pressure for exemptions from the PRT for 'marginal' fields, a desire to see these 'marginal' fields developed; or was it a desire to reduce the impact of oil taxes on the highly profitable projects which was the motivating force?

5.2. 'Marginal' Fields and the Question of Rent Capture: Prelude to Negotiations

While the names of the firms and the groups working in the North Sea are generally known, there is little public recognition of the various industrial organisations which represent the interests of these firms and these groups *vis-a-vis* the government. Of those who know about such interest group activity, few think of it as being both political as well as technical. Yet North Sea groups are well organised politically, and were so in 1974 when the Oil Tax Bill was first discussed.

This political organisation did not occur overnight. Early in the 1960s the British state tended to go to individual firms for information and advice, with BP and Shell perhaps consulted most. By 1973-4, however, the situation was considerably different. The United Kingdom Offshore Operators Association had taken the spotlight. Originally formed as the UK Offshore Operators Committee, the organisation's founding had preceded the 1964 act establishing the ground rules for British offshore policy. By the fourth licensing round, the group, now designated the UKOOA, was deeply involved in its advisory role to government policy-makers. UKOOA should be distinguished from two other oil industry groups also involved in policy-making, the Petroleum Industry Advisory Committee (PIAC) and the Oil Industry Taxation Committee (UKOIT). PIAC is concerned with downstream activities; its role is to provide industry viewpoints on refinery runs, product markets, and the like. UKOIT, as we have noted, deals with taxation at all levels. In contrast, UKOOA deals with the 'upstream' activities of the oil industry. The association nevertheless consists of a goodly number of committees concerned most notably with safety, engineering, environment, and legislation. Their work has not been inconsiderable. (It was UKOOA that stood behind the first inter-industry Offshore Pollution Liability Agreement of 1974, for example.)[2] Of these committees, by 1977 only one was designated as 'political' by the oil industry, the legislative committee, although the more 'technical' committees can, it might be argued, serve a political purpose in representing industry's views regarding technical matters to politicians.

The primary impetus for oil taxation reform, oddly enough, did not stem from the enormous price increases of 1973 and 1974, but rather from a series of hearings by the House of Commons' Public Accounts Committee. With the discovery of significant oil reserves in the British sector and with the initial oil price increases stemming from the OPEC negotiation rounds (resulting in theTehran-Tripoli Agreements), oil company interest in the British sector tended to increase. Unfortunately, the fourth round of licensing in the British sector was badly muddled. Of the 436 blocks offered, 421 through normal British licensing procedures and another 15 through an experimental block auction, 286 blocks were applied for, and 282 were awarded. The question arose as to whether the system of auctioning blocks off might not lead to better results than the alternative, the awarding of blocks on company pledges to explore them. In money terms the 15 auctioned blocks brought the Treasury about £37 million, roughly £2.5 million per block; the other 271 blocks went according to the work programme which companies were willing to implement, work programmes to the value of over £200 million or around £740,000 per block. The questioning into the practice of granting block licences against work programme pledges and into several other matters led the government to place North Sea policy under the surveillance of the House of Commons' Public Accounts Committee.[3]

The hearings brought to light some serious omissions in British royalty and taxation policy. Testimony from the Department of Trade and Industry supported the view that the government could gain considerable revenue by 1980 from the capturing of North Sea rents. Inland Revenue witnesses differed sharply. By using transfer prices for crude oil, and building up allowances on various capital items, tankers and the like, the UK affiliates of the oil companies together could utilise some £1.5 billion in historic losses, together with £500 million of annual trading losses. These threatened, when offset against North Sea oil and gas revenues, to reduce the total government tax revenue to zero. 'Indeed, even in the period 1965 to 1972, UK registered oil companies had paid only one-half million pounds in corporation taxes.'[4]

These revelations sparked a minor political furore. In September, the oil companies received a letter from Under-secretary Tuck of the Department of Trade and Industry outlining a dozen points where changes in legislation would be made. Ironically, the date set for introducing this legislation was mid-October 1973, by which time the first of many OPEC price increases was on the way. These increases made revision of government legislation more imperative than ever. The issue became less one of 'plugging' loopholes, than of capturing 'excess' rent. Tuck's promised legislation was postponed for 13 months. A White Paper issued by the Department of Energy in July 1974, spelled out the government's intention to 'secure a fairer share of the profits for the nation and to maximise the gain to the balance of payments' on the one hand while, on the other, to allow the oil companies a suitable 'return' on their investment.[5]

The groundwork had been well prepared for the Oil Tax Bill of November 1974. Nevertheless, the original proposal had little that would resemble the Oil Tax Act of 1975. It proposed to levy a Petroleum Revenue Tax on production, field by field. Originally, a figure as high as 60 per cent was mentioned, but lower figures were also suggested early on. This tax would be charged in addition to the normal corporation tax, but the PRT could be deducted before payment of the latter (unlike the process in Norway). There were some interesting changes with regard to interest payments on project loans. The reader may recall that these interest payments can reduce the incidence of corporate tax significantly, one of the features of the licensing costs discussed in Chapter 3. Interest payments while still deductible before payment of corporate taxes were not deductible before payment of the new PRT. Here rather than allow interest deductions before taxes, the depreciation of capital equipment was increased to 150 per cent of the value of the equipment — a so-called 'uplift' of 50 per cent. Other features incorporated in later versions of the bill and in the Oil Tax Act itself were absent in this early version. There were no oil allowances; there were no signs of the 'tapering' provisions. These features were to result from a round of negotiations between government and industry.

When the oil companies finally concluded they would be hard put to live with the proposed legislation, time had become limited. The government insisted they make their representations by early January. Mr J. Reynolds of Conoco organised and chaired a special UKOOA committee to draft a response. Work in the committee, the Industrial Committee, was thorough. Unlike the other committees in UKOOA, it was composed of company heads. They had very good access to leading figures in the government, both individually and collectively: Sidney Dell, Lord Balogh and others. Nevertheless, the committee had to work through New Year's Day to meet the government's deadline.

The committee's response to the proposed Oil Tax Bill for the first time highlighted the role of 'marginal' fields. It was generally thought that the government officials had focused their tax proposal on capturing the rent (or windfall profits) from the major North Sea fields. Their proposals were based on a 'model' field which many in the committee recognised as the Piper field — a very profitable project.[6] Clearly Montrose, Heather, Hutton, Alwyn and many other fields did not fit into the Piper class. The committee prepared a draft meant in part to convince the government of this point. This was the first emphasis on 'marginal' fields. Although never released in full, extracts of the UKOOA response including the main arguments were published in the respected Norwegian journal *Noroil* (February 1975).

The response dwelt on the number of 'smaller and medium sized' fields which were being discovered in the North Sea, and the impact the PRT would have on these fields. It also argued that such a burden would make it difficult to explore for and develop anything but extremely large fields.

The points about small and medium sized fields were both general and particular. The report is quoted by *Noroil* as declaring:

> Analysis of the UK North Sea fields and their reserves found to date shows that more than 50% of total reserves occur in medium and small field categories.
>
> Development of similar sedimentary basins elsewhere in the world suggests that the percentage of small and medium fields will tend to increase by the time the North Sea is fully explored.[7]

This declaration was supported with data (see Table 5.2) defining what the UKOOA meant by large, medium, and small fields. The response then pointed out that cost increases in the development of fields already planned meant that many of the estimated 14,000 million barrels of oil reserves which might have been forthcoming, were now of questionable value. 'Because of sudden changes in economic climate

Table 5.2: UK North Sea Fields Classified by Size

Size of fields (millions bbls.)	Total reserves (millions bbls.)	Percentage reserves by size of field
Large (600 and over)	6,300	45
Medium (350-600 and over)	3,000	21
Small (100-350)	4,700	34

Source: Quoted in *Noroil*, III, 2 (February 1975), p. 17.

in the past year, and specifically the anticipated negative impact of PRT, many of the North Sea fields will not be economic.'[8]

These general points were elaborated in more detail. A rough sensitivity analysis of four model fields was included to show the impact of a 25 per cent PRT and a 45 per cent PRT. (We will note this analysis in our discussion of the PRT rates proper.) A more threatening tone was struck with reference to oil fields which might not be developed under a PRT system:

> Some small fields could not be considered economical and others economically marginal if development was starting at today's construction costs with the additional burden of PRT. These include Alwyn, Andrew, Argyll, Auk, Beryl, Claymore, Cormorant, Dunlin, Heather, Hutton, Maureen, Montrose, and Thistle.[9]

After pointing out the onshore effects of a decline in offshore exploration and production, the industry response concluded its analysis of small fields by stating simply, 'The Government and industry need a taxation system which will not discourage exploration for and development of these smaller and marginal fields.'[10]

5.3. Marginal Fields and the Capture of Rent: The Negotiated Results

Given the force of the industry representations, it was not too surprising that in the ensuing months the government modified the proposed Oil Tax Act considerably. The result was announced on 26 March 1975. The PRT was set at 45 per cent, but there were a number of 'marginal field safeguards'. As the Treasury indicated in its press brief: 'the Government have indicated from the start that it would be necessary to design provision to ensure that the rate of return on marginal fields was sufficient to encourage their full development.'[11] Although these discretionary and non-discretionary 'safeguards' were for the purpose of benefitting 'marginal' fields, it was readily admitted that the provisions would also benefit all fields by exempting part of their revenue from PRT. Who did benefit from the negotiated results announced in March? To what degree did 'marginal fields' really figure in the discussions?

Negotiations focused on a number of specific items. There were discussions about the rate of taxation which any PRT should entail. Secondly, there was the issue of an 'oil allowance', which was to benefit 'marginal' fields proportionately more than 'economic' fields. The question of what the 'uplift' should be to compensate oil firms for their loss of interest payment deductions for PRT purposes came up as well. The famous tapering provision was created and finally the government agreed to remit royalty payments on a 'discretionary basis'.

(a) The Discussion of Petroleum Revenue Tax Rates

Disagreement over PRT rates was a fundamental bone of contention between government and industry throughout the negotiations. The oil industry favoured a lower PRT: 25 per cent rather than 45 per cent. This was indicated in the industry's January 1975 response, a sensitivity study demonstrating what a 45 per cent PRT would do to the profitability of model fields of 30, 40, 50 and 60 million tons of recoverable reserves. The results, reproduced in Table 5.3 are somewhat misleading, however. In part, this was due to the method by which the industry calculated cash outflows and inflows: all investments were over a seven-year period; the timing of cash inflow was not specified; the parameter of the investment costs were not made precise. In part, this was due to the inflation of capital costs (by ten per cent *per annum*) and of operating costs (by five per cent *per annum*), while holding all revenue at constant prices.[12] Under these circumstances the 'Profit/ investment' category in Table 5.3 does not mean very much.

Why didn't the government accept the oil industry's arguments for a lower 25 per cent PRT rate? The answer must be found in the overall compromise which was struck, particularly in the adoption of the one million ton *per annum* oil allowance. This was then thought to be of more benefit to smaller marginal fields.

Yet the government's failure to incorporate the oil industry's point of view into its legislation might also have resulted from the marked contrast between the industry's sensitivity analysis and what the government knew about the fields. First, development plans were

Table 5.3: Returns to Fields of 30, 40, 50 and 60 Million Tons Recoverable Reserves. Sensitivity Analysis Examining Effect of No PRT and 25 and 45 PRT Rates at Prices of 9, 12 and 15 US Dollars per Barrel

Reserves (MMT)	I 30			II 40			III 50			IV 60		
PRT Rate (%)	0	25	45	0	25	45	0	25	45	0	25	45
$9/B Crude price												
Profit/investment ratio	0.48	0.42	0.37	0.77	0.64	0.53	1.03	0.83	0.68	1.43	1.13	0.89
Present Value (£mm)												
10% discount	8.3	2.2	(2.6)	48.6	33.9	22.1	85.3	62.4	44.0	126.2	93.2	66.8
15% discount	(18.5)	(22.5)	(25.8)	10.5	0.6	(7.4)	36.4	20.9	8.5	62.0	40.1	22.6
DCF return (%)	11	10	9	17	15	14	21	19	17	23	21	19
Government take (%)	66	70	74	64	70	75	63	79	76	62	70	76
$12/B Crude price												
Profit/investment ratio	1.00	0.81	0.66	1.42	1.13	0.89	1.81	1.42	1.10	2.34	1.81	1.39
Present Value (£mm)												
10% discount	72.5	52.8	37.2	129.8	96.9	70.7	182.9	137.7	101.6	239.0	180.0	132.8
15% discount	30.0	16.6	5.9	71.0	48.4	30.3	108.3	77.3	52.5	143.9	103.8	71.9
DCF return (%)	20	18	16	26	23	21	30	27	24	33	29	26
Government take (%)	62	69	75	61	69	76	61	79	76	60	69	76
$15/B Crude price												
Profit/investment ratio	1.51	1.19	0.94	2.07	1.62	1.25	2.58	2.00	1.53	3.24	2.49	1.89
Present Value (£mm)												
10% discount	135.2	101.3	74.0	210.2	158.7	117.0	278.7	210.6	156.2	350.2	264.3	195.3
15% discount	77.0	53.6	34.9	130.6	94.5	66.0	178.7	131.1	93.2	223.8	165.1	118.3
DCF return (%)	28	25	22	34	30	27	38	34	30	40	36	32
Government take (%)	61	69	76	60	69	76	60	69	76	59	69	76

Source: *Noroil* (February 1975), pp 21-2.

already well underway for many of the 'marginal' fields, plans based on completely different calculations from those in the industry's sensitivity analysis. Secondly, there was good reason to doubt whether the 45 per cent PRT with a 150 per cent uplift, the original government proposal, would really have rendered these fields uneconomic. This is borne out by the subsequent development of these 'marginal' fields. Table 5.4 shows the net present value (NPV) of eight fields based on a 150 per cent uplift and tax rates of 25 per cent and 45 per cent respectively. Also shown are the differing Internal Rates of Return.

These were all calculated by the author on the basis of figures current in 1977. These figures are included in the Appendix to this chapter. Although not strictly necessary, the figures were rendered comparable to those in Table 5.3. It is therefore assumed in Table 5.4 that operating costs increase at a compounded rate of five per cent *per annum*, capital costs at a compounded rate of ten per cent *per annum*; prices in contrast are held to $12 per barrel and are constant throughout. The base year is 1976.

With a $12 per barrel price, as shown in Table 5.4, the effect on all Internal Rates of Return is insignificant. For those 'marginal' fields on which the IRR would have been low in any case, most notably Heather, the impact of a 45 per cent PRT is only slightly negative. For a series of marginal fields – Montrose, Auk and Cormorant – all of which had around 20 million tons of reserves or less, the IRR figures are the same or slightly higher than for much larger 30 million tons fields in the industry analysis, as can be seen from Table 5.5. With the exception of Heather, where the IRR would be 12.8 per cent and 11.1 per cent respectively for a 25 per cent and a 45 per cent PRT system, the Internal Rates of Return for the smaller marginal fields have turned out to be significantly higher than the gloomy figures forecast by the industry in 1974.

It is probably safe to say that irrespective of whether the government had persevered with its original 45 per cent PRT across the board or not, most of the fields in Tables 5.4 and 5.5 would have been developed. Yet it is also equally likely that the heightened atmosphere of tension would have had a counterproductive effect as well. Given the economic consequences of the latter, the government negotiators probably acted wisely in deciding to pursue a conciliatory course. One significant compromise was that of the oil allowance.

(b) The Oil Allowance

The Oil Tax Act of 1975 contains a provision exempting the first one

Table 5.4: Effect of the Proposed 25 Per Cent PRT Rate and 45 Per Cent PRT Rate on Fields Designated 'Marginal' in 1974-5 (150 Per Cent Uplift, $12 per bbl. Oil in All Cases)

	Auk		Beryl	
Proposed PRT rate (%)	25	45	25	45
IRR (%)	40.7	35.3	40.3	36.2
NPV at 15%	$62.1m	$44.6m	$376.8m	$275.9m
NPV at 20%	$43.6m	$35.3m	$242.7m	$171.1m
	Claymore		Cormorant	
Proposed PRT rate (%)	25	45	25	45
IRR (%)	26.6	23.5	25.3	22.7
NPV at 15%	$206.0m	$114.4m	$154.7m	$104.5m
NPV at 20%	$93.6m	$45.7m	$65.2m	$30.4m
	Dunlin		Heather	
Proposed PRT rate (%)	25	45	25	45
IRR (%)	21.8	19.6	12.8	11.1
NPV at 15%	$172.7m	$106.3m	−$25.9m	−$44.1m
NPV at 20%	$37.3m	−$8.0m	−$66.5m	−$77.5m
	Montrose		Thistle	
Proposed PRT rate (%)	25	45	25	45
IRR (%)	25.0	22.3	30.5	27.2
NPV at 15%	$87.6m	$57.4m	$455.7m	$318.1m
NPV at 20%	$35.9m	$14.9m	$253.5m	$155.4m

*All investment and production profiles based on Appendix 5B. Capital costs from based year 1976 assumed to increase at a compounded rate of 10%. Operation costs assumed to increase at a compounded rate of 5%.

Table 5.5: Group I (30 Million Tons) Fields Compared with 'Marginal Fields' of 20 Million Tons or Less

	Fields							
	Group I example		Auk		Cormorant		Montrose	
Proposed PRT rate (%)	25	45	25	45	25	45	25	45
IRR (%)	18	16	40.7	45.3	25.3	22.7	25	22.3
NPV at 15% (mill.)*	16.6	5.9	25.8	18.6	64.5	43.5	36.5	24.0

*In US dollars at £1.00 = $2.40.

million tons of oil produced from a field from the Petroleum Revenue Tax. This provision was a direct outcome of the PRT discussions, the result of an idea advanced by the UKOOA. The first UKOOA *demarche* of January, as cited by *Noroil*, makes no mention of the provision. As advanced by the industry in the winter of 1975, this allowance was not to be a per field allowance; it was to be a per platform allowance. The implications of this argument are significant. To argue that one million tons was to be adempted from PRT *per annum* for ten years on a field-by-field basis tends to favour the small one-platform fields (although it also undoubtedly helps the larger fields). To argue that one million tons per *platform* was to be allowed tax free definitely places large highly profitable multiple-platform projects such as Ninian, Brent and the Forties in a much stronger position. That this was the precise intention of the UKOOA committee is arguable. It is likely that the industry, concerned about the steadily rising costs of the mammoth platform systems of the central British North Sea, were looking for another form of tax relief. It is none the less curious that the oil industry has justified the oil allowance as being particularly beneficial to smaller 'marginal' fields. That this was the case in the end was not due to oil industry arguments. Rather the consequence of the industry arguments was to allow a large four-platform field four million tons of oil *per annum* exempt from PRT and a smaller 'marginal' one-platform field only one million tons *per annum*.

Yet whatever the merits and demerits of the UKOOA's case, it was evidently rejected. A one million ton oil allowance was allowed free of PRT *per annum* for a period of ten years in the provisions of the Oil Tax Act.

(c) Depreciation and 'Uplift'

If the UKOOA's intent was to favour large economic fields, not small marginal fields, through the oil allowance, it had no such worries about the depreciation 'uplift' for the PRT. The uplift favoured all fields, 'marginal' and highly profitable alike. We have noted that the uplift, an increasing of depreciation to 150 per cent of the value of the capital equipment on a project was a palliative for the fact that interest payments would not be deductible for PRT purposes. The government's proposal of a 50 per cent uplift was used in the *Noroil* analysis of February 1975. This did not mean that the UKOOA thought the uplift was sufficient for their purposes. The UKOOA members all agreed that the government's original proposal was too low a compensation for the loss of interest deductions. Smaller firms dependent on loans available only at higher interest rates pushed for a 100 per cent uplift — the depreciation of 200 per cent of the value of platform, wells, pipelines installed on a field. The bigger firms did not disagree although their support for a 100 per cent uplift was reportedly 'lukewarm'. The compromise arrived at, a 75 per cent uplift (175 per cent depreciation) should not be understood as a government 'gift'. (A nine per cent loan with three per cent principal repayment per year takes only seven years before the cumulative interest is equal to 75 per cent of the original principal.) This solution had the further benefit of being 'free' and could be applied wholly to the initial years of a project thereby increasing the 'net-of-tax return' early in the life of a field. This allowed considerable 'front-end loading', an important factor in oil field economics especially regarding the Internal Rate of Return. It did not, however, particularly favour 'marginal' fields over other fields.

(d) The 'Tapering Provision'

This provision is perhaps the only one directly to benefit both small and 'marginal' fields. The oil industry was interested in placing a 'floor' under the amounts the Petroleum Revenue Tax could collect. The floor they favoured was adopted; if in any given year the income from a field was less than 30 per cent (after deduction of royalties, operating costs and oil allowances) of the total historic capital costs incurred, the Petroleum Revenue Tax would be refunded. For a truly 'marginal' field, irrespective of whether there were oil allowance provisions or not, this feature clearly provided relief. It also ensured the oil industry of a corresponding safety net for more economic fields should the price of crude decline world-wide. Yet while the 30 per cent base provided security for 'marginal' projects, its counterpart, a provision that only 80 per cent of the difference between the 30 per cent base and the income of the field would be collected in any one year, in effect placing a ceiling on the PRT 'take' of the government, had a two-edged effect. While it placed a ceiling on the 'take' from 'marginal' fields such as Heather, it also put a limit on government income from the highly profitable projects such as the Forties field.[13] According to industry sources, the tapering provisions were a direct result of the period of government-industry negotiation. The idea of an 80 per cent limit to revenue collections over and above the 30 per cent historical capital expenditure apparently originated in government circles.

(e) Discretionary Refund of Royalties

Arguably, the provision with potentially the most positive effect on revenues is the discretionary refund of royalties. The reason can readily be appreciated. Royalty is calculated on the basis of the value of oil or gas at the well-head, calculated before any significant cost deductions. A refund on royalty therefore has the maximum effect on profitability. On the other hand, royalty is relatively easy to collect; it is payable almost immediately, unlike corporation taxes, within two months after every six-month period. Curiously, although mentioned in the publicity surrounding the Oil Tax Act, the discretionary power to refund royalty payments was not included in that Act but in the Petroleum and Submarine Pipelines Act,[14] passed in the same year.

The existence of this possibility has presented government bureaucrats with a monumental headache. 'Every unoccupied accountant or restless mind in the industry writes of possible government guidelines for the implementation of the royalty discretionary clause,' commented one bureaucrat to the author. 'We spend an inordinant amount of time analysing these ideas and reporting on them to our bosses.' One idea known to have been explored subsequent to the 1974 negotiations was to link royalty refunds to the 'Capex'-provision, the 'tapering provision' mentioned previously. Here should the profitability of a field fall below the floor set by the tapering provision (30 per cent of historical capital expenditures), not only the PRT but also the royalty sums would be refunded. This suggestion would undoubtedly reinforce the profitability of many fields, not only 'marginal' ones, but also those characterised by declining production rates late in their producing lives.

5.4. 'Marginal' Fields and the Oil Tax Act of 1975 — Some Retrospective Conclusions

What ultimate role did 'marginal' fields play in the OTA negotiations? The answer to this question must remain tentative. Still some conclusions would appear justified.

Overall, by the criteria of what the government originally set out to do, there can be little doubt that the companies wound up with a great deal. Table 5.6 shows that for those marginal fields chosen from the industry's list, the Oil Tax Act significantly improved their Internal Rates of Return not only in relation to the government's original proposals, *but also in relation to the original 25 per cent counter-offer by the industry*! In six of the eight cases examined the OTA gives the companies a better deal than that for which they had originally asked. For one of the remaining two, Thistle, the values are basically unchanged. Only for Beryl is the DCFR appreciably lower with the Oil Tax Act (37.4 per cent), than with the companies' original 25 per cent PRT counter-proposal. Clearly, in terms of the original government proposals, the Oil Tax Act was a suboptimal result.

Table 5.6: The Industry's 25 Per Cent PRT, the Original Governmental 45 Per Cent PRT, and the 1975 Oil Tax Act Provisions (OTA) — The Results Compared (Price = $12.00/bbl.)

	Auk			Beryl		
Proposed PRT rate (%)	25.0	45.0	OTA	25.0	45.0	OTA
IRR (%)	40.7	45.3	45.0	40.3	36.2	39.7
NPV at 15%*	$62.1m	$44.6m	$75.4m	$376.8m	$275.9m	$368.0m
NPV at 20%*	$43.6m	$29.4m	$54.4m	$242.7m	$171.1m	$213.4m

	Claymore			Cormorant		
Proposed PRT rate (%)	25.0	45.0	OTA	25.0	45.0	OTA
IRR (%)	26.6	23.5	26.8	25.3	22.7	25.6
NPV at 15%*	$206.0m	$114.4m	$212.8m	$154.7m	$104.5m	$177.1m
NPV at 20%*	$96.3m	$45.7m	$100.3m	$65.2m	$30.4m	$70.4m

	Dunlin			Heather		
Proposed PRT rate (%)	25.0	45.0	OTA	25.0	45.0	OTA
IRR (%)	21.8	19.6	23.4	12.8	11.1	14.1
NPV at 15%*	$172.7m	$106.3m	$231.9m	−$29.9m	−$44.1m	−$10.5m
NPV at 20%*	$37.3m	−$8.0m	$77.1m	−$66.5m	−$77.5m	−$56.8m

	Montrose			Thistle		
Proposed PRT rate (%)	25.0	45.0	OTA	25.0	45.0	OTA
IRR (%)	25.0	22.3	26.6	30.5	27.2	29.6
NPV at 15%*	$87.6m	$57.4m	$107.1m	$455.7m	$318.1m	$413.6m
NPV at 20%*	$35.9m	$14.9m	$49.6m	$253.5m	$155.4m	$222.9m

*All net present value figures are in millions of US dollars. All assumptions behind the figures are the same as in Table 5.4.

Yet the results could have been worse. The Oil Tax Act should also be seen in conjunction with the profitability of major fields, fields which were not 'marginal' by the oil companies' own admission. To the extent that the UKOOA negotiators may have wished to utilise 'marginal' fields arguments as a 'Trojan Horse' to reduce the government's PRT citadel through cunning, they were unsuccessful. The best example of this Trojan horse strategy was the industry argument for allocating the one million ton exemption to platforms rather than fields. We have noted previously that such a provision as that favoured by the UKOOA would have favoured the larger multi-platformed fields. What if the government had given in on this demand? Table 5.7 shows the possible results of such a surrender. It demonstrates the effects of two scenarios to contrast with that of the Oil Tax Act. The first might be called the optimum company scenario, a 25 per cent PRT with a 100 per cent uplift and a per platform allowance (Scenario A). The second (Scenario B) demonstrates the effect of a per platform allowance on the PRT and uplift established by the Oil Tax Act. As can be seen, the impact of the uplift and the per platform allowance is minimal in the case of Auk and virtually non-existent with Heather. The most interesting case is that of the Forties field. Here, depending on the scenario, a per platform allowance would have lifted the Internal Rate of Return from around 35.2 per cent to between 36.7 and 37.8 per cent. Nor is this impact confined to Internal Rates of Return; the present value of the project discounted by 15 per cent increases by 13 or 20 per cent depending on the alternative scenario.

Although these scenarios contain a speculative element, they

Table 5.7: Oil Tax Act 1975 and Alternative Scenarios*

	Fields					
Scenarios	Auk		Heather		Forties	
	IRR (%)	NPV at 15%	IRR (%)	NPV at 15%	IRR (%)	NPV at 15%
Oil Tax Act (OTA)	44.5	$75.4m	14.1	−$10.5m	35.2	$1,087.0m
Scenario A (200 % depreciation/ 25% PRT)	40.9	$62.1m	12.8	−$29.9m	37.8	$1,323.6m
Scenario B (per platform allowance otherwise as with OTA)	44.5	$75.4m	14.1	−$10.5m	36.7	$1,240.0m

*Assumptions: as with Tables 5.4 to 5.6.

demonstrate the very real danger of the Trojan horse strategy. Had the government accepted the 'marginal' fields arguments uncritically, it would have in fact granted relief which would have benefitted all fields, 'marginal' and highly economic alike.

'Marginal' fields, it might reasonably be argued, entered the PRT negotiations less from an intrinsic interest in them by either government or industry as from an opening gambit in a complicated chess game. Ultimately, only the tapering CAPEX provision and the discretionary refunding of royalties can be said to have direct relevance to the development of future high-cost sources of oil (and gas, for all contracts signed after 31 May 1975).

That the Oil Tax Act negotiations resulted in a somewhat less than satisfactory outcome, given the goals of government and of industry, should not surprise us. Any outcome of negotiations of this sort tends toward compromise. That this compromise was highly unsatisfactory from the government's point of view would subsequently emerge. In the summer of 1978, the Department of Energy announced a revision of the Petroleum Revenue Tax. Another chapter was about to begin.

5.5. 1978-9, 'Marginal' Fields Again — A Case of *Deja Vu*?

In November, 1978, three years after the OTA negotiations, *Noroil* published the contents of yet another UKOOA paper. This paper, 'The interdependence of government policies and industry effort in optimising the potential benefits of the UK continental shelf', was issued six weeks before the deadline for Sixth Round applications. It stressed the need for increased exploration and production to avoid shortfalls in British self-sufficiency by 1990. In contrast to Department of Energy predictions that two million barrels per day needed be produced in the mid-1990s, the UKOOA pointed out that existing fields would yield only 400,000 barrels per day.[15] To attain the projected end of two million barrels per day in 1990, the UKOOA paper argued that between 18 and 32 new fields would need to be developed. In order to develop these fields, two concessions were needed: 'The government's priority should be provision of sufficient acreage, including deep water areas to sustain the drilling of 60 to 95 exploration wells annually'; and secondly, 'The government must provide fiscal policies and incentives to ensure sufficient funds for exploration and reduce the threshold size of which fields become commercially exploitable.'[16] A final argument for the development of more liberal rent-capture policies was also made. If the minimum size of commercial fields were reduced from 250 million barrels to 150 million barrels, the additional oil to fulfil governmental self-sufficiency objectives would drop from 13,700 million barrels to 9,200 million barrels.[17]

What provoked this outbreak of oil industry concern? At issue were British licensing policies and a revised PRT system.

Ostensibly, the attack was directed at the number of blocks offered in the Sixth Licensing Round. Blocks were no longer being granted on the scale of the 1960s. The number of blocks offered were not the best of the remaining blocks either. They numbered 45 and were concentrated in the Channel area and further off the Shetlands. Lord Kearton, then chairman of the BNOC, and other critics were quick to counter-attack. Lord Kearton, in particular, noted the tendency of the oil companies to 'sit' on unrelinquished areas in the North Sea: 'The amount of acreage lying fallow from previous rounds is enormous', Kearton is reported as saying. 'The area that has never been explored using today's more modern technology is very big and far greater than what is being presented in the present Sixth Round.'[18] Indeed, there is considerable evidence to support Kearton's view, as has been noted in Chapter 4. Nevertheless, it was not enough to prevent Esso from ostentatiously passing in the Sixth Round out of protest. (It might be worth noting in this context that this company, together or with others held no fewer than 55 blocks, 22 of which had never been the subject of an exploration well.)

In reality, more may have been at stake than just the number of blocks. The criteria by which licences had been allocated had been getting progressively tougher. In the First Round (1964), five criteria were suggested by F.J. Errol, the Minister of Power in the Conservative Government:

> First, the need to encourage the most rapid and thorough exploration and economical exploitation of petroleum resources on the continental shelf. Secondly, the requirements that the applicant for a licence shall be taxed here. Thirdly, in cases where the applicant is a foreign-owned concern, how far British oil companies receive equitable treatment in that country. Fourthly we shall look at the programme of work of the applicant and also at the ability and the resources to implement it. Fifthly, we shall look at the contribution the applicant has already made and is making towards the development of resources of our continental shelf and the development of our fuel economy generally.[19]

By the Fifth Round the list had grown considerably longer and more precise. In addition to the ones mentioned above (that concerning rapid and thorough exploration and production was dropped), the criteria in 1977 included: the overall performance by the applicant with regard to other areas on the British Shelf held under licence, exploration 'relevant to the areas applied for', the degree to which the applicant had been willing on existing licences to concede to the state a majority share in discoveries already made, the degree to which the applicant subscribed to a Memorandum of Understanding between the Energy Secretary and the UKOOA to 'ensure that full and fair opportunity is provided UK industries to compete for orders of goods and services', and whether or not the applicant was willing 'to grant reasonable access to representatives of independent trade unions to his offshore installations. . .' Licences granted were conditional on the applicant's arriving at an operational agreement with the BNOC, and together they should work out an 'acceptable work program'. Fulfilment of these conditions had to be to the satisfaction of *both* the BNOC and the Secretary of State for Energy.[20] Unfortunately, it is impossible to ascertain the degree to which licensing conditions were responsible for the concern expressed by the oil industry.

Another irritant was the proposed revision of the Petroleum Revenue Tax. Policy-makers announced in August 1978 that beginning in 1979 PRT rates would be increased from 45 to 60 per cent; the tax-free exemption would fall from one million tons *per annum* to 500,000 tons; and the uplift for PRT purposes would be reduced to 35 per cent from 75 per cent (giving a PRT depreciation of 135 per cent rather than 175 per cent). There was a mix of cost perspective, rent capture, and timing in this move. British officialdom had long suspected that North Sea fields represented a much better investment than the oil companies had publicly admitted. Further the problems of enforcement (elaborated in Chapter 4) worked so that the British state was collecting nowhere near the 66-7 per cent proportion that had been an unannounced aim. Much of this shortfall was due to the impact of financing. (Of particular concern was the reported wide use of investments in one field as a pre-tax deduction from income from an already producing field — which meant that the British state was financing a substantial portion of the more recent projects.)

By November 1978, the detrimental aspects of this increase in PRT were somewhat superfluous, given the imminent rises in OPEC North African crudes. The impact of the changed PRT legislation on the Heather field (as posited in the Appendix to this chapter) with constant costs and prices is shown in Table 5.8. The retention of the 'tapering provision' considerably softens the impact of the new PRT rates. While there could be little doubt that the profitability of Heather fell, it did not do so significantly. The Finance Bill containing these adjustments never made it to the House of Commons, a victim of the Conservative victory. However, by June 1979, the implementation of the new measure was really inconsequential given the enormous increases in the price of OPEC oil. As can be seen from a $17 per barrel price, the profitability of Heather is not significantly affected *vis-a-vis* the old PRT system and a $14 per barrel price (Table 5.9). The subsequent decision of the Thatcher Government to shelve the reinstatement of the old PRT system was really quite academic, given that the price of North Sea crude could then be expected to increase to $22-4 per barrel.

Table 5.8: Heather Field under 1975 Assumptions — Impact of Increased Take ($14.00 bbl. Constant Prices and Costs)

	Profitability under revised PRT regime	Profitability under pre-'79 PRT regime
Internal Rate of Return (%)	19.3	20.84
Max. negative cash flow	$282m	$282m
Payout period (from initial investment)	5.65 years (out of 15 years total)	5.65 years (out of 15 years total)
Government take	$1,190.6m	$1,130.7m
Royalties	$324.6m	$324.6m
CT	$581.0m	$645.9m
PRT	$285.0m	$160.2m
Corporate take	$536.34m	$596.3m

Table 5.9: Heather under Contrasting PRT Regimes with Contrasting Prices

	Profitability at $14 per bbl. pre-'79 PRT regime	Profitability at $17 per bbl. under revised PRT regime
Internal Rate of Return (%)	20.84	22.83
Max. negative cash flow	$282m	$272.9m
Payout period (from initial investment)	5.65 years (out of 15 years total)	5.13 years (out of 15 years total)
Government take	$1,130.7m	$1,651.4m
Royalties	$324.6m	$394.2m
CT	$645.9m	$684.8m
PRT	$160.2m	$572.4m
Corporate take	$596.3m	$632.1m

5.6. 'Marginal' Fields and the Development Decision — The Case of British Oil

In Chapter 4 government policy was criticised for not tackling directly the problems associated with high-cost resources. In particular criticism was focused on the indirectness of government policies. This chapter provides support for the thesis. Through granting exemptions or preferences for 'marginal' fields, the UK authorities had to tread warily to avoid giving too much to the companies. The UKOOA through arguing its points for a per platform one million ton annual exemption, for higher uplifts, and the like, eventually gained their way on so many points that the original government proposals were almost unrecognisable (and the UKOOA received more than they asked for in the first place). Did these policies lead to the development of high-cost resources which would otherwise not have been developed? This is an unanswerable question. But there is room for doubt that any of the projects mentioned in the UKOOA January representations to the government were high-cost. It could be claimed that it was only because of the revised PRT that these fields were developed. On the other hand, it could be as convincingly argued that decisions were pending or already made on most of the fields. This point of view is supported when one looks at the minimal changes in profitability of most fields which revision of the original government proposals engendered. This point of view is further supported by comparisons of the various proposals in this chapter, notably that in Table 5.6.

Added to the fact that the industry may have gained rather too much in the winter-spring of 1974-5 were the problems of enforcement and administrative definition described in Chapter 4. The issues of the period 1975-8 were the minutiae of detail: assessing the value of the oil, checking corporate costs, judging 'real' versus 'nominal' government 'take'. The upshot of these considerations was the revision of the PRT in August 1978, a revision against which the industry protested vehemently. But where in all this were high-cost resources?

In spite of all the evidence, British authorities perceive a dilemma. On the one hand they perceive a domestic need for North Sea resources. Currently 40-50 per cent of all British energy comes from the North Sea as well as governmental hopes for eventual self-sufficiency. On the other hand, the exploitation of the oil on the Shelf yields a considerable rent, in 1975 not inappropriately called a 'windfall' profit. Clearly the British state must also act as a rent captor — a role which is perceived to be at odds with the development of high-cost ('marginal') resources. One end precludes the other. In 1978 the stakes were perceived in a slightly different manner; licensing policy was added to 'rent-capture', but the predicament was perceived in the same terms.

The perception that this dilemma exists is predicated on the assumption that through tax exemption and other breaks, North Sea groups can be induced to develop high-cost resources. Yet although evidence is hard to come by, there is a good deal in the 1974-5 government industry negotiations to indicate that the industry was using the arguments with regard to 'marginal' fields not because it was interested in such fields, but because the industry was interested in reducing the impact of the PRT on highly profitable fields.

This evidence coupled with the institutional viewpoint of this book points to another equally plausible possibility: the oil industry does not develop high-cost resources — not yet at any rate, although there are probably a few exceptions such as Heather. (One should note these exceptions are due more to error, accident and delay than to intent.) Yet so long as the perception of British authorities remains as it is, the need to develop 'marginal' fields enables the oil industry to provide bureaucrats with a useful windmill at which to tilt while giving industry increased profits on already profitable fields.

Notes

1. Interview, London, 27 September 1977.

2. The Offshore Pollution Liability Agreement (OPOL) was formed in response to rising environmental concern both on the part of government and citizenry. Under OPOL the oil companies operating in the British North Sea sector have agreed to accept strict liability of up to $16 million (US), half to pay for pollution damages and half to pay for the cost of remedial measures. OPOL has been since overtaken by a series of international agreements covering the problems of North Sea pollution.

3. See Kenneth Dam, *Oil Resources: Who Gets What How?* (Chicago: The University of Chicago Press, 1976), pp. 32-43 for a trenchant analysis of the predicament in which the lack of a British (vs. foreign) response for the 15 blocks placed the Ministry for Trade and Industry.

4. J.R. Morgan, 'The Promise and Problems of Petroleum Revenue Tax', Department of Economics, University of Surrey, unpublished paper, 1975, p. 6.

5. Ibid., p. 8.

6. Interviews with various corporate executives, London, September 1977. This has been denied by official interviewed in the Department of Energy.

7. *Noroil* III, 2 (February 1975), pp. 17-18.

8. Ibid.

9. Quoted in ibid., p. 18.

10. Ibid., p. 19.

11. Press Office, HM Treasury, 'Taxation of North Sea Oil' (26 March 1975), p. 4.

12. Nor was it specified whether these were current costs/prices or real costs/prices. An indication of how this accounting practice affects cash flows can be seen in the impact of such rates of inflation of capital and operating expenses of Dunlin field (see Appendix 5B). At constant costs and prices these are $850 million (including 50 millions for dismantling) and $520 million for capital and operations costs respectively. At the proposed rates of inflation, the costs become $1,244 million for capital costs and 867 millions for operating costs. This is $741 million added to costs and $741 million subtracted from revenues or a total $1,482 million difference in cash-flow terms. It would take an incredibly good investment to survive such treatment.

13. Heather only qualified for PRT one year in its productive life and that year the PRT take was limited by the 80 per cent provision. Forties qualified for PRT for the bulk of its producing history. The government 'take' from the Forties field is limited by the 'Capex' provision for all but its final years.

14. Section 41, para. 3.

15. 'Policy Options', *Noroil* (November 1978), p. 19.

16. Ibid.

17. Ibid.

18. Kevin Done, 'Licensing Policy under the Microscope', *Financial Times* (31 March 1979), p. 6.

19. As quoted in Dam, *Oil Resources*, p. 25.

20. *Development of the Oil and Gas Resources of the United Kingdom* (London: HMSO, 1977), p. 42.

6 'MARGINAL' FIELDS — THE CASE OF SOUTHERN NORTH SEA GAS

6.1. Introduction

As pointed out in Chapter 5, issues surrounding the development of natural gas fields are characterised by a symbiotic relationship between buyer and purchaser. This symbiotic relationship introduces another institutional element into the picture. In addition to intra- and inter-company dynamics, opportunity costs, preferences, group behaviour, and the like, a new factor comes into play, the conflict of institutional interests between the sellers of natural gas and the buyers. In the case of southern North Sea gas fields, this clash was caused by the divergent commercial interests of the groups selling the natural gas and the Gas Council (later the British Gas Corporation), a state-owned entity since the end of the Second World War. These interests have both strategic and tactical aspects.

The strategic aspects of natural gas bargaining are illustrated in Table 6.1. Here it is assumed (which is *not* always the case) that the oil companies selling the gas have considerable interests in the energy markets into which natural gas is to be introduced. Oil companies desire to sell natural gas not only to the highest bidder, a strategy which specifically excludes the *de facto* monopsony position of the BGC, but also to sell it on terms that will hurt their own competing oil product markets as minimally as possible. It matters little if natural gas displaces coal or hydro-electric power; it is of vital concern if natural gas displaces a highly profitable oil product. The purchaser's interests are to limit competition in natural gas bidding, to obtain it at the lowest possible price, and to introduce it into the most highly profitable sectors of the energy market in question. These strategic differences stand out clearest in the negotiation stage when the terms of introducing natural gas into domestic markets are worked out. Later in the relationship, tied together through the mutual quest for profit, the conflict of interests subsides but still remains in a somewhat more latent, dampened form.

These strategic interests are manifest in a multitude of tactical issues which, while they may seem somewhat minor, in the North Sea context have major implications. These are illustrated in Table 6.2. Each of these tactical issues must be settled at one time or another during the negotiations, in this case the period 1967-72. As can be seen, 'price' is

Table 6.1: The Institutional Relationship — Strategic Interests

Issue	Seller's interests	Purchaser's interests
Ability to offer gas to several national markets	Capability to induce purchaser competition for the natural gas on offer will maximise the profits of the seller	Capability to restrain purchaser competition for the natural gas on offer will enable its purchase at a somewhat lower price
Competition with oil products	Price should be set to enable orderly introduction of natural gas into the market without displacing more profitable oil product markets	Price should be set so that the more profitable portions of the energy markets will be open to the introduction of natural gas

not the only issue. Other institutional factors play a significant role, one generally unrecognised in the discussions about British North Sea gas. The cost to the companies of producing and selling natural gas can either be high or low depending on factors which those unfamiliar with the 'game' of gas negotiations seldom take into account. Price *per se* plays a role, but as important (or more so) are escalation clauses, production profile, load factor, length of contract, penalties, and the like.

Whether the terms of a natural gas contract are acceptable or not may depend less on a 1.2p per therm vs. a 1.4p per therm price than on a 60 per cent versus an 80 per cent load factor. At least on one occasion elsewhere in the North Sea, the actual *price* offered for natural gas has meant less than the other terms. (This involved the sale of Placid gas to Germany. Placid, an American company, refused an offer from the Dutch state — NAM corporation, Gasunie, preferring to sell its gas to Germany. The dispute in this case was over terms of delivery, *not* price, according to correspondence furnished to the author.)[1]

If 'price' alone does not determine whether a natural gas project is high-cost or not, then what does? Here, as with oil, it is opportunity cost. In this case the preferred markets were those on the European continent, markets which would have offered higher load factors, accelerated production, more advantageous escalation clauses. These markets had to be sacrificed in favour of the UK market, a market to which the oil companies felt forced to sell. Here the issue was not one of initial prices, but the terms of delivery to the Gas Council. In the southern North Sea the development of a gas field did not depend simply on oil company preferences and options. As important as these

Table 6.2: The Institutional Relationship — The Tactical Issues

Issue	Seller's interests	Purchaser's interests
Load factor*	High as possible. Reduction of cost of development; limits introduction of natural gas to more flexible energy markets	Low as possible. Eases marketing and guarantees entry into flexible energy markets
Production profile	Quick start-up of production will increase IRR on investment. High annual rate of production enables stronger cash flows	Slow start-up gives an opportunity to establish markets for gas domestically. Lower annual rate of production ensures longer period of selling gas
Price	High initial price ensures quick return on capital and limited inroads on oil product markets	Low initial price enables establishment of domestic gas markets
	Price escalation clause tied to oil products so that important product markets are not threatened	Price escalation clauses formulated to allow inroads on important oil product markets
	Base price increases at a constant compounded rate	Base price increases irregular and if regular increase arithmetically
Length of contract	Depending on terms as long/short as possible	Depending on the terms as long/short as possible
Penalties	'Take or pay'*	'Deliver or pay'*
Amount of gas covered in contract	Limited amounts as seller may hope for better terms later/is responsible for delivered amounts agreed upon	Unlimited amounts to enable better long term planning of gas marketing in the domestic economy

*Load factor, 'take or pay', 'deliver or pay', are defined in the text.

factors was the willingness of the Gas Council to take the supplies involved and the terms on which the supplies could be sold. In the later sixties and early seventies the opportunity cost was defined by the greater profitability of the European market. In later years, opportunity cost was the perception that if a group waited for old contracts to expire rather than producing new gas under old contract terms, it would procure considerably better terms.

6.2. The Conflict of the 1960s: The Position of the Parties

The amount of recrimination and bad feeling linked to the natural gas negotiations of 1967-71 is sufficient even today to render the objective situation at that time very difficult to ascertain. Briefly, however, the facts are as follows.

Natural gas was first discovered at West Sole in 1965. In the subsequent period of rapid exploration, additional fields were found, most notably Viking (discovered in 1965, but developed after its neighbours), Leman, Indefatigable, and Hewett; these are all illustrated in Map 6.1. Consequent to their discovery, negotiations about natural gas from these fields began between the groups of companies which had discovered the fields and the Gas Council. The latter occupied a *de facto* monopsony position.

Map 6.1: General Location Map of North Sea Fields

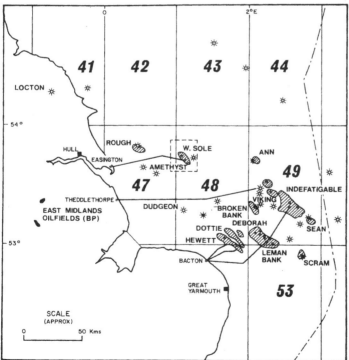

Source: J.B. Butler, 'The West Sole Gas-Field', in Austin W. Woodland (ed.), *Petroleum and the Continental Shelf of North West Europe*, vol. I (Essex: Applied Science Publishers, 1975).

According to the regulatory authority vested in the Minister of Power, all petroleum (including natural gas) discovered in the British area should be delivered onshore in the United Kingdom unless the Minister of Power consented to its delivery elsewhere. According to the Continental Shelf Act of 1964, neither a licence holder nor anyone else can supply natural gas to a buyer in the United Kingdom without the further consent of the Minister of Power. Here the Gas Council and the Area Boards had first option; although consent could be given to a third party *if* the Minister was satisfied (1) that the supply was for industrial purposes, and (2) that the Area Board concerned[2] had already refused a reasonable offer.[3]

The effect of these two statutory provisions was to place wide discretionary power in the hands of the Ministry of Power. To the oil companies, this discretionary power meant a *de facto* if not a *de jure* monopsony position for the Gas Council in the negotiations over gas price and delivery terms, if not over the manner in which the gas fields were developed. There is some substance to this point of view. All the contracts examined by Sullivan, virtually the only published authority on contract terms, contained juridical provisions strengthening the hands of the Gas Council after agreement was struck.

First, these contracts all contain a clause authorising the Gas Council to negotiate on behalf of the relevant Area Boards (the regional gas authorities), of which there were 12. Such a clause would prevent Area Boards' competitive bidding for natural gas supplies. That an offer by the Gas Council was deemed to be an offer by the relevant Area Boards greatly solidified the Gas Council's hold over the negotiating procedures.[4]

Secondly, and more importantly, each contract contained provisions that it was in conformance with Section 9 of the Continental Shelf Act — that section which juridically weakened the position of the Gas Council *vis-a-vis* the Minister of Power and the alternative industrial use of natural gas. The gas negotiation process generally begins with the exchange of contract drafts, the prospective purchaser and seller including in their respective drafts all the provisions deemed essential. Factors such as prices and the like come into the negotiating process somewhat later. It is quite possible, therefore, that the companies were required to include in their draft contracts clauses with respect to Section 9 before settling issues such as price, escalation clauses, load factor and so forth. Such a formulation would weaken their hand in a confrontation of interests with the Minister of Power acting as the ultimate arbiter. In any case, it is revealing that in interviews, those engaged in the negotiating process on the companies' behalf stated it was their impression that the Gas Council and the government of the day were one and the same.

The views of the Gas Council were necessarily different. While the companies tended to look at the Gas Council and the government in terms of complete unanimity on various issues of concern to the companies, members of the Gas Council are quick to maintain that the statutory discretion of the Minister of Power was a real power and in fact influenced the negotiations considerably. If the selling companies were unhappy with the price offered by the respective Area Boards, it must be remembered that they could ask the Minister for consent to supply the gas themselves directly to customers. Consent could be given if the Minister felt that the Area Board (Gas Council) had made an 'unreasonable' offer:

> It is important to note that reasonable price was entirely a matter for the Minister's judgement and he did not even have to disclose it to either of the contending parties. Furthermore the Minister retained his discretion to refuse consent even though he thought in his heart of hearts that the Gas Council had had a reasonable offer and refused it.[5]

The company points of view and those of the British Gas Corporation diverge considerably. With regard to the negotiations in the late sixties, the companies argue that British Gas had a *de facto* monopsony position; British Gas argues that it did not have a *de jure* monopsony position and largely ignores the *de facto* arguments. It is not unlikely that there is some truth to both positions. British Gas has gone on record as saying that the Minister of Power used his discretionary powers in the negotiations.[6] Yet through interviews the author ascertained that this happened only twice and 'the Government mucked it up both times'. On the other hand, it is doubtful whether the companies made as much use of the option to go to the government with the charge of unreasonable prices. In fact, British Gas executives contend that the companies have never formally done so. This is no doubt because the sale of natural gas directly to the British market would have entailed heavy capital outlays. More important from the companies' point of view at the time is that they were denied the possibility of selling at a higher price to another non-British market. Here there is record of an attempt by the Viking Group to market Viking gas to a continental group of purchasers, an attempt which was blocked by the British Government.[7] Throughout this period, company weakness resided in the inability to sell to multiple buyers, to the various Area Boards, rather than to the Gas Council itself, and in an inability to use continental gas prices as a lever to improve their contract terms with the Gas Council.

The results of the negotiations were therefore somewhat predictable. Yet why was the resulting conflict so bitter? Various authorities have stressed that this bitterness arose from a Gas Council attempt to capture the rent involved in natural gas exploitation.[8]

There are two ways of capturing rent, the argument runs: through reducing 'windfall' profits through taxes (the PRT and the oil fields of the North Sea) or through paying low prices for what is exploited (southern British gas fields). Profits undoubtedly entered the picture. But what an emphasis on rent capture involves is ignoring the very real problems inherent in distributing and marketing the natural gas within the UK. The Gas Council, and its successor the British Gas Corporation, have consistently emphasised their marketing position to the detriment of rent collection. There was rent capture in 1968-72, but it was more the product of historical accident and gas marketing requirements than of deliberate policy. (Later, with regard to the Petroleum Revenue Tax, the British Gas Corporation was to fight against its application to natural gas.)

Rather, the Gas Council assumed the position of gas marketer. To begin with, the Council was faced with an increase in the supply of gas, making it several times larger than the existing market. Consequently, the Gas Council wished to match supply and demand as much as possible. Gas prices should be predictable and determinable at all times; the amount of gas and its introduction to the British market should be as gradual as possible and allow for considerable flexibility; depletion of the gas fields should be as slow as possible to secure supplies for the British market. Furthermore, there should be a great flexibility as to day-to-day and seasonal variations in the natural gas supplied, in this case a 60 per cent 'load factor.'

> As to load factor of supply the Industry [Gas Council and Area Boards] was serving a predominantly domestic residential demand with a load factor very much lower than that which the oil industry wished to supply...The Industry was interested in having a detailed specification to ensure the quantity of the gas and were much more interested than their American [oil industry] counterparts in day to day flexibility in output and day to day security of supply.[9]

There can be little doubt that the companies negotiated with an eye to getting the best possible Internal Rates of Return from their project investments. In negotiating terms this concern was reflected in such issues as when the production of gas would begin (start-up date), the rate of production build-up (production profile), the period of production before reserve depletion, the load factor, and prices — in particular the price review mechanism.[10] These issues collectively affected company profits more than the initial negotiated prices, although it is these latter which have attracted the bulk of attention the last ten years. This contention will be the next focus of our attention.

6.3. The Conflict of the 1960s: The Question of Prices

There is a tendency to characterise the prices set in the negotiations in the period 1966-72 as being 'non-market' prices — with no relation to 'market' prices, however this latter term is defined. Similarly imprecise is the characterisation that the prices settled upon were 'cost-plus' prices — prices which enabled the companies to cover costs (say around a 10-15 per cent Internal Rate of Return) plus a little more to keep them 'in the game.'[11]

It is probable that both these theoretic ideals were considered during the negotiations, and that both were then rejected. Indeed there are indications that the final outcome was a mix of these policies. This is for several reasons: first, the terms 'cost-plus' and 'market' prices are singularly imprecise and could cover a multitude of differences. For example a 'market' price for natural gas from the companies' point of view was defined for industrial purposes as 'parity with fuel oil' plus a slight reduction for natural gas to be supplied on an 'interruptible basis'.[12] Given the enormous capital expenditure British Gas would necessarily have to commit in furnishing this bulk market, the 'slight' reduction might not be enough for effective competition with fuel oil. Thus while companies with significant oil markets in the UK would have one view of 'parity' with fuel oil, the Gas Council would of necessity have had quite another. As Dam himself admits: 'One must conclude that the concept of a market price in the absence of a true market is a difficult tool to use for making public policy decisions.'[13] 'Cost-plus' is a no less complicated concept; what is the minimum acceptable rate of return for a company: 15 per cent? 20 per cent? What should the premium above cost be? Given the difference between corporations and within single corporations regarding measures of this kind, it is highly doubtful that 'cost-plus' was ever really seriously considered by the Gas Council:

> It is sometimes asked whether these were 'cost-plus' or 'market related' prices. Certainly none of them was cost-plus. We have never undertaken to pay an agreed rate of profit irrespective of the cost. Of course the prices paid for gas delivered at the beach had to cover the estimated cost of delivery and to enable us to sell the gas in the market at a profit. More than that is hard to say. . .Neither term is susceptible of precise definition.[14]

A second factor mitigating against the adoption of a hard-and-fast price setting doctrine was the group dynamics within the companies involved in negotiations. Acrimony developed not only between the Gas Council and the oil companies but also among the oil companies themselves. Negotiations were highly strenuous, the discussions within the various groups being so intense at times that the Gas Council representatives left the room to allow the companies to iron out the difference among themselves. The Gas Council also utilised these divisions constructively, building a basis of consensus through piecemeal bargaining, taking care of individual preferences, allowing for different objections and the like. A rigid policy either with regard to desirable marketing goals or with regard to a cost-plus policy would have seriously impaired this negotiation process. Indeed much haggling had little to do with price but instead dealt with such hot issues as capital expenditures, unitisation, production profile and the like.[15]

Further, the historical record speaks against any price dogma. The first price settled upon was 5d per therm for natural gas from West Sole. This price, as we shall note, was well above that prevailing on the European continent at the time, and was temporary in intent. It was to be decreased if it turned out that the quantities of gas available exceeded 50-100 million cubic feet per day. The high price initially offered BP for West Sole would provide the oil companies with a very good base to argue for similarly high prices in the negotiations of 1967/8.[16] It was widely reported at the time that the 5d per therm price was imposed on the Gas Council by the Ministry of Power.[17]

The next series of prices were those negotiated by the Gas Council with the Hewett Group. Indefatigable and Leman followed in summer 1969; Viking in 1972 and Rough in 1974. It is hard to see how the widely varying prices for gas from these fields as shown in Table 6.3

Table 6.3: Initial Prices for British North Sea Gas — Southern Basin

Field	Price per therm (10^5 BTU)		
	d/therm	p/therm	US cents/therm
West Sole			
1967-70	5.0	2.08	5.01
1971-		1.12	2.39
Hewett			
Base price	2.87	1.195	2.83
Valley gas	2.025	0.844	1.997
Leman[a]			
First 600 million cubic feet per day (mcfd)	2.87	1.196	2.83
Second 600 mcfd	2.85	1.1875	2.81
Remainder	2.83	1.792	2.79
Indefatigable[b]			
All gas to 1983	2.90	1.208	2.89
Viking (1972)	3.6	1.5	3.5
Rough (1974)	—	3.4	7.87

Notes:

a. These prices are for the first 15 years only. After that the prices are 2.87d, 2.80d, and 2.75d per therm respectively for the specified amounts produced per day.

b. These prices as well are applicable for the first 15 years of production. Afterwards the price will be 2.90d for the first 600 mcfd, 2.83 for the next 600 mcfd, and 2.78d per therm for the balance.

represented a consistent policy either of 'cost-plus' or of 'market-related' prices. Doubtless the prices paid for Leman, Hewett, and Indefatigable gas are very similar — leading to the impression that rather than individual costs per field, the price is set with respect to developing inland markets. The prices paid for Viking gas and Rough gas in the succeeding years have been interpreted both as a response to the price of competitive fuels (which rose) and as a response to increasing development costs (particularly in the case of Rough).[18]

And finally, the pattern of pricing both with respect to the prices natural gas was commanding on the continent and with respect to competitive fuels — most notably fuel oil — is indeterminate. If there was really an attempt to 'capture rent' or to adopt a 'cost-plus' strategy, one might expect prices to have been well out of line with those on the continent. If there was a deliberate attempt to match a market price, one might expect a price per therm close to that of heavy fuel oil. In

Table 6.4: Initial Gas Prices, British North Sea, Compared to Natural Gas Prices in International Continental Deals/Price of Fuel Oil ex Rotterdam Spot (Prices in US Cents/Therm)

Year	Initial UK price	Continental gas prices	Average price per therm fuel oil Rotterdam Spot Market
1966	–	Holland-France: 3.67 Holland-Belgium: 3.32	2.99
1967	5.01 for Initial West Sole contract		3.09
1968	2.83 for Hewett/Leman 2.89 for Indefatigable	–	3.08
1969	–	Holland-Belgium: 3.7	2.67
1970	–	Holland-Germany: 3.85 Holland-Italy: 4.37 cents/1000 cu. ft. (but no escalation)	4.88
1971	Viking: 3.5	–	5.75
1972	–	Norway to Continental consortium: 4.33	5.52
1973	Frigg: UK contract 5.02	–	n.a.
1974	Rough: 7.87	Frigg (Petronord-Norway contract): 6.2	n.a.

Source: M. Valais and M. Durand, *L'Industrie du Gaz dans le Monde*, 2nd edn (Paris: Editions Technic, May 1975).

fact neither of these two indicators point to one form of pricing strategy or another. Table 6.4 compares British gas prices with prices of continental deals and the per therm price of duel oil on the Rotterdam spot market.

With the exception of the original West Sole contract, the prices per therm for British gas versus continental gas tended to be low, approximately 0.5 cents per therm lower than continental prices as of 1968. But if these gas prices were low in this respect, they tended to be

0.2 to 0.3 cents per therm higher than fuel oil on the Rotterdam spot market. Indeed, in one year, 1969, the average price per therm on the Rotterdam spot market was significantly lower than the price per therm paid for British North Sea gas. Given that British Gas was facing a massive reconversion of existing town gas facilities, writing off recent investments in capital plants, and developing markets for natural gas, it should be surprising that the price of gas was a shade lower than that for fuel oil. It can be objected that the Rotterdam spot quotation has little to do with fuel oil prices in Britain, particularly since transportation costs are not taken into account. Yet at the same time, the Gas Council had contracted to receive natural gas which had not only to be transported but marketed in an unknown market; the size of the job to be done can be seen by the estimated £1,207 million which the Gas Council (BGC) invested in the period 1964/5 to 1975.[19] The discrepancy between natural gas prices in the UK and on the continent grew in the years 1969-78. It is in that growth that much of the oil company grievance lies. In fact, although the oil companies may have hoped for continental prices in 1968-72, given the undeveloped British market, they could not be too terribly disappointed with the prices they received.

Yet, appearances can be deceiving. Initial (or base) prices alone tell little. They must be seen in conjunction with other aspects of the cost of developing a gas field: the rate of start-up, the rate of depletion, the load factor involved, and last but not least the price escalation clauses involved. In these areas, the Gas Council got a very good deal indeed.

6.4. The Conflict of the 1960s: The Issues of Production

To clarify the sort of opportunity costs imposed by the Gas Council with respect to load factor and production profile, let us consider an illustrative example, a model of a not atypical southern North Sea gas field. The data on which this model is based are derived partially from the Indefatigable field (primarily the price of 2.9d per therm) and from the West Sole field (general investment allocation in the first decade). Cost data, time pattern of investment, production variations, and the like are derived from the author's experience with such data elsewhere in the North Sea (primarily Denmark). The figures are probably overly conservative; platform and well costs are largely those of 1974/5, for example. But the model represents a state of affairs not too unlike that of a field brought into production in the period 1968/9.

Table 6.5: Model Field — The Conflict of 'Optimum' Production Plans

	Companies' development plan	GC development plan
Reserves	2,467 X 10^9 cubic feet	2,196 X 10^9 cubic feet
Production period	18 years	25 years
Capital costs	$105,730,000	$128,750,000
Annual operation costs	$6,200,000/year	$6,400,000/year
Period of peak production	10 years at 173 Bcf/year[a]	6 years at 125 Bcf/year[a]
Period to peak production rate	5 years[b]	9 years[b]

Notes:
a. Bcf = billion (thousand million) cubic feet.
b. Including the period of investment (3 years for both plans).

(For further details of the assumptions in this model, the reader should refer to the Appendix to this chapter.) The overall capital costs, peak production rates, operating costs, and the like for this field from both the company and the Gas Council side are summarised in Table 6.5. What is the explanation for the differences represented in Table 6.5, and how are these differences reflected in increased costs to the companies owning the hypothetical field?

(a) The Question of 'Load Factor'

Normally defined as 'the ratio of the average quantity [of natural gas] taken per day to the maximum taken on any day in the year',[20] 'load factor' has other meanings as well. (It may for example be taken as peak vs. average daily demand within a 24-hour period.) There is a considerable lack of information regarding 'load factor' in the 1968 negotiations, other than that it was 60 per cent. This was largely a seasonal definition rather than a 24-hour definition. The Gas Council was required to accept a minimum amount per day, generally 25-33 per cent of the daily contracted amount, or pay a penalty. On the other hand, it had rights to 100 per cent of the daily contracted amount during the three summer months, 167 per cent of the daily contracted amount during the six winter months, and 130 per cent during the balance of the year. If the companies selling the natural gas ·could not come up with these contracted amounts as demanded by the Gas Council, they would be penalised.

Such a range of possible daily takes provided the Gas Council and the Area Boards with considerable flexibility in marketing the natural gas purchased from the North Sea. Elsewhere in the world, the growing practice was the requirement to accept 80 per cent of the daily delivery capacity and to take no more than 125 per cent of capacity. (This corresponds to an 80 per cent load factor.) An additional irritant to the negotiated contracts was that penalties for the failure to purchase the minimum amount required per day (25-33 per cent), the 'take or pay' provisions, were reciprocal; the companies were subject to a 'deliver or pay' clause which would cost them should they be unable to deliver the amounts demanded.[21]

The low load factor penalised the oil companies in two ways. It could well have deprived them of markets for gas oil or fuel oil, in that the Gas Council's new flexibility enabled it to furnish markets with considerable variation in daily and seasonal demands — markets which might otherwise have purchased oil products. More importantly, however, for our purposes, a low load factor diminished the overall reserves available, and increased capital and operation costs. The latter was due to the need to place extra capital equipment on the fields to provide for the large daily and seasonal variations in supply. This was particularly reflected in additional compressor needs, stronger platforms to support the compressors, and the like. Operation costs would increase due to the additional manpower and fuel needed to service the additional equipment. More controversial, perhaps, is the contention that a low load factor ultimately reduced the overall reserves of a field. Such a contention of course depends on engineering evaluations and such evaluations will vary from field to field; but load factor is connected with total recovery elsewhere in Europe and the United States, and it would be surprising if the reverse were uniquely true of the southern UK fields. These factors explain some of the differences in Table 6.5.

(b) Production Profile and 'Start-up'

With regard to the overall production profile, the companies desired a quick start-up, a rapid progression to peak production, and a shorter producing life for the fields, generally 15-20 years. Such expectations were not misplaced given practices elsewhere in the world. (In the US, for example, there are provisions for accelerated 'takes' during the early years of a contract.[22])

In contrast, the Gas Council insisted on longer periods of production, normally 25 years; this insistence of course cut down on the rates of peak production throughout the history of the field. Furthermore, the Gas Council insisted on gradual build-up periods, with durations of four to six years not uncommon.

Two reasons were advanced for this insistence. First, the Gas Council was concerned about the difficulties of marketing gas domestically. Characteristically, the Gas Council insisted on knowing the quantities to be delivered (and the price of delivery) as precisely as possible. Daily contract delivery was a fraction of the total production period (in days) and although publicly expressed in standard cubic feet per day, daily contract delivery was denoted as a fraction: 1/5833; 1/7300, 1/7292 and so forth, of the total quantity of gas remaining. A second reason for gradual start-ups was 'queuing'. Five large gas fields were to be brought into production. The only manner in which this could be done at the same time would be to limit the amount of gas bought from any one of them in the early production years. Such insistence was correct, of course, but only fully acceptable if the companies involved in the five fields wished to begin production immediately – irrespective of the production profile, the length of time in the contracts, and the prices, and if the companies desired only to sell to the United Kingdom. Manifestly, these desires were not shared within all the developing groups, or at least not shared with equal enthusiasm, as the attempt of the Viking group to sell to the continent demonstrates. The 'queuing' argument is very definitely two-edged, and some oil executives may be forgiven if they felt that they were trapped in their bargaining position with the Gas Council.

The results of these differences in opinion are expressed in our model field. The longer start-up period (which in Table 6.5 also includes three years of investment before production begins) and the lower annual production rate have already been mentioned. The differences on a year-to-year basis are illustrated in the Appendix to this chapter. Particularly notable is the difference in the start-up in the two production plans, a difference reflected in a higher rate of return and quicker payout time.

What are the results of these two differences, isolated from other variables with prices held constant at 2.9d per therm? The results are summarised in Table 6.6. Perhaps no summary illustrates more aptly the general points in this chapter on opportunity cost than that presented by Table 6.6. The difference in Internal Rates of Return between a company-type production plan and the Gas Council's is around 100 per cent: 14.79 per cent versus 29.54 per cent. Other

Table 6.6: Differences in Profitability — Model Field. GC and Company Production Plans with Price Held Constant 2.9d[a] per Therm throughout Production Periods

Investment measure	Companies' plan	GC plan
Internal Rate of Return (%)	29.5	14.79
Actual Value Profit	$286.1m	$207.3m
Present value disc. at 15%	$51.1m	negative
Present value disc. at 10%	$91.6m	$28.7m
Payout period[b] (years)	4.46	7.8
Maximum negative cash flow	$59.4m	$70.5m
Net income ratio	2.75	1.59
Government 'take'	$429m	$330m

Notes:
a. 1.34 cents per cubic metre. Based on upper heating value.
b. As defined in this context, 'payout' includes the entire investment period of three years in both cases.

cash-flow measures confirm this difference; payout period, 4.46 years versus 7.8 years; present value discounted at 10 per cent, $91.6 million versus $28.7 million. The total maximum negative cash flow is also considerably lower in the companies' plan — a not unimportant aspect regarding the problems of financing the project. Net income ratio also shows a notable discrepancy. Clearly, price is not the only parameter. In this case, a very attractive project by company criteria is made 'marginal' if the criteria of the Gas Council are adopted. (The figure of 14.79 per cent as a company IRR should not be taken as meaning that the GC was aiming for a 15 per cent IRR for the companies.) *It is important to note in this context that the figure of 14.79 per cent for our hypothetical project has nothing to do with real oil company profits.* According to sources within the BGC a more accurate rate of return would be double the 14.79 per cent of this example. This does not detract from the obvious point that the oil companies desired even better IRRs than this and were disappointed. They had hoped for much more — which they ultimately did not get.

Yet one can claim that this comparison really means little. Nobody in the negotiations of 1966-70 would have been content with fixed prices. Another technical element in the negotiations and one on which there must have been bitter differences, was that of escalation causes.

6.5. The Conflict of the 1960s: The Issues of Price Escalation and Currency Stability

Evidence as to price escalation clauses in the negotiations of 1966-70 is highly sketchy. There are infinite variations of price escalation formulae. The Southern Gas Basin negotiations were no exception. Prices in all cases were adjusted according to formulae which varied from contract to contract. All contracts specified price reviews at intervals in the life of the agreement. 'One contract specified for a price review based on [specified commercial] indexes at three-year intervals.'[23] Another, according to Sullivan, provided for an index trigger which upon movement of the relevant index a certain percentage up or down would untrigger a price change. 'At least one contract has a minimum floor price' as well (that of valley gas).[24] Virtually all contracts provide for price redetermination.[25] The problem with this fragmentary evidence is that it really tells us little about price escalation.

At the same time of the southern North Sea gas contracts, there were two practices. The first was to link the price of gas to the price of competitive fuels — generally various grades of fuel or gas-oil. The second was to arrange for a certain price rise every year. In the US, for example, a flat 0.5 cent, 1 cent, or 2.5 cents per thousand cubic feet *per annum* were not untypical price escalation clauses. Price escalation could also at times be connected to other measures — consumer price indices, for example. An increasingly common practice was to include two or more price formulae, and then adopt the price formula yielding the higher return. Thus a contract price (at time 'n') could be either the result of price formula (a) or of formula (b) in Figure 6.1 whichever was the higher. As can be seen, formula (b) would put a floor to minimum prices. The negotiated prices (price$_o$) could be the same for

Figure 6.1: Pricing Formula: (a) Connected to Fuel Oil and Gas-Oil Price; (b) Connected to an Automatic Escalation Rate

(a) $\text{Price}_n = \text{Price}_o \left[0.5 \times \left(\dfrac{\text{gas-oil}_n}{\text{gas-oil}_o} \right) + 0.5 \times \left(\dfrac{\text{fuel-oil}_n}{\text{fuel-oil}_o} \right) \right]$

(b) $\text{Price}_n = \text{Price}_o \ (1.005)^N$

*Where Price$_n$ is the price paid at n, price$_o$ is the original contract price. Gas oil prices and fuel oil prices are prices paid in a particular geographic market, for example fuel oil number 6 in Rotterdam. N is the number of years elapsed since the signing of the contract.

both equations or different prices. Thus, the one minimum floor price in the British southern North Sea of which we have record, adopts the price of valley gas as a floor.

The degree to which the British contracts of 1967-72 possess such clauses is uncertain for two reasons. First, although there is evidence that the prices are linked to fuel oil prices to some degree, the exact formulae are not publicly available.[26] Secondly, although it is reported that in 1974, the average price of North Sea gas was in the order of 1.9d (up about 58 per cent from the 1968 levels), it is hard to tell whether this price increase is due to escalation clauses or the difficulties of the pound. The latter problem, although undiscussed, is significant, as we shall see in the discussion of price escalation and currency provisions.

(a) Escalation Clauses

There is much to indicate that the escalation clauses agreed upon from 1967 to 1972 have been a prime irritant to the companies. This is openly admitted by British Gas:

> [T]he price escalation provisions in the Southern Basin contracts have contributed enormously to the Industry's commercial success. . . At the same time it must be said that none of the Southern Basin contracts have become unprofitable to the seller. They made *a lot of early money from the contracts and the overall return to date, though less than they would have liked and less in real terms than they hoped for*, has been satisfactory.[27]

What is the impact of differing escalation clauses on the return of our model field? For the purposes of illustration, let us look at the returns on the field at the end of 1972. There are two price formulae involved, cited in Figure 6.2.

For the sake of argument, it is assumed that the companies' production plan and the British Gas production plan are being implemented. This indicates how escalation clauses can further increase the companies' impression of cost. Initial price is the same. The results are presented in Table 6.7. How they would look to the corporate executive is summarised in Table 6.8. Clearly, Table 6.7 represents the actual state of affairs better than the tables based on data which do not take escalation into account. As can be seen, in terms of every investment measure, the two escalation formulae increase overall corporate profits. Yet, the optimal corporate case is rendered even more attractive by the price escalation provisions. Table 6.8 represents the

Figure 6.2: Company Price Formula versus Gas Council Price Formula*

(1) Company formula: $Price_n = Price_o \left[0.5 \left(\dfrac{\text{gas oil Rotterdam}_n}{\text{gas oil Rotterdam}_o} \right) \right.$

$\left. + 0.5 \left(\dfrac{\text{fuel oil Rotterdam}_n}{\text{fuel oil Rotterdam}_o} \right) \right] \times (1.005)^N$

(2) Gas Council formula: $Price_n = Price_o \times (1.005)^N$

*Note that in both of these formulae, price is defined as the price at time of payment, n. $Price_o$ is initial (base) price negotiated, at time o. Fuel Rotterdam and gas oil Rotterdam subscripts indicate the same points in time, as those for the natural gas prices. All Rotterdam prices utilised are from M. Adelman, *The World Petroleum Market* (Washington, D.C.: The Johns Hopkins Press, 1972), pp. 343-82.

Table 6.7: Differences in Profitability II — Model Field. GC and Company Production Plans with Different Escalation Clauses

Investment measure	GC plan	Corporations' plan (linked to oil products: 1968-72)
IRR (%)	15.35	34.22
Actual Value Profit	$227.2m	$339.7m
PV disc. at 15%	$1.5m	$70.5m
PV disc. at 10%	$33.2m	$117.8m
Payout period	7.71 years	4.35 years
Net income ratio	1.75	3.27
Government 'take'	$357.8m	$503.3m

Table 6.8: Increase in Corporate 'Take'

	GC plan		Corporate plan	
	Without escal. (1)	With escal. (2)	Without escal. (3)	With escal. (4)
IRR (%)	14.79	15.35	29.5	34.22
AVP	$207m	$227.2m	$286m	$339.7m
Net income ratio	1.59	1.75	2.75	3.27
Government 'take'	$330m	$357.8m	$429m	$503m

greater impact of tying natural gas prices in 1968 to fuel oil prices and gas oil prices. This is reflected in the higher profitability in columns 3 and 4 than columns 1 and 2. And this is only part of the picture. The additional income from this linkage is only included for the years 1968-72. Using the price formula specifying the linkage with gas oil and fuel oil, the price per therm in 1972 was 4.94 cents. The price per therm in terms of 1977 prices would have been 15.94 cents! Given a base 1968 price of 2.89 cents per therm, this is an enormous increase. An escalator provision of 0.5 per cent without relation to fuel and gas oil would yield 1972 and 1977 per therm prices of 2.948 cents and 3.02 cents respectively. The degree to which the Gas Council could successfully tie gas prices to a fixed escalator must in retrospect have been enormously costly to the companies with whom they were negotiating. The illustrative escalation clauses and the results in Table 6.7 are a somewhat academic exercise. Yet available evidence indicates that there is in fact a critical difference between fuel oil linkage escalator clauses and the escalator clauses in the 1967-72 contracts. This contrast is provided by the difference between the overall increase in the average price of those contracts to about 1.7p (3.9 cents) per therm in 1974 and the known increase in Frigg prices — prices definitely tied to competitive fuels. This contrast is illustrated in Table 6.9, in which the results should be viewed with care in that much of the escalation could be in the form of currency clauses. Still it could reveal a significant cause of company discontent.

Table 6.9: Effects of Escalation — Prices of Southern Basin Gas Contrasted with Frigg Gas (Cents per Therm, US)

Date	Reported price of Frigg Gas[a]	Average price of Southern Basin Gas
1968	—	c. 2.83 cents[b]
1971	6.2 cents	—
1974	16.1 cents	c. 3.93 cents[b]
Per cent change	+159.7	+38.9

Source: Valais and Durand, *L'Industrie du Gaz.*
Notes:
a. Frigg gas sold from the Norwegian sector (Petronord).
b. Prices are converted at then current exchange rates, British pound to US dollar.

(b) Southern British Gas and Currency

The effect of currency clauses on prices paid is mentioned nowhere in the literature on the 1967-72 contracts. Until now, the prices quoted have been in US dollars for two reasons: first, the US dollar was a firm currency in the late sixties; secondly, the majority of the companies involved in developing North Sea gas fields were American. Even when not American, they would have had reason to distrust the British pound. Therefore, although it is unlikely that payments to the oil companies made by British Gas were made in anything other than pounds, it is highly likely that the pounds were linked to dollars (and perhaps the Deutschmark) either directly or indirectly. Although ostensibly a means of stabilising income, these arrangements, depending on currency linkages, can impose considerable costs.

A somewhat academic example shows the impact of currency provisions. Let us assume three regimes: the first (column 1 in Table 6.10) has no provisions for currency linkages but allows a cumulative two per cent *per annum* escalation of prices; the second regime allows the two per cent *per annum* escalation and additionally ties the price of gas to the American dollar (column 2); and the third regime is similar to the other two but ties the price to a 'currency basket' consisting of the American dollar and the German mark.

As can be seen, depending on the currency linkage, the prices can become widely disparate, compounding the impact of the escalation clause. (The possibilities with regard to currency clauses are virtually limitless; for example the formulae used in our illustration could be varied considerably to suit the objectives of the negotiating parties. Particularly remarkable are differences between the price systems in columns (2) and (3). First, these illustrate the degree of difference which contract currency clauses can have; more importantly, however, they could represent the opportunity cost in selling to the British market—(columns (1) or (2) versus selling to the continental market (column (3)).)

The example used is purely illustrative. The compounding effect of currency baskets can be higher depending on the price formula used. Should use be made of the 'company formula' in Figure 6.1, the differences would be more significant by far. An oil company position in 1968 could have been an insistence on parity with fuel oil and gas oil prices *plus* a currency basket including strong currencies such as the German mark. The degree to which they failed in achieving such objectives must remain a matter of speculation.

Table 6.10: Impact of Currency Baskets on Price, Pence Per Therm
(Escalated by 2 Per Cent *Per Annum* 1.2p Per Therm in 1968)

Currency regime: Year	(1) None	(2) Tied to US $	(3) Tied to US $ and German mark 50/50
1968	1.2	1.2	1.2
1971	1.27	1.288	1.449
1974	1.35	1.3465	1.727
1977	1.721	2.385	3.214

Note the formulae used in this example are as follows:

Column (1) : $P_n = P_o \times (1.02)^N$

Column (2) : $P_n = P_o \times (1.02)^N \times \dfrac{K_t^{\$,\,£}}{K_o^{\$,\,£}}$

Column (3) : $P_n = P_o \times (1.02)^N \times \dfrac{\dfrac{K_t^{\$,\,£}}{K_o^{\$,\,£}} + \dfrac{K_t^{DM,\,£}}{K_o^{DM,\,£}}}{2}$

in which P_o is the 1968 price; P_n is June price for the given year: 1971, 1974, 1977. N is the number of years elapsed; and the expression: $K_t^{\$,\,£}$ stands for dollar/pound exchange rates in June of the given year, $K_o^{\$,\,£}$, for the dollar/pound exchange rates in June 1968, respectively. (The same applies to the German mark.)

6.6. The Aftermath of Conflict — Southern British Gas in the 1970s and 1980s

That the critical difference between the Gas Council and the West Sole, Leman, Hewett, and Indefatigable groups was not over initial price but over production profiles and price escalation clauses is perhaps fortunate. The contracts signed in 1968/9 were to be of 25-years duration, but were also to be highly flexible, within limits, subject to future discussions on delivery conditions to British Gas, discussions which could profoundly alter the production profile and/or the price escalations formulae. This flexibility has led after a period of time to a degree of accommodation between seller and purchaser.

The period to 1978 has been characterised by a high degree of caution among the oil companies in the Southern Basin. This was reflected in the slow rate of exploration and in the emphasis on the costliness of the 1968/9 agreements. The issue with regard to the continued marginality of the Southern Basin discoveries — both those associated with the developed fields and the developed fields themselves — was not so much whether further development could be profitable, but rather one of *when* such development should occur. The question of cost is that of the opportunity cost of developing a field under unfavourable contract conditions today, versus development under more favourable contract conditions tomorrow. The Appendices to this chapter list the major Southern Basin fields, together with their associated structures and other finds. The one theme running through the decision on whether or not to develop is revision of contract conditions — in many instances, one suspects, not only of the smaller fields, but also of the larger.

Complementing this oil company insistence on 'waiting for better days' has been an undenied reserve with regard to exploration. The argument is normally advanced that the BGC through appropriating rents from existing fields has deprived the oil companies of the incentive to continue exploration. Evidence is often presented in the form of comparative drilling activities in the Dutch and the British sectors. The Dutch sector is implicitly tied to a continental system of prices and affords better opportunities. There are arguments against making such a correlation between cost and rate of activities, illustrated in Table 6.11. First, one must recognise that the rate of successful drilling in the Dutch sector is much the higher of the two. The Dutch have 49 discoveries out of 140 exploration wells, versus 33 out of 173 for the British sector. Secondly, many of the companies holding Southern Basin blocks are also exploring in the northern North Sea sector, with a wide range of much plusher pickings. Nevertheless, the decline in exploration efforts in the British Southern Basin is particularly notable after 1969.

On the buyer's side, the energy markets quickly felt natural gas from the North Sea. This development could be seen both from the rapidly growing share of the British energy market held by natural gas as opposed to other energy forms, but also in the price development of various fuels. In the energy market, natural gas increased both its absolute and relative market share. From a low of 1.4 per cent in 1968, natural gas was providing about 17 per cent of all British needs seven years later (see Table 6.12).

In prices as well, it was obvious that natural gas could and did compete favourably with other fuels, displacing first coal and, later — much to the chagrin of the oil companies — petroleum products. This

Table 6.11: Comparative Drilling Rates and Success Ratios —
Southern North Sea Basin

	British sector		Dutch sector	
Year	No. exploration wells commenced/drilled	Success ratio	No. exploration* wells commenced/drilled	Success ratio
1968	30	3/30	7	2/7
1969	34	5/34	16	4/16
1970	12	3/12	14	7/14
1971	7	1/7	19	4/19
1972	8	3/8	17	10/17
1973	7	0/7	19	5/19
1974	4	0/4	17	9/17
1975	2	1/2	18	7/18
1976	3	2/3	16	5/16

*Dutch sector for period 1968-75: figures for this period include the drilling of
nine appraisal wells of which four were successes.

Sources: Kenneth Dam, *Oil Resources: Who Gets What How?* (Chicago: The
University of Chicago Press, 1976), p. 97. More recent British figures from Dept.
of Energy, *Development of the Oil and Gas Resources of the United Kingdom*
(London: HMSO, April 1977.) Dutch figures from Ministerie van Economische
Zaken, *Aardgas en Aardolie in Nederland en op de Noordzee 1976* (March 1977).
There is confusion in the figures used in this source. According to p. 10, there
were 11 discoveries made in the period 1968-70; on p. 24, a count of discoveries
gives 13 which is in accord with Dam's figures.

Table 6.12: UK Market Shares (Per Cent) — Gas and Competitive Fuels
1968-75

Year	Coal	Petroleum	Natural gas	Nuclear energy	Hydro-electric power
1968	53.5	41.0	1.4	3.3	0.7
1969	50.6	42.7	2.6	3.3	0.6
1970	47.0	44.4	4.8	2.8	0.8
1971	42.9	45.6	7.9	3.0	0.6
1972	37.0*	48.1	11.2	3.2	0.6
1973	37.6	46.5	12.5	2.8	0.6
1974	34.8	45.3	15.7	3.6	0.6
1975	37.0	42.0	17.0	3.4	0.6

*Coal strike.

Source: Table is calculated from UK energy consumption given in million tons coal
equivalent. Central Statistics Office, *Monthly Digest of Statistics* (London: HMSO,
1968-76).

Table 6.13: Retail Price of Natural Gas and Competitive Fuels
(Indexed, 1962 Price Index = 100)

Year	All fuels (incl. oil)	Coal/coke	Gas	Electricity
1968	133.7	131.1	124.6	145.0
1969	136.0	137.6	126.5	144.7
1970	145.0	159.6	126.0	145.7
1971	162.9	180.3	138.6	165.6
1972	174.0	199.4	146.0	173.7
1973	177.2	203.6	146.0	175.1
1974	217.2	233.6	153.9	228.8
1975	291.6	318.6	179.1	335.3
1976	347.4	386.7	214.6	n.a.

Source: Calculated from Central Statistics Office, *Monthly Journal of Statistics* (London: HMSO, 1968-76).

trend can be seen in Table 6.13. Although the base year of the index used in that table is 1962 (and reflects the higher price of town gas at that time), the table gives a good impression of price evolution in the period after North Sea gas was introduced to British markets. While the price of all fuels (including both oil and gas) increased about 160 per cent during this period, the price of gas alone increased no more than 70 per cent.

The cause of this underpricing cannot be laid at the BGC's door alone. The Corporation has been one of the most insistent on the need for fuel price increases both to promote conservation, and, more importantly, to bolster its own profit position. Because of its overall investments and the increase of interest rates, the BGC reported a loss of £41.3 million in 1973/4. The problem, of course, was political. Raising gas prices would be inflationary, something the Prices Commission wished very much to avoid. As a consequence, in a year in which the BGC reported a turnover of £1,000 million, it reported a deficit. The result was perhaps inevitable; the Prices Commission in 1974 allowed charges for non-domestic use to increase by 40 per cent, although in the very important domestic (household) market, the allowed increase was 12 per cent.[23]

Nor was the picture all that bright for additional gas supplies. Contracts after those of 1968/9 increased prices considerably (to 1.5p per therm for Viking), and in one case very substantially (a reported

3.6p per therm for Rough gas in 1974). The problem with these later contracts is that it is unknown what the other critical factors may have been: production profile, escalation clauses, load factor, and the like. British Gas bid for and failed to obtain Norwegian gas from Ekofisk. The reason, reportedly, was a failure to agree on an escalation formula.[29] The need to find supplementary gas led to the successful bidding for Frigg gas. The price was set differently for gas from the Norwegian sector and for that from the British sector (see Table 6.9). Additionally, efforts were made to acquire associated gas from the Brent and other northern North Sea oil fields. The price of Frigg gas was many times that of gas from the southern North Sea, and very importantly, it was bought at a very high load factor. Associated gas, too, had its problems. It is often mixed with condensate which can lead to operation difficulties on pipeline maintenance. (Condensate can form 'slugs' which block up the line.) Furthermore, this associated gas can vary greatly in supply, being dependent on gas-oil ratios of a large number of oil fields. The combination of continental purchasing conditions and high load factor (Frigg) and the need for more flexibility (associated gas) has led both the British Gas Corporation and the oil companies to re-examine their positions in the Southern North Sea Basin.

6.7. 'Marginal' Fields as a Fulcrum?

To what extent could 'marginal' fields — or 'marginal portions' of established producing fields, be said to have acted as an oil industry 'fulcrum' in the same manner as oil? The analysis in this chapter began by disproving the notion that the 'marginality' of the southern British gas fields was due not only to low initial prices offered by a monopsonistic Gas Council. Other factors were also significant, in particular load factor, production profile, and price escalation clauses. The resulting 'package' was highly unattractive from an oil company point of view. A calm then set in on the Southern Basin area. The question remains: can the marginality of the undeveloped areas of the Southern Basin be linked with oil company pressure to better overall contract terms?

Evidence on this point remains scanty. It would be wrong to place too much weight on the decline in exploration activity, for reasons previously elaborated. It is notable that many of the undrilled/ unexplored blocks still in the hands of the oil companies from the early licensing rounds are located in the Southern Basin. It is not impossible that there are good prospects as yet not investigated: the oil company practice of 'sitting', in the words of Lord Kearton.

The oil companies are quite open about the need for higher prices to enable the development of 'marginal' Southern Basin fields. Does this mean that 'marginal' gas fields are hostages to be retained unless the government (in this case, the BGC) comes up with better terms? It would seem that any parallel with the 1975 PRT negotiations is somewhat tenuous. This is primarily because nothing thus far has affected the *de facto* monopsonistic position of the British Gas Corporation. The Corporation simply does not *need* the natural gas at present. Even if companies with smaller undeveloped gas fields were willing to develop them, they would have to go to the end of the queue. Rather, the BGC has set about diversifying its sources of supply, either by collecting associated gas from northern North Sea oil finds, or purchasing the immense quantities of new gas from the Frigg field. This led to a somewhat constrained marketing position in so far as the BGC was concerned. The additional sources of natural gas could not only extend the lives of the Southern British Basin fields, but also imposed great uncertainties. Unless the British Gas Corporation were very careful, its gas supplies might possibly become too inflexible to allow continued market expansion.

The oil company determination to wait on better times and the BGC policy of diversification have led to a new equilibrium in the southern North Sea. British Gas wished to increase the flexibility of its gas supplies and could do so by negotiating with the companies for lower load factors from the already existing producing fields. The groups owning these fields could argue for better prices and financial terms in return for a lower load factor. The resulting equilibrium was achieved in a series of negotiations from 1977 to 1979. Under these negotiations the companies promised to invest in additional compressors (needed for a change in load factor) and accept a lower load factor in return for a 'slightly higher' price.

It is clear what this equilibrium means with respect to load factor. For their portion of Indefatigable field, for example, the operators Amoco will deliver an average of 368 million cubic feet a day. Under the present contract, it could provide up to 646 million cubic feet per day in the hard winter months. Similar contracts are reported in hand for Leman and Viking. As of this writing, negotiations are in progress with the operators of Hewett and West Sole fields.

Also known are the size of investments which the operators are making. Amoco and Shell on Leman are reported to be spending £105 million on a programme which will increase compressor capacity on the Leman field by about 173,000 horsepower. For Indefatigable (shared once again by the Shell and Amoco groups), £60 million will be invested in 120,000 horsepower of increased compression. The Amoco/BGC group has agreed on a 15,000 horsepower compressor (at £8.7 million) in return for a new contract on the very costly Rough field, which while not expensive in capital outlay is proving very difficult to produce from. Finally, the BGC has arrived at a new contract with Conoco, the operators at Viking; in return, some £7.7 million worth of compressor capacity will be added.[30]

Also public is the fact that these contracts will extend the life of the producing fields:

> The length of contracts has also been extended so that they will not terminate while there still is gas remaining to be recovered. There have always been elements of flexibility in the contracts. . .But nothing on the scale of the new agreements.[31]

Prices, as expected, were lower than the companies would have liked. As we have noted, this can mean very little. Far more important than initial prices will be escalation clauses (and to only a slightly lesser degree, currency provisions). On this nothing is said. It would be difficult to insist that the companies got nothing from the new arrangements. What remains to be seen is whether the new contractual

Table 6.14: Reserves — Southern North Sea Gas Fields (Billion Cubic Metres)

Status of fields		Reserves		
	Proven	Probable	Possible	Total
Fields under contract to BGC	421	14	25	460
Fields believed to be commercial	51	65	—	116
Other discoveries	—	31	40	71
Total	472	110	65	647*

*This is 41.2 per cent of the overall total of 1,546 billion cubic metres for the entire British North Sea (and Irish Sea — in the case of the Morecombe field).

Source: Kevin Done, 'British Gas Wins Room to Manoeuvre', *The Financial Times* (1 December 1978), p. 8. Note that these figures are marginally lower than those of Wood MacKenzie for the same area.

terms will encourage further development of the reserves listed in Table 6.14. The degree to which the Southern British Basin will continue to remain 'marginal' from an oil company viewpoint will depend on future events.

To what extent have the smaller undeveloped gas fields in the Southern Basin been used as a 'fulcrum' to improve oil company profits in the southern British North Sea? It is apparent that any 'fulcrum' theory would have to be modified to accord with the dynamics of the natural gas industry. To begin with, it has been impossible for the oil companies to use the threat of not developing these fields, largely because the British Gas Corporation has ample supplies of gas from the northern North Sea. Rather the BGC need for greater flexibility of supplies, for a lower load factor, has provided the companies with the 'fulcrum' in this case. The issues to date have little to do with 'marginal' fields. The institutional context has not radically altered for undeveloped gas fields as yet; but it shows signs perhaps of doing so in the future.

Notes

1. Letter, State Mining Department, Ministerie van Economische Zaken, to author, 2 June 1978.

2. The nationalised gas industry was at the time structured into 12 Area Boards with a co-ordinating body, the Gas Council. This organisational structure became more centralised with the formation of the British Gas Corporation and the abandonment of the Area Boards.

3. Robert L. Sullivan, 'Comparison of North Sea Gas Sales Contracts with US Contracts', *Journal of Petroleum Technology* (October 1973), p. 1130.

4. Ibid., pp. 1130-1.

5. J.F. Allcock, 'Natural Gas Purchasing', Communication 1062, The Institution of Gas Engineers, 16-18 May 1978, pp. 2-3.

6. Ibid., p. 3.

7. Keith Chapman, *North Sea Oil and Gas* (Newton Abbot: David & Charles, 1976), p. 135.

8. See for example, Kenneth Dam, *Oil Resources: Who Gets What How?* (Chicago: The University of Chicago Press, 1976).

9. Allcock, 'Natural Gas Purchasing', p. 8.

10. Ibid.

11. Clearly the best discussion of the problems involved in these twin price conceptions is that of Kenneth Dam, *Oil Resources*, pp. 82-92.

12. Ibid., p. 84.

13. Ibid., p. 86.

14. Allcock, 'Natural Gas Purchasing', p. 4.

15. Unitisation was such a hot inter-company issue that it is rumoured that one of the fields, Hewett, was never properly unitised.

16. It is curious how observers have bought the oil companies argument that

they were justified in the 4d and 5d initial offers for natural gas and that any price lower than those offered was a form of 'cost-plus' pricing. For an exception to this point of view, see Dam, *Oil Resources*, p. 77.

17. Ibid.

18. See Chapman, *North Sea Oil and Gas*, p. 134, for the first impression, and Dam, *Oil Resources*, p. 96, for the second.

19. *Financial Times* (23 January 1975), p. 14.

20. Dam, *Oil Resources*, p. 87.

21. Sullivan, 'Comparison of North Sea Gas Sales Contracts', pp. 1133-4. In the US for example, the producer insists on a 'take or pay' obligation but has limited liability if unable to deliver the amount required. Punishment in this case merely is that the purchaser can automatically set the amount he is required to take downwards. See Sullivan for the technical details: ibid., p. 1134.

22. Ibid.

23. Ibid.

24. Ibid.

25. This redetermination could depend on 'favoured nation' clauses — clauses which provide that if the gas purchaser pays a third party more for natural gas, the higher price would also apply to earlier prices set in earlier contracts. Such clauses are not unusual and could perhaps explain the reticence of the BGC with regard to issues of price.

26. This is in any case implied by Allcock, 'Natural Gas Purchasing', p. 3, in discussing the relatively low prices of oil products in 1968 in the midst of the negotiations.

27. Ibid., pp. 3-4. Emphasis added.

28. *Financial Times* (23 January 1975), p. 14.

29. This is a rather mystical note. Ekofisk gas is tied to number 2 and number 6 fuel oil within Germany. The only other escalation clause to the author's knowledge was an automatic *per annum* 1.8 per cent increase in an initially very low base price. If this is right, it is easy to understand why the companies are less than enthusiastic with those escalation clauses which they have in the Southern Basin context.

30. Kevin Done, 'British Gas Wins Room to Manoeuvre', *The Financial Times* (1 December 1978), p. 8.

31. Ibid.

PART FOUR

THE DANISH SHELF

7 DENMARK – THE DEVELOPMENT DECISION IN ABSENCE OF POLICY

7.1. Introduction

In 1974 officials responsible for implementing Danish North Sea hydrocarbons policy – the Supervisory Authority within the Ministry of Commerce[1] – undertook a review of previous Danish concessionary commitments. Apparently they were unable to find any original assessment of the reservoir size, production characteristics, and the like for the Dan field – the only producing formation in Danish waters. A request was forwarded to the Danish Underground Consortium (DUC) for the original assessment – 'such as it appeared to the concessionaires in connection with the planning of production in 1971'.[2] This request, in October 1974, occurred three years after the Danish Government had initially approved production plans for the Dan field. This episode is illustrative of the state of Danish North Sea policy at the time.

Yet the episode also underlines the special character of the Dan field, one of the most costly North Sea fields ever to be developed. The Dan had been developed so rapidly that the DUC itself in 1971 may well have been ignorant of the information requested by the government three years later. Had the information been available then, it is questionable whether this field would have been developed at all.

As can be seen, Danish policy is in interesting contrast to UK policy. In the preceding section the political economy of high-cost fields centred on the issues of rent capture – and the discretionary provisions of the UK licensing system. In Denmark to date only one field is in production (although several are stated for development). Furthermore the focus here is on the access provisions of the North Sea 'contract'.

In contrast to the closely policed British licensing system, the Danish concession until 1976 can be characterised almost as having no policy at all. This is of course amply illustrated by the Dan example. In contrast to the British system, there is no extensive rent-capture mechanism in the Danish sector. Neither can there be said to be state participation. The nature of the Danish concession is perhaps unique in the world in this regard. Yet, while not possessing many of the policy instruments characteristic of the Norwegian and British licensing systems, the Danish concession does have one access requirement – that a production of one hydrocarbon be commenced within ten years

of the concessionary award and that a production of the other
hydrocarbon be started within five years of the production of the first.

The emphasis on the North Sea 'contract' struck in this analysis is of
interest here. If, as has been posited in Chapter 3, the nature of the
contract will lead to a particular pattern of oil industry behaviour,
there should be a contrast between oil company behaviour in the British
sector and that in the Danish sector. To the degree that there has not
been any relinquishment (relinquishment provisions were only
introduced in 1976), there would be little incentive to explore as
thoroughly or adequately as is the case in the British area. To the degree
that there is little rent capture, there should be no great complaints as
to the 'marginality' of the Danish projects.

Yet a critical contrast was introduced in Chapter 3. There is a
contrast between access provisions which act as a 'spur' to rapidity/
efficiency – most generally the various relinquishment policies – and
policies which seek to induce a particular form of behaviour – the
discretionary economic incentives which we have analysed in the British
context. The Danish concession has no discretionary economic
incentives such as those set up in Britain for 'marginal' fields. But the
Danish concession does have a 'spur' – the requirement that both
hydrocarbons (oil and gas) be produced within 15 years of the
concessionary awards. In the absence of such a production, the
concession to one or both hydrocarbons would expire. This requirement
is not dissimilar to a relinquishment policy. In Chapter 3, note was
made of how differing relinquishment requirements in the British and
Dutch sectors led to differing patterns of drilling activity in the two
areas. In the Danish area, one can note a similar phenomenon, only in
this case the issue is that of the development decision, a far more costly
undertaking than the drilling of an exploration well or two. In 1971 the
DUC undertook to develop the Dan field rather than forfeit the Danish
concession – the topic of Chapter 8. In 1978 the DUC bowing to
considerable pressure undertook to develop a series of Danish gas
fields – again the alternative was forfeiture of the concession for natural
gas. This is the focus of Chapter 9. But before proceeding to these
issues, a brief review of the Danish concessionary policy is necessary.

7.2. The Absence of Policy

The 'absence' of policy on the Danish Shelf lies in the complicated
relationship existing between the A.P. Moeller company[3] – which

possesses what has been called the 'world's best concession' – and the Danish state. Through a series of flukes, incremental policy-making and errors, A.P. Moeller received the concessions to the entire Danish North Sea Shelf plus Jutland and the Islands on terms more favourable than even those of the first Danish concession of 1932. The folklore behind this sequence of events, although classic, need not concern us here.[4] Essentially, the American wildcatter Frederic Ravlin, Gulf Oil, and Esso in turn unsuccessfully explored the Danish Islands and Jutland for a period of 30 years. In 1962, the Danish shipowner Arnold Peter Moeller undertook the concession. As a Danish industrialist, he argued, he could not be given terms worse than those given the oil companies. The government authorities agreed. The difference in concessionary terms are given in the appendix to this chapter. Essentially, the terms are illustrated in Table 7.1, organised as to access, timing and benefits.

The only snags in the concession were the requirements that one hydrocarbon (oil or gas) had to be produced within ten years or the concession would be revoked, and that a second hydrocarbon (oil or gas) had to be produced within five years of the first or rights to that hydrocarbon would revert to the state. As will be noted, these two provisions were the only ones which secured any degree of state control over the concession. The provisions were weakened by a curious change in 1962. Production of a hydrocarbon could be initiated by the concessionaire if it thought production was 'economically defensible'. This did not automatically ensure the extension of the concession. Such extension depended on a 'commercial production' of hydrocarbons, the determination of which was clearly the prerogative of the state. In the 1962 concession (retained in 1963), the state's capacity to determine what qualified as commercial production, the basis for concession extension, was weakened. 'Commercial production' was struck from all provisions and replaced with the term 'production' alone. In the light of the earlier provisions on 'economic defensibility' as the criterion to initiate production there is no separate legal foundation for state supervision/interference. 'Commercial production' is no longer required for concession renewal, but only whatever production the concessionaire considers to be 'economically defensible' *as the concessionaire defines the term*. Not only does the production of a few barrels of oil per year qualify as 'economically defensible' when it is clearly not 'commercial' in international industrial terminology, but the contract terms place the concessionaire as the only juridical authority capable of terminating its own concession. The abandonment by the Danish state of its other rights in the earlier concession pales to insignificance beside this

Table 7.1: Concessionary Terms — 1962/3

State policy	Provisions	Notes on provisions
Access	Danish land area + 56,000 km^2 Shelf area for 50 years	Land area granted 1962. Shelf area granted 1963. Access controlled by concessionaire alone with approval of Danish state
Timing	One hydrocarbon should be in production within 10 years or concessionary rights revoked. Second hydrocarbon within 5 years or rights to that hydrocarbon revoked. No production regulations in force	Concessionaire is given the right to determine what 'production' is. (Definition of 'economically defensible production')
Distribution of benefits	Royalties on shelf : 5% first 5 years; 8.5% thereafter	Royalties charged after deduction of transportation costs
	Corporation taxes of 37%	No special regulations applying to income from offshore operation. Actual incidence of taxes second only to Switzerland within Europe
	No state participation	5% state participation required in 1950 concessionary law abandoned in 1962
	No special petroleum revenue tax	

arrangement. Anthony Sampson's succinct characterisation of the A.P. Moeller concession: 'The Danes even awarded the entire plans for offshore exploration to a single consortium as if they were Arabs in the 1930s',[5] is doubtless over-dramatic, but the concessionary law covering the Danish area is undoubtedly the exception to North Sea practice.

As might be predicted, there have been attempts to adapt the Danish concession more to the advantage of the state. Generally these attempts fall into two categories: those to reinterpret the concession where it is less than clear as to the concessionaire's rights, and those to enforce the provision requiring 'defensible production' within ten years.

The only notable attempt to interpret the concession in favour of the Danish state occurred in 1972, the year in which the Danish Underground Consortium — at that time also including Gulf —

announced that it might consider selling natural gas to Denmark. Danish authorities quickly acted to form a state-owned gas transportation company, the Danish Natural Gas Company later renamed the Danish Oil and Natural Gas Company (DONG).[6] Formation of a transmission company was justified on the grounds that the 1962/3 concession was unclear as to whom could market natural gas, despite its clarity as to the DUC's production rights. This may have seemed a logical move at the time, but it may have considerably reduced DUC's interest in gas.

In 1971 and 1976 attempts were made by the Danish state to amend the concession. In both years attention focused on whether or not the DUC had established the necessary production to retain the concession. In 1971 the rights to oil were the subject of negotiation; in 1976 it was the rights to natural gas. Although these negotiation rounds may have been instrumental in establishing oil and gas production, they were lean on results for changing the concession. After the 1976 negotiation round, the Danish Shelf was divided into blocks, but the blocks were very sizeable (15 times larger than British blocks), the rate of relinquishment slow. Most importantly, the DUC held on to the promising South-west Sector in its entirety until the year 2000 and would retain half of the area to the expiration of the concession in the year 2012.

Up to the year 1978, in fact, there was no real political backing for any government move to change the policy base of Danish North Sea activities due to the party constellations in the Danish Folketing (Parliament). The DUC had thus been free to do as it pleased, provided either oil or gas production commenced within ten years of the concessionary award. It is this period of company/group behaviour with which we are concerned.

7.3. The Presence of High-cost Fields

As can be seen in Table 7.2, the total estimated reserves on the Danish Shelf are not inconsiderable, about 50 to 60 million tons of oil and around 100 to 110 billion cubic metres of natural gas. The problem is that these finds, when separated, amount to considerably less oil and gas per field than is normal in the North Sea. There are exceptions in the Dan, Vern and Cora fields, but these are still smaller than the North Sea 'giant'. There can be little doubt that the Danish sector is characterised by a plethora of small, high-cost fields. The term 'cost' is meant here in the sense of opportunity cost, as the fields are cheap in

Table 7.2: Oil and Gas Resources — Danish North Sea Shelf, 1963-78

Field name	Date of find	Estimated reserves Oil 1,000 tons	Natural gas 10^6 cubic metres	Status
Anne	1966	2,250	1,011	Unknown
Cora	1968	6,700	43,200 to 51,200	To be developed 1984
Bent	1969	1,200 to 1,700	16,000 to 32,000	To be appraised after 1990
Arne (I)	1969	—	—	Unknown
Dan field	1971	8,116 to 23,700	10,000 to 15,000	Production began in 1972
Vern (Gorm)	1971	16,000 to 22,000	c. 10,000	To be developed by 1981
Gwen (Q)	1973	—	—	Unknown
North Arne	1974	—	—	Unknown
Ruth Skjold)	1976	—	—	Proposed development plan abandoned in 1977. Under continuing appraisal?
Adda	1977	—	—	Under appraisal. Possible future delineation
Tove	1978	—	—	Gas find under appraisal. Development unlikely before 1995
Nils	1978	—	—	Under appraisal. Most promising find to date

Source: Jerome D. Davis and Ib Faurby, 'The Paradox of Danish Offshore Policy: A Deviant Case in North Sea Oil and Gas Exploitation', in Martin Heisler and Robert Lawrence (eds.), *International Energy Policy* (Lexington, Mass.: D.C. Heath, 1980).

terms of direct development outlays, due to the shallow depths on the Danish Shelf.

Unfortunately evidence is lacking as to the reserves in many of the Danish fields. This is in part due to the general corporate secretiveness on such figures; but it is also in part due to an absence of delineation drilling. This latter factor is a function of a fundamental lack of interest in those finds which have been made to date.

7.4. Conclusion – The Danish Sector and the 'Contract'

Chapter 2 and the analysis of British policy stressed the 'institutional' aspects of corporate behaviour. Oil companies have varying interests in the North Sea. They are also quite definitely important political actors. There should be little surprise in discovering that in line with these observations, the DUC has not only not been terribly innovative in its exploration and development programme, but has also created political difficulties for Danish policy-makers. A lack of supervisory authority does not necessarily mean that Danish activities are problem-free. Rather it is seen by the managers within the industry itself that Danish policies are to blame for Danish problems – rather than the oil industry. Or, in the words of one industry observer, 'The Danish Government gets what the Danish Government deserves'.

It is in this context that the Danish 'contract' should be of interest. For despite its lack of specificity it has led to progress in the development of high-cost fields. Given the emphasis in this book on the dichotomy between access provisions and discretionary economic incentives – the difference between the stick and the carrot – the circumstances under which this progress was made is of considerable interest.

Notes

1. These are translated from the Danish 'tilsynet' and 'Handelsministeriet', respectively.
2. Handelsministeriets Tilsyn, *Rapport om Eneretsbevilling af 8. Juli 1962 med senere aedringer til efterfarskning og indvinding af kulbrinter m.v.* (Copenhagen: Handelsministeriet, October, 1975), p. 47.
3. Actually the concession is held by a number of companies within the A.P. Moeller group of shipping firms. To avoid confusion between this group and the DUC, we will refer throughout to the 'concessionaire' or the 'A.P. Moeller'.
4. For an authoritative version of the history of the Danish concession see J.D. Davis and Ib Faurby, 'The "World's Best" Oil Concession: A Critical View of Danish North Sea Offshore Policy', Århus, Denmark: unpublished manuscript, December 1976.
5. Anthony Sampson, *The Seven Sisters* (London: Hodder and Stoughton, 1975), p. 180.
6. The renaming took place at the time of the 1973/4 OPEC price hikes. It reflects the authorisation of DONG to purchase crude oil and products on behalf of the Danish state. Little of this activity has been performed, however.

8 THE DEVELOPMENT DECISION AND DANISH OIL

8.1. Introduction

If it is true, as stated in Chapter 7, that the Danish concession — seen in contractual perspective — is unique in the freedom it gives the oil multinational companies, the development decision in the Danish context can provide valuable insights as to how companies behave in the absence of the normal North Sea licensing requirements. This is particularly true in the case of the Danish oil fields as high-cost resources. They are much smaller than the gas fields.

Contractually speaking, the Danish concession is a monopoly concession. With one or two exceptions — e.g. the requirement of production within ten years — the firms comprising the DUC can set their own tempo and decide their own rate of development. In Chapters 1 and 3, it was argued that it was 'bounded rationality' which in the last instance characterised firms' behaviour in the North Sea. How do firms' organisation, oligopoly market control and political activity

Table 8.1: Danish Oil Reserves, 1979 — DeGolyer and MacNaughton Estimates (Millions of bbls.)

Fields	Proved reserves	Potential reserves	Possible reserves	Totals
Dan	120	—	—	120
Gorm	160	—	—	160
Skjold	35	36	—	71
Anne	14.5	—	—	14.5
Adda	8.3	62.2	—	70.5
Nils*				
Bo*				
Gwen*	—		280-560	280-560
Lulu				
Uffe				
Totals	337.8	98.2	280-560	716-996

*Drilled structure awaiting evaluation.

Source: DeGolyer and MacNaughton, *Report on the Feasibility of Installing an Oil Pipeline to the Danish North Sea Oil Fields* (January 1979).

affect their economic behaviour not only in a regime characterised by its leniency but also in a North Sea sector where most fields are high-cost (or 'marginal')? A study of the Danish case can be instructive in this regard, first because the relevant group, the DUC, has existed continuously since 1962/3 and secondly because there have been no fewer than three development decisions concerning 'marginal' fields. The first of these was in 1970/1 and dealt with the Dan field. The second decision concerned the Vern/Gorm field in the period 1975-9; the third, the Ruth/Skjold structure in 1977.

But before we turn to these decisions, a brief review of the nature of the DUC is necessary.

8.2. The DUC, An Institutional View

'With regard to the production of hydrocarbons', the Danish Government report stated gently, 'the committee [DUC's management committee] decides how large such a production should be. The size of any such production *should alone be limited by good production practice and by the partners' mutual economic differences*.'[1] There exists considerable evidence as to decision-making difficulties within the DUC.

A major source of disagreement within the group has been the interpretation of the various Danish offshore sectors. These differences have been reflected in the changing corporate ownership patterns. In the beginning, the concessionaire, A.P. Moeller, shared Jutland and the Islands with Gulf exclusively (July to autumn 1962). This 50:50 partnership was altered in late 1962 to include Shell. The new distribution of shares was A.P. Moeller 40 per cent, Shell 30 per cent, and Gulf 30 per cent. This situation existed when the concession was extended to include the North Sea Shelf in November 1963. Gulf was operator on the subsequent exploration surveys and drillings. Prior to commencement of offshore drilling, however, the group was further extended to include Chevron and Texaco. These two firms acquired 7.5 per cent shares apiece from A.P. Moeller's 40 per cent holding, reducing the concessionaires' share to 25 per cent of the total. The reason behind this move was an evident need for the concessionaire to reduce its share of the burden prior to active exploration. The initial exploration wells were successful, showing signs of both oil and gas (notably wells A1 and A2, the first two in the Danish sector). In 1967, the partnership again changed to increase Chevron's and Texaco's holdings to ten per cent apiece. A.P. Moeller's holdings fell to 20 per cent.

Further drilling revealed strains in the DUC. First the operator Gulf, disappointed with the results in the North-east Shelf Area, desired to pull out. The concessionary area was then divided into three sectors: the South-west Area, the North-east Area, and the Subsoil/Inner Waters. Gulf withdrew from the newly created North-eastern Area, Chevron assumed operator privileges for this area alone, and Gulf remained as the operator for the rest of the concessionary area. This adjustment was clearly not enough. On 1 January 1975, Gulf withdrew from the Danish Area entirely, its interests being divided among the remaining partners. This rather confusing progression of interest shifts within the concession is illustrated in Table 8.2 and the accompanying Map 8.1.

These concessionary changes clearly reflect differing preferences among DUC members. White, Kash, *et al.* have argued that the rate of activity in the Danish sector is higher than it should be due to A.P. Moeller's direct influence.[2] However, this contention would seem to be belied by the minority share which the concessionaire holds in the critical South-west Area. Three of the DUC partners, Gulf, Texaco and Chevron, are not noted for their commitment to the North Sea (see Chapter 3).

Co-operation with the DUC has been facilitated by a management committee of six members, originally comprising two members apiece from Gulf, Shell and A.P. Moeller. It is known that Chevron and Texaco upon their subsequent accession to the DUC, were regarded as being part of the A.P. Moeller vote, the latter firm representing them on the management committee. Changes must also have occurred upon Gulf's 1971 withdrawal from the North-east Area. But the only certain change took place in 1975, when Gulf's total withdrawal from the Danish Area meant that Chevron (now operator) and Texaco were given committee representation (one apiece). If this situation still prevails, the Danish Underground Consortium curiously allows the operator for the majority of the area represented one vote, while the other partners (with the exception of Texaco) retain two apiece.

That this situation is acceptable is due to another factor. Unlike the majority of groups in the North Sea, decision-making in the DUC is based on unanimous agreement. Should differences occur, the issues are 'ironed out' among the partners. An exception to this rule is that the Dansk Boreselskab (The Danish Drilling Company, an A.P. Moeller firm that represents the latter in the DUC) has final say when the 'life of the concession is at stake'. How well this oil industry version of the

Table 8.2: Changes in the Composition of the DUC

Date of change	Nature of change	Percentage of ownership	Operator status
July 1962	A.P.M. partnership with Gulf	A.P.M. — 50% Gulf — 50%	Gulf
Autumn 1962	Partnership revised to include Shell	A.P.M. — 40% Shell — 30% Gulf — 30%	Gulf
November 1963	Concession extended to Continental Shelf and Danish inland waters (incl. Baltic)	A.P.M. — 40% Shell — 30% Gulf — 30%	Gulf
January 1965	Partnership revised to include Chevron and Texaco (wio. voting privileges)	A.P.M. — 25% Shell — 30% Gulf — 30% Chevron — 7.5% Texaco — 7.5%	Gulf
January 1968	Partnership revised to increase Chevron and Texaco holdings	A.P.M. — 20% Shell — 30% Gulf — 30% Chevron — 10% Texaco — 10%	Gulf
January 1970	Major revision Danish concessionary area divided into 3 portions	South-west Area A.P.M. — 20% Gulf — 30% Shell — 30% Chevron — 10% Texaco — 10% North-east Area A.P.M. — 20% Shell — 30% Chevron — 25% Texaco — 25% Subsoil/Inner Waters A.P.M. — 40% Gulf — 30% Shell — 30%	South-west Area Gulf North-east Area Chevron Subsoil/Inner Waters A.P.M.
January 1975	Gulf withdraws. Proportional redistribution of ownership	South-west A.P.M. — 30% Shell — 40% Chevron — 15% Texaco — 15% North-east Same as in 1971 Subsoil/Inner Waters A.P.M. — 57% Shell — 43%	South-west Chevron North-east Chevron Subsoil/Inner Waters—A.P.M.

Map 8.1: The North Sea Concession, 1971-6

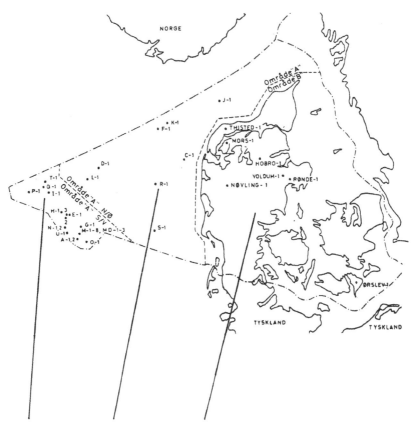

North Sea South-west	North Sea North-east	Subsoil and Inner Waters
A.P.M. — 20%	A.P.M. — 20%	A.P.M. — 40%
Gulf — 30%	Shell — 30%	Gulf — 30%
Shell — 30%	Chevron — 25%	Shell — 30%
Chevron — 10%	Texaco — 25%	
Texaco — 10%		

Revised Holdings after 1 January 1975

A.P.M. — 30%	A.P.M. — 20%	A.P.M. — 57%
Shell — 40%	Shell — 30%	Shell — 43%
Chevron — 15%	Chevron — 25%	
Texaco — 15%	Texaco — 25%	

Source: Jerome D. Davis (ed.), *Danmark og Nordsøen II. Olie og naturgas* (Copenhagen: Informations Forlag, 1980), p.47.

eighteenth century Polish *liberum veto* has worked out in practice is uncertain, but there are clues that there have been unhappy experiences.

A major conflict area has undoubtedly existed between A.P. Moeller and the other partners, particularly the operators. There is no record of whether A.P. Moeller speculated in concessionary territory. There is similarly no record of payment for operator privileges — a common occurrence elsewhere in the North Sea. Questions remain, however. Did A.P. Moeller profit through awarding operator privileges to Gulf? Did A.P. Moeller profit by the various 'farm-ins' to the Danish concession by Shell, Chevron, and Texaco respectively? (The implication here with regard to the second two partners is that originally they bought shares in the A.P. Moeller holdings — otherwise why should they be represented by A.P. Moeller within the management committee?) Finally, did A.P. Moeller profit from the sales of its ownership shares subsequent to the 'farm-ins' — notably in 1967? There is no evidence available possibly because of a lack of Danish government concern in these areas — another notable exception to the North Sea practices elsewhere.

A much more certain source of strain between A.P. Moeller and its consortium partners has been that of concessionary revisions. The revisions of 1971 and later of 1976 were basically to A.P. Moeller's advantage *vis-a-vis* their offshore partners, rather than to the advantage of the Danish state *vis-a-vis* the DUC. The 1972 revisions, for example, pledged the concessionaires to explore with Danish platforms, use Danish labour and helicopters, and construct Danish bases. A.P. Moeller complied, certainly to the disadvantage of the operator who was then forced to utilise A.P. Moeller equipment, a proposition which was probably suboptimal for the company at the time. The operator, Gulf Oil, reportedly opposed these arrangements, but eventually gave in.[3] With this guaranteed market as a base A.P. Moeller has since expanded world-wide as a concession-holder (in Tunisia, Egypt, Korea) and offshore equipment firm (with three semi-submersibles, six jackups, five self-contained platforms, six inland barge rigs, and a considerable number of supply vessels and barges).[4] Nor is this role fully over. With the increasing attraction of production in the Danish Area, A.P. Moeller's Lindoe shipbuilding subsidiary has been among the leaders in designing offshore production platforms which fit the special requirements of Danish offshore conditions. Clearly, A.P. Moeller has in effect delegated to itself the same procurement privileges which most countries demand of offshore operators *vis-a-vis* domestic onshore offshore construction industry and procurement. In this instance the

A.P. Moeller group performs the function of the state, with the exception that the benefits go directly to the group whereas elsewhere the benefits are indirect, the state merely ensuring that contracting does go to the most competitive domestic firms rather than to firms overseas.

A good final illustration of the group dynamics within the DUC could be seen in the results of the attempted government revision of the concession in 1976. The then Social Democratic Government attempted to change certain concessionary terms as well as start natural gas production from finds already eight-years-old. Among the more nominal changes (another change was the division of the Danish Shelf into blocks), was the introduction of the 'self-risk' clause into the intra-company agreements:

> Concessionaires and their partners will change their joint venture agreements in order to secure that one or more of the DUC partners can carry through an exploratory well or develop an oil or gas field on their own responsibility without participation of the other partners.[5]

This language sounds unequivocal. Unfortunately the implementation of the provision was not. The provision was a compromise, resulting from a government insistence that the DUC agree to some form of government participation. When it came to implementing the substance of this article into the inter-corporate agreements, the author was informed, it was found that A.P. Moeller as concessionaire had to be included in whatever project might be envisaged by its partners. The result has been that this 'self-risk' clause further enhances the power of the concessionaire which can block any progress by its partners. 'Self-risk' in this case does not prevent deadlocks fully; rather 'self-risk' like virtually all the other provisions of the Protocol of 15 July 1976, strengthens the hand of A.P. Moeller in dealing with the other members of the DUC.

8.3. The Decision to Develop the Dan: North Sea Activity and Options

On 29 March 1971, the concessionaires informed the Ministry of Public Works that they intended to begin production from a field in the Danish area (thereby fulfilling this requirement of the original concession agreement). The interesting part of this letter was an admission from the concessionaires that they were uncertain as to where production was to begin. Enclosed with the letter was an ambiguous production plan, probably aimed at the first structure explored in the Danish area, the A or 'Anne' structure, the site of two wells drilled in 1966/7. The letter was, however, ambivalent:

> The production system can be used on structures A, M or N. . .in that the water depth at each is about the same. Wells 'Dansk Nordsoe A-1' and 'Dansk Nordsoe A-2' established oil in the A structure, but in so far as presently undertaken exploration work might succeed in discovering oil under better geological conditions, the production platform will be installed on that structure instead [of A structure].[6]

The enclosed production plan was equally obscure:

> Priority is being given to the establishment of production from a geologic structure in the area of the previous discoveries. From previous studies of the deposits of hydrocarbons discovered to date, it has been concluded that these are not of sufficient magnitude to justify the cost of constructing a pipeline for production from these deposits. Nevertheless, from a recent feasibility study, a system has been devised to make it possible to commence the recovery of oil from a structure to be selected when the current exploration drilling is completed.[7]

At the time of announcement, the DUC had drilled 14 exploration wells, 12 wildcats and 2 step-outs. Some 12,000 miles of seismic profiles had been accumulated, and some discoveries had been made. The first exploration well offshore (August 1966) discovered natural gas and traces of oil. DUC efforts during the period concerned were not insignificant. The Danish offshore area was carefully explored with particular attention paid to the Central Graben (where all significant discoveries have taken place) and to the deep sandstone reservoirs of the Danish Basin (Dansk Saenkningsområde) which has been the subject of investigation of an additional land-based wells. Perhaps less thoroughly explored than desirable was the Danish extension of the northern German Basin, the source of only one well Oerslev-1. Particular attention was paid to the Danish chalk strata (Danian/Higher Chalk) particularly in 1970/1. Not until 1973 would the DUC begin looking at possible Jurassic strata — the source of the major British and Norwegian finds, but which is thin or non-existent in the Danish North Shelf area.

Map 8.2: Geological Regions in the Danish Offshore

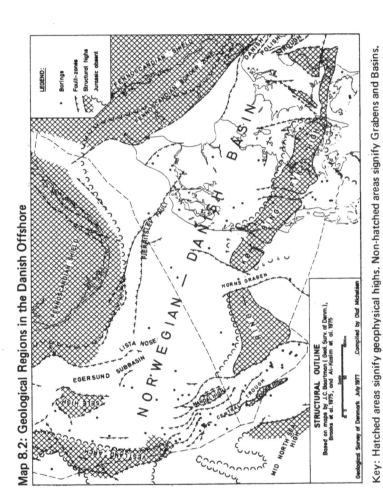

Key: Hatched areas signify geophysical highs. Non-hatched areas signify Grabens and Basins.

Source: Olaf Michelsen, 'Stratigraphy and Distribution of Jurassic Deposits of the Norwegian-Danish Basin', *Geological Survey of Denmark*, Series B, no 2, (Copenhagen, 1978).

Table 8.3: Structures under Consideration — Danish North Sea Area, December 1970

Name of structure	Wells	Flow rate (bbls./day)	Reserves (millions bbls.) Probable	Possible[b]
Anne	A-1, A-2	1,022[a]	5.7	16.4
Cora	E-1, E-2	n.a.	41.3	102.2
Bent	H-1	n.a.	16.7	36.7
Arne	I-1	n.a.	n.a.	n.a.

Notes:

a. Calculated from production plans, 200,000 tons per 270-day year from five wells.

b. Or defined as maximum/minimum in Letter Uggi Engle (DUC) to Hagen Jørgensen, 15 September 1976. Later defined in terms of possible and probable, but not along the normal usage of these terms.

At the time of the DUC planning, it was clear that an economically defensible production should be started by 1972, or at the very least by 8 July 1973, in order to retain the concessionary privileges. Yet the alternatives first considered in 1970/1 were not particularly attractive. These are illustrated in Table 8.3.

One can easily see the sources of the DUC's lukewarm enthusiasm for establishing production in the Danish Area. Feasibility studies done by the Gulf Development Corporation indicated that A-structure should be the best. This is a somewhat strange conclusion given the much larger reserves of Cora. It is possible, given the date of the reserve figures in Table 7.6, that Anne's reserve were subsequently downgraded relative to those of Cora. No information on Arne exists at all, but it is thought to be a smallish structure with a flow rate of up to 300-400 tons of oil per day.

This picture changed somewhat with the results of drilling on Abby-Dan and Vern in the period of March to June, 1971. Suddenly it appeared that the DUC had discovered structures which were rather large, particularly in comparison to the Anne option. Activity must have been fast and furious for four days after completion of the Vern drilling, the drill rig *Britannia* was drilling the first of the five production holes on the Dan structure. (Given the juxtaposition of events, it is highly likely that the well results from Vern were not investigated thoroughly before the decision was made to commit the platforms on order to the Dan structure.) The picture had changed somewhat; the four fields in contention were Anne, Cora, Dan and Vern.

Table 8.4: The Basis of the Dan Decision, June 1971

Structure	Flow rate (bbls./day)	Reserves (millions bbls.) Probable	Possible	Calculated IRR (%)
Anne	1,022	5.7	16.4	n.a.
Cora	n.a.	41.3	102.2	19.0[c]
Dan	2-3,000	58.3	170.6	18.3[b]
Vern	3,240	n.a.[a]	n.a.[a]	n.a.

Notes:
a. The only source for Vern's reserves gives the total of these reserves after a *second* well, appraising the structure in 1975. These are therefore excluded. The other reserve figures are for comparison's sake only.
b. Calculated by author on the basis of the $10 million original production plan with five wells.
c. Figure furnished by the DUC, production of oil alone at a cost of $20 million.

On the basis of the information in Table 8.4, it becomes clear why Dan became the preferred alternative. Cora was the only other field which possessed anything approaching the reserves of the Dan field. But there were two outstanding deficits with Cora: (a) a production system for oil alone from Cora would cost $20 million (vs. $10 million for the Dan); and (b) Cora was largely a gas structure, but the production of both oil and gas from Cora would result in an IRR of only 10.3 per cent on an investment of over $90 million.[8] The return on Anne was worse than that for Cora, but the overall capital costs of Anne were only half as large. Anne would suffice to fulfil the letter of the concessionary agreement and turn a small profit besides. Dan on the other hand could be exploited at a higher rate of profitability and with a smaller investment. A decision was taken for Dan.

On 4 July 1972, a few days before the concession was originally due to expire (it had been extended due to *force majeure* and the Danish-German dispute over the delineation of their respective shelves), production of oil was inaugurated on the Dan field. The irony of the Dan decision is that both Cora and Vern (later renamed Gorm) were actually better structures. But this would not be discovered until 1975-7. The lack of caution exhibited by the DUC was remarkable. The Dan was started to fulfil conditions of the concession. No time was allowed for several confirmation wells. A platform destined for another field was installed and production begun.

Under these circumstances it should come as no surprise that the Dan field was a disaster. The production system should have cost $10 million, an extremely low figure even in 1971 dollars. Operating costs would be $1,850,000 *per annum.* The field was to yield 350,000 tons of oil *per annum.* The best the DUC could have hoped for was a 23.6 per cent DCFR, given a 300-day producing year and a $2.50 per barrel price of oil.

By the time the production system was ready in July 1972, it had cost something in excess of $26.4 million.[9] A second phenomenon that production tests should have revealed was that the permeability of the Danish chalk reservoir was considerably below the predictions. Far from yielding the anticipated 350,000 metric tons of crude per year, the production rates for the first two years were as follows: 94,000 tons (1972), 134,000 tons (1973). In 1974, the DUC companies undertook to add three additional platforms to the field, an expenditure of roughly $70 million. Installation interfered with production but by 1977 the wells were producing 510,000 tons of oil. Capital expenditures on the field and subsequent profits are illustrated in Table 8.5. But, as can be seen, the project will break even sometime in 1980/1. The Dan, despite its problems, should therefore be giving good profits until abandonment in 1993. In no other way are its earnings even comparable to other North Sea fields.

Table 8.5: Capital Investment and Before-tax Income, Dan Field 1972-8 (Millions US Dollars)

	Invested sums (1)	Sales (oil) (2)	Operations cost (3)	Royalties (4)	Balance (5) (2) − (3+4)
1972	25.7	0.4	2.5	0.05	−2.15
1973	—	3.2	5.53	0.154	−2.48
1974	10.3	9.35	7.64	0.465	+1.245
1975	8.1	13.25	6.04	0.604	+6.61
1976	42.1	20.4	9.05	0.944	+10.41
1977	20.5	50.4	11.7	3.64	+35.03
1978	11.6	44.5	19.7	4.67	+20.23
Totals 1972-8	118.3	141.5	59.6	10.48	68.9

Source: Company accounts as reported to Danish tax authorities.

8.4. The Decision to Develop Gorm Field

Vern (later renamed Gorm, after a legendary Danish king)[10] was one of the fields considered by the DUC at the time of the decision to develop Dan. The sequence of exploration/development wells gives a good indication of how Vern was overlooked in the haste to develop Dan. The *Britannia*, a jack-up, was the only piece of equipment in the Danish area at the time:

Well No.	Purpose	Drill rig	Dates on location
M-1 (Dan)	exploration	*Britannia*	1971-03-08 to 1971-05-08
N-1 (Vern)	exploration	*Britannia*	1971-05-11 to 1971-06-19
M-2 (Dan)	production	*Britannia*	1971-06-23 to 1971-07-19

Four days after completing the first exploration well at Vern, *Britannia* 'spudded' the first of the six Dan production wells! And this despite the fact that the maximum flow from the Vern exploration well was somewhat higher than from the Dan well.

The second drilling at Vern was not made until late April 1975. A subsequent confirmation well was put down in 1976. Not until spring 1978 would the DUC announce its intentions of developing the Vern field — now renamed Gorm. There are a host of questions which could be asked about Gorm/Vern. Why did the DUC not develop Gorm instead of Dan? Why did the DUC wait four years before drilling its first confirmation well on the structure? Why, after the favourable results of the confirmation wells, did the DUC wait until 1978 before announcing its decision to go ahead with the Gorm project?

The reasons for the choice of Dan over Gorm/Vern are undoubtedly rooted in haste and in a basic lack of awareness on the nature of Danian chalk as a reservoir rock. There was simply no time to conduct lengthy well tests from the first Dan well. Only after the platforms were installed on the field would the DUC firms recognise the extent of their error. Since that period the DUC has poured money into the Dan. Additional platforms, frequent redrillings, mooring buoy repairs notwithstanding, the DUC can hardly hope to get Dan production above 500,000 tons *per annum*. This is surely a North Sea low.

Having established an 'economically defensible' production from the Dan in conformance with the letter of the concession, there was no need for the DUC to develop the Gorm field, or even to confirm the extent of the structure. Money which could have been used to this end was drained away to the Dan. Another reason for not going ahead with the test wells at Gorm could have been reluctance on the part of the DUC operator, Gulf. Gulf withdrew from the Consortium on 1 January 1975. The Gorm confirmation well was drilled four months later. This sequence of events may not have been purely coincidental.

The curious aspect of Gorm is that the field promised almost as good returns on investment in 1972 as it did in 1978 when the decision was made to go ahead and develop the field. Table 8.6 shows that with essentially the same plan as that of 1978, Gorm could have returned 30 per cent plus (IRR) in 1972 with a $3.00 per barrel price.[11] (Assumptions behind Table 8.6 are given in the Appendix to this chapter.) Even at 1972 crude oil prices, it would be hard to characterise Gorm oil as 'marginal' or costly. Compared with other fields in the British sector in 1972, its rates of return were as good or better. In terms of capital costs, Gorm developed in 1972 or 1973 would have cost about $2.62 per barrel. This compares with around $3.66 per barrel for the Forties field, developed at the same time.

Gorm clearly presents a better investment prospect in 1978 than in 1972 — even with considerably increased capital costs. But does this improvement 'justify' the four-year interval between the first Gorm discovery well and the first delineation well? One could make this case for virtually any of the North Sea fields. Ekofisk, for example, makes better returns in 1978 than it would have in 1972, even with the Norwegian petroleum taxation arrangement.

In the period after the first delineation well, development of Gorm was evidently delayed by another matter — that of natural gas. The natural gas question, to be discussed in Chapter 10, arose in 1975. At issue was whether or not the DUC would develop the Cora and Bent fields and utilise the associated gas from Dan and eventually Gorm. The application to develop Gorm occurred within days of the delivery of the DUC's *Gas Report of 1978* reporting favourably on the prospects for natural gas production. That this is not coincidence is explicitly noted by Clifford Browne's 1977 discussion of the 'Vern' field:

> Development of Vern is being considered but commercialization is not anticipated until the Danish natural gas situation is more clearly defined. Platform installation and oil production at Vern could preceed complete resolution of the natural gas issue if gas reinjection is feasible since flaring is unlikely to be permitted.[12]

Once the application to develop Gorm had been submitted, Danish authorities tied this to a successful resolution of the natural gas price

Table 8.6: Gorm (a) Developed in 1972; (b) Developed in 1978;
Measures of Profitability

	(a) $3.00 per barrel	(b) $14.00 per barrel
DCFR (%)	30.8	43.1
Payout period*	5.1 years out of 23	4.4 years out of 28
Net income ratio	3.03	5.07
Corporate take	$169.7m	$957.08m
Government take	$126.57m	$752.7m

*Including entire period of investment.

Sources: Production figures from the two cases are from DeGolyer and
MacNaughton, *Rapport om Tilvejebringelsen af et Beslutningsgrundlag Angående
Produktion af Naturgas fra Cora, Dan, Vern og Bent Felterne i den Danske
Nordsø Sektor* (1 May 1978), Table 8. Investment figures calculated from
J.D. Davis, B.A. Svendsen, with T.S.F. Knudsen and K.L. Lau, *Dansk Naturgas —
Problemer og Muligheder i 80'erne* (Åarhus, Denmark: Forlaget Politica, 1978),
pp. 150-3, for the $14.00 per barrel case. For the $3.00 per barrel case,
reinjection costs and costs of living quarters removed from investments and the
investment sums are discounted backwards to 1972 dollars. Both cases assume
constant prices and costs.

issue. In a remarkable retreat however, production permits were granted
for Gorm field on 13 July 1978. It would take a further seven months
to negotiate the natural gas question.

   Gorm is scheduled for production in 1981. Delays in developing the
field had two causes. The four-year gap between discovery and the first
appraisal well was most likely due to the impact of the Dan field. Dan
affected corporate perspectives towards the entire North Sea sector,
so much so that 'Danian chalk' was one of the major reasons Gulf
withdrew from the DUC in 1975. Gorm fell within these perspectives.
Its development was unnecessary in 1972. The DUC 'sat' on Gorm.
The delay between the two successful appraisal wells of April 1975 and
of September 1976 respectively and the application in February 1978
is traceable not only to the need to evaluate the well results. This had
been done by autumn 1977.[13] It was also tied to developments with
regard to natural gas. The DUC 'sat' on Gorm once again.

8.5. The Decision to Develop Ruth/Skjold

The events surrounding the small Danish field originally called 'Ruth', but renamed 'Skjold', are in striking contrast to those influencing Gorm. Ruth was discovered in March 1977. Less than six months later, a production application had been filed with the Danish Ministry of Commerce for the commercial development of the field in its new incarnation Skjold. The haste calls for some explanation.

Skjold is a small field located about 10 kilometres from Gorm. The discovery well encountered oil which flowed at rates up to 5,000-6,000 barrels per day. These rates were a considerable improvement on anything found in the Danish sector at that time. (By contrast, the maximum rates from Gorm were around 3,300 barrels per day.) The DUC drilled no confirmation or appraisal wells, proceeding with a production application directly.

How could the DUC do this? The answer to this question lies in the nature of the Danish Shelf and of production technology. The oil fields on the Danish Shelf are characterised by shallow water depths contrasting greatly with oil fields elsewhere in the North Sea. Fulmar, a British field which excited Shell/Esso, due to its reserves (250 million bbls.) and also to the shallow depth of water in the area, a depth of 83 metres (270 feet) is more than outclassed in this respect by the Danish fields, Gorm with 39 metres (128 feet) and Dan with 43 metres (140 feet). This makes the Danish fields highly commercial if oil is discovered in sufficient quantity. Danish platforms have averaged anywhere from $7 million to $14 million apiece — a far cry from the hundreds of millions required for platforms elsewhere in the northern North Sea.

Technologically, Chevron had developed the idea of a movable production platform. The idea was that an old 'jack-up' platform could be hired or leased, rebuilt, and used as a production platform on the Danish Shelf. Wells would be drilled and be serviced by the redesigned 'jack-up'. Should the structure prove unprofitable, little money would be lost. The 'jack-up' could be removed from the field and used elsewhere. A further advantage was that a 'jack-up' could be installed on a field and its first wells could also serve as appraisal wells. Savings would be immeasurable.

Yet there were disadvantages as well. The 'jack-up' reportedly envisaged for such reconditioning, the *Orion*, was not suited for gas reinjection on the Skjold field — a complicated process requiring heavy compressors. Furthermore, nobody really knew much about the size of the Skjold field. The exploration well had not yet found the oil-water contact which normally marks the bottom of the North Sea fields. The DUC stressed the disadvantages of developing the field, repeatedly stressing the 'thin' oil column.

Government authorities were not sure. DeGolyer and MacNaughton were called on for advice. The opinions of the Houston-based consultants would not make the DUC particularly happy. To begin with, DeGolyer and MacNaughton evaluated the field much more positively than did the Consortium. The 'thin column' was repeatedly evaluated as being about 300 feet thick with no bottom. (Evaluations in this regard can very easily differ in the absence of appraisal wells.) The DUC had claimed there were only 30-45 million barrels in the field. DeGolyer and MacNaughton's figures were twice as high (around 71 million barrels). The DUC proposed initial production rates of one million tons *per annum*; DeGolyer and MacNaughton found that 750,000 tons *per annum* was the maximum which the structure could tolerate. As a clincher, DeGolyer and MacNaughton argued that oil recovery would be considerably enhanced if the associated gas were reinjected into the structure. This would make the use of the 'jack-up' difficult if not impossible.

The resulting conflict between the DUC and the ministerial authorities broke into the papers. Columns stressed the pros and cons of gas reinjection. The DUC stressed the benefits for Skjold oil for the Danish balance of payments. The Danish authorities found themselves locked in a struggle. The question of how the field should be exploited was shelved in favour of a public confrontation over whether the DUC should be allowed to 'flare' natural gas or not. A compromise solution was suggested. Skjold would be developed, and the associated gas could be reinjected at Gorm field, which all expected would be developed. Although the costs of such an arrangement were minimal, about $10 million, this alternative was rejected. By the time a study team from Aarhus University published the results of an analysis undertaken there, pointing out that the prospective IRR of 82 per cent for the field was a North Sea 'high', the DUC had withdrawn its application.[14]

One reported reason for the furore over the field is that the A.P. Moeller group and the other DUC partners were relying on the profits from Skjold to provide capital for investing in Gorm and the gas project. There can be no doubt that the project was a money-maker: it would cost about $32 million in capital costs and although operation costs were high — estimated in the region of $24 million *per annum* — these would be more than made up in positive cash flows from the field. The profitability of the field is given in Table 8.7, both in terms of the $14.00 per barrel price at the time (1977) and the more recent $22.00 per barrel price characteristic of 1979. (The project would have

Table 8.7: Skjold — Measures of Profitability for the Original Project*
(750,000 mt. *per annum*)

	(a) at $14.00 per bbl.	(b) at $22.00 per bbl.
DCFR (%)	106.8	145.9
Payout period	2.35 years (out of 8)	2.28 years (out of 8)
Net income ratio	5.45	8.66
Corporation 'take'	$178.5m	$335.5m
Government 'take'	$141.5m	$266.3m

*For specification of assumptions, see the appendix to this chapter.

commenced in 1979 had permission been forthcoming.) The Internal
Rates of Return are impressive. Yet it is important to remember that
they are very sensitive to time. A one-year delay in the project reduces
its IRR (at $14.00 per bbl.) from 107 per cent to around 60 per cent.
The addition of a pipeline to transport associated gas similarly affects
profits. Assuming that the pipeline costs $7 million, causes operations
costs to rise by $2 million *per annum*, and delays the project by an
additional six months, then the DCFR falls to 54.5 per cent, the
payout period increases to 3.32, and the net income ratio falls to 4.95.
(All this is based on the assumption that the natural gas is not sold
further, but is instead reinjected at Gorm.)

Since the withdrawal of their application, the DUC have been
somewhat ambivalent about the Skjold project. It will undoubtedly be
submitted again, although in a considerably revised form. The DUC
has since let it be known that the 'jack-up' was never intended as a
permanent arrangement, but was a means of delineating the field whilst
establishing production. Why this sentiment was not expressed in 1977
is not known.

8.6. Conclusion — The Development Decision: The Institutional Approach Reconsidered

To what degree have different corporate opportunity cost and
preference rankings affected the development decision in the Danish
cases examined in this chapter? Given the nature of group activities in
the North Sea, differences among their members are a matter of secrecy.

With the DUC, the evidence surrounding the Dan, Gorm and Skjold decisions must remain largely circumstantial. This evidence is bolstered by oblique government commentaries as to inter-group/management committee differences, and by the pattern of Gulf's withdrawal, finally accomplished in 1975. More recently, this circumstantial case has been somewhat strengthened. It is a fact that intercorporate differences were to plague the natural gas negotiations in 1978/9, as will be discussed in Chapter 10. It is a fact that development plans as first elaborated by some of the DUC partners do not conform to the development plans generally presented later to the public. Notable in this regard were the development plans for the gas fields. The Riggs National Bank Report of 1977, based largely on Chevron sources, suggested that the natural gas fields would be developed with three four-well platforms. The final plan suggested four eight-well platforms. Earlier, a Gulf Development Corporation report had suggested one single twelve-well platform. That these changes occurred without some differences within the DUC is difficult to believe. Inter-group differences require much further investigation. With present sources, it is difficult to get beyond the type of evidence presented in this chapter. Until knowledgeable persons are willing to confide the nature of these decision-making processes beyond the level of vague generalities, inter-group differences will remain an area of rumour, gossip, and conjecture in the Danish North Sea and elsewhere.

Less susceptible to speculation is the sequence of development decisions in the Danish North Sea. The DUC first developed a highly costly field, one which they should not have developed. That this was done and done in a hurry was to fulfil the sole concessionary obligation of any significance — that of establishing an 'economically defensible' oil production within ten years of the concessionary award (later prolonged to twelve). The DUC did not develop a far more attractive structure that would have yielded a considerable income, i.e. Vern/ Gorm. In a pure opportunity cost perspective, the DUC should have developed Vern/Gorm (even without pressure to do so). In fact the field was bypassed for years and then held hostage to the natural gas discussions. Finally, the third development decision, involving a small but highly rewarding field, was revoked when the DUC found automatic government approval not forthcoming. Here the opportunity cost perspective would have led to the development of the field in any case. Instead the DUC decided to wait till better times — even semi-publicly acknowledging that they were waiting for a change in government.

One would be hard put to find a series of development decisions made under more widely diverse circumstances. Yet, the question as to how the institutional approach modifies an economic perspective remains to be answered. One can, on the basis of Danish evidence, deduce several contributing factors.

First, an economic approach assumes near perfect information. In practice this information can be difficult to obtain. Had it been available in 1971, the Dan field would never have been developed. It would (quite rightly) have been classed as a 'marginal' high-cost field. Development efforts should have been concentrated on Vern/Gorm in the first instance. The decision to proceed with Dan and not with Vern/Gorm probably had more to do with the seismic estimates of the size of the two respective structures, the Dan structure being considerably larger. Further, to turn this argument around, if the DUC had not been so adversely affected by the Dan, it might have investigated the Vern/Gorm structure earlier than 1975/6. There can be little doubt that Dan occasioned considerable gloom within the DUC in the period until 1975. This gloom would 'rub off' on corporate perspectives regarding the prospects of the Danish sector. The DUC partners lost interest in this sector, so much so that the operator in fact abandoned the group rather than proceed. The Danish case is perhaps extreme in this regard, but it is not unlikely that the sequence of events has been repeated elsewhere, in the Norwegian, the British, and the Dutch sectors.

Secondly, the economic perspective is significantly affected by the political environment, as reflected in each of the three development decisions. The Dan decision was clearly influenced by the need to establish an 'economically defensible' production to secure the concessionary rights. The Gorm decision, when finally made, was withheld pending successful resolution of a controversy over natural gas. The Skjold decision was withdrawn when the partners, most notably the concessionaire, objected to the government's conditional acceptance of their production plan. Here again, the absence of policy could have led to considerably more politicisation than would otherwise have been the case. The DUC was not used to fulfilling political/economic preconditions from the government's side. None had existed prior to 1971/2. There was therefore a considerable amount of 'testing' of governmental will, when preconditions began to be attached after 1975. Still the Danish case does lend support to arguments made elsewhere that the political environment is a critical factor in the development decision.[15]

Thirdly, the interaction of institutional factors and economics

Table 8.8: Rates of Activity — Wells Drilled by the DUC in the Danish Sector Compared to Wells Drilled by Shell/Esso, Amoco Groups in the UK Sector, 1964 to 1978

Group name		Well categories		Wells total
	Exploration	Confirmation/ appraisal	Production	
DUC (Denmark)	28	6	18	52
Shell/Esso (UK)	65	45	251	361
Amoco Groups (UK)	39	23	132*	194*

*Of which 72 are at Leman.

Source: Offshore Promotional Services Ltd., *European Continental Shelf Guide, 1979* (London: OPS, 1979).

affects the development decision perhaps more than exploratory expenditures. Table 8.8 compares the rates of drilling activity between the two of the more active groups on the UK Shelf and the DUC. Although the DUC has been criticised for its lack of exploratory activity, it compares rather favourably in terms of exploration wells. (It should be noted that Table 8.8 does not specify well depth, however.) Where Danish activity falls short is of course in the confirmation/appraisal and production categories. Of the six confirmation/appraisal wells only one was drilled before 1974. This picture conforms to that presented in this chapter.

Fourthly, Table 8.8 raises the problem of access. The DUC's 'wildcatting' rate may approach that of the Amoco groups but the Amoco groups are only several of many different licensed groups in the British North Sea. The DUC has monopoly rights on the Danish concession essentially until the year 2012. Might not the *admission of yet more groups have improved the Danish rate of exploration substantially?* The same can be asked of the development decision. One of the institutional factors mentioned previously, information, comes in here. With more groups drilling for different structures of different geological strata, the amount of information relevant to development decisions would increase. If, furthermore, the DUC were forced to relinquish land on which an Adda or Skjold were discovered and developed by another firm, would this not reinforce the DUC incentive to examine already discovered fields more closely? Had Vern been discovered by another group, it is quite likely it would have been developed by this time. Its production history would also have increased

DUC knowledge about other similar structures such as Cora and Bent. The most critical failure of Danish policy is this failure to provide more open access. The development decision could thus become the sole prerogative of a single group – in this case the DUC.

Although it can be argued that the institutional approach modifies the pure 'opportunity cost' perspective of the economists, the question remains: is there any indication that the institutional aspects of the DUC in fact delay development progress in the Danish Area more than would be the case for any other group? This question is difficult to answer. Not only must an alternative group of companies be found for the Danish area, but one must prove the willingness of this alternative group to invest in prospects the DUC has decided to ignore for the time being.

While this notion must remain hypothetical, given the concession terms, have there been any actual instances where prospects straddling the frontiers Norway-Denmark, UK-Denmark, or West Germany-Denmark have excited interest in the foreign sector but not the Danish? There has already been one such case. The Norwegian Hod field discovered by the Amoco/Noco Group and the object of no fewer than three appraisal wells, may in fact extend into the Danish sector.[16] This, despite some contrary evidence and denials, first became public in 1975:

> Did the last few days of 1974 rekindle hopes of interesting hydrocarbon discoveries in the Danish sector? It now seems certain that the Amoco/Noco structure on block 2/11 which appears very promising extends into the Danish sector.[17]

There are two possibilities: either the Hod structure does extend into the Danish sector, or it is cut off by a fault very close to the frontier.[18] For obvious reasons, the Amoco/Noco Group is keeping quiet. Whether the Hod does or does not extend across the frontier may be immaterial. The field (or that share of it in Norway) is too small to be a producing unit in and of itself. Before proceeding to a development decision, the Amoco/Noco Group was also interested in the nature of structures similar to Hod on the Danish side of the frontier, the existence of which is publicly known.[19] Approaches have reportedly been made to the DUC about the possibilities of a common project. There is no record of a response. The DUC has neither evinced an interest in a co-operation with the Amoco/Noco Group nor recognised publicly that some geological structures in the area might be of interest.

Notes

1. Handelsministeriets Tilsyn, *Rapport om Eneretsbevilling*, p. 40. Author's translation and emphasis.

2. Ibid., p. 17. The source for this argument was an interview with the officers of A.P. Moeller in August, 1973.

3. See *Information* (29-30 November 1975).

4. Operating in the North Sea, E. Malaysia, Singapore, Gulf of Mexico, Louisiana, and Brazil. *Danshore* (July/August 1976), p. 46. Note that these rigs and vessels are owned by diverse A.P. Moeller firms: Maersk Drilling, Asia Pacific Marine, Aquadrill. Two of the semi-submersibles are held in partnership with ODECO.

5. Article 6, Protocol of 15 July 1976, as quoted in *Danshore* (September-October 1976), p. 37. (Trans. is *Danshore*'s.)

6. Handelministeriets Tilsyn, *Rapport om Eneretsbevilling*, Appendix 66. (My translation.)

7. Ibid., 'Dansk Undergrounds Consortium: Production Plan, 25 February 1971', pp. 1-2.

8. A.P. Moeller, 'Remarks to the Tilsynet Report', II, p. 10 is the source for the figures for Cora.

9. This and other data are from DeGolyer and MacNaughton, *Report on the Results of a Study of the Dan Field, 'E' Structure and 'H' Structure North Sea Continental Shelf Denmark* (March 1975), Table 5.

10. 'Dan' is also the name of a Danish king.

11. This is based on the assumption of a $56 million capital investment (1972 prices). No reinjection wells are included − the price of oil not justifying the added investment.

12. Clifford Browne, *Status Report on the North Sea Development Drilling Market* (Washington D.C.: Riggs National Bank, September 1977), p. 270.

13. Industry sources.

14. 'Dansk olie-felt bedst', *Politiken* (6 October 1977), p. 18.

15. See, especially, Jon Morgan and Colin Robinson, *North Sea Oil in the Future: Economic Analysis and Government Policy* (London: Macmillan, 1978).

16. The Amoco/Noco group consists of Amoco Norway (25 per cent), Amerada Petroleum Corp. of Norway (25 per cent), Texas Eastern Norwegian Inc. (25 per cent) and the Norwegian Oil Consortium (25 per cent).

17. *Noroil* (January 1975), p. 53.

18. See for example, Browne, *Status Report*, isopachous map p. 184.

19. Of particular interest is the 'Lone' structure which straddles the frontier in this area. See DeGolyer and MacNaughton, *Report on the Feasibility*, Figure 6.

9 THE PROBLEMS OF DANISH GAS

9.1. Introduction

Perhaps no better example of the politics of 'marginal' fields in the North Sea exists than in the Danish gas fields. These fields show clearly the interplay between government and corporate preferences, and represent no fewer than six years of political manoeuvring, controversy, and concentrated efforts.

As with high-cost fields elsewhere, there is considerable evidence that the DUC deliberately attempted to avoid producing from the gas fields it had discovered. The first significant discovery was the E-structure, later known as the Cora field. This structure was first investigated 29 May-15 August 1968, with the drilling of the exploratory well, E-1. Five days later, the *Maersk Explorer* drilled a confirmation well, E-2, and found sizeable quantities of natural gas. That this was not recognised at the time was in part due to the press release confirming the find. It tersely stated that 'some oil and gas was found, but to such a limited quantity that commercial exploitation possibilities are doubtful.'[1] DUC interest subsequently waxed and waned with regard to this field, due largely to institutional conditions (the formation of the state owned Dansk Naturgas Company) and to various testing results. Although at one time the Consortium argued that recoverable gas reserves at the field were between 7,800 million and 10,800 million cubic metres, it is now agreed that the field actually contains a minimum of 45,000-50,000 million cubic metres – a five- to six-fold increase.

The second gas discovery of any importance was the Bent field (H-structure). Although considerably smaller than Cora, it could represent a significant supplemental source of natural gas. At the time of its discovery (December 1968-January 1969), the DUC declared, 'To all appearances', both the oil and the gas found, 'were so limited in extent that commercial production must be assumed doubtful in the extreme.'[2]

Although the DUC estimated the reserves at this field at from 8,284 to 14,058 million cubic metres, their true extent is unknown. This is because no confirmation drilling of any sort has been made on the structure.

In addition to these fields, there are considerable quantities of natural gas associated with oil in the finds listed in Table 8.1. The total recoverable gas reserves in the Danish area could well be as high as 150 billion cubic metres, but the exploitation of much of this must be regarded as highly uncertain.

As in the United Kingdom, institutional factors have played a considerable role in the development/non-development of Danish natural gas. To begin with, the operator for the Danish area was Gulf Oil, a firm which has not been particularly noted for its enthusiasm for North Sea natural gas. Not only did this firm voluntarily surrender its rights on the British Rough field rather than co-operate with Amoco and the BGC in its development, but it let its discovery of the Morecombe field pass virtually unchallenged into the hands of the BGC. Secondly, the brief interest exhibited by the DUC in 1971 in developing these gas fields passed when the Danish state established a state-owned privately incorporated gas company, Dansk Naturgas A/S, to purchase and transport North Sea gas. Later renamed Dansk Olie og Naturgas (DONG), in 1974, the monopsony position intended for this company was never in doubt.[3] Thirdly, the discussions over natural gas grew out of a badly-conceived attempt to alter the concessionary terms, terms on which the institutional interests of the DUC and Danish Government were in open conflict. As a result the negotiations over the purchase of Danish gas were preceded by a threat to the DUC gas concession, much too-ing and fro-ing by both the DUC and the Danish authorities, and the establishment of terms for contract negotiation. Similarly, the contract negotiations were a marathon affair stretching over eight months and only accomplished with much hardship.

9.2. The Background to Negotiations: I. The Initial Impasse

Danish government interest in the potential of North Sea gas was from the first considerable. As early as 1967/8, the Danish Ministry of Commerce investigated the potential of natural gas for the Danish market. Nor was this interest misplaced. The Phillips Group's discovery of Ekofisk led to that Group's application for sale and transit (to Germany) of approximately 10-12 billion cubic metres of natural gas *per annum.* The quantity of gas was far too high for the Danish authorities to consider purchasing anything but a small portion of the available quantities. Nor was the price the Danish authorities could offer as attractive as that of Ruhrgas, the principal German purchaser. Still, for a considerable period of time it was planned that the gas line from Ekofisk to Germany would cross all or a portion of Jutland. It was about this time that the DUC made the startling revelation that they could produce one to one and a half billion cubic metres of gas per year from the Cora structure. The gas, of course, would be delivered via the major pipeline. The Ekofisk pipeline route never came to anything, a direct route to Emden being chosen instead. But the joint applications of the Phillips Group and the DUC had led to the Danish authorities to take up the problems of gas sales seriously.

The initiative apparently was taken by the concessionaires, the A.P. Moeller group. Meetings with the Department of Commerce took place on 3 September 1969; 13 August, 4 September, 12 October, 1970, and 13 and 16 January 1971. Additionally, Maersk McKinney Moeller, the son of A.P. Moeller (and heir to the latter's industrial empire), discussed the matter with the then Minister of Trade, Knud Thomsen, even going so far as to mention details of the establishment of a gas transmission company and the terms under which the concessionaires would be prepared to participate in such a company.[4]

It was with something akin to shock that the concessionaire discovered on 7 March 1972, that the Social Democratic Government was about to establish a national gas transmission company. This company would, in connection with Ruhrgas, bid for Ekofisk gas. The A.P. Moeller group argued that the concession not only gave them the right to discover and produce hydrocarbons, but also the right to process, transport and sell them.

Government deliberations were begun on this representation, and it was eventually agreed that the establishment of a state-owned gas transmission company did not infringe upon the concessionary rights granted in 1962/3. Despite protests from the concessionaires party, the government proceeded with its plans. The Dansk Naturgas Company was formed shortly thereafter with a capitalisation of 5 million Danish kroner.

Did the authorities in 1972 realise the problems involved in enforcing monopsony purchasing powers? It is unlikely that they did. In this period the decision to form a state company was envisioned more in terms of limiting the extensive concessionary powers given the A.P. Moeller group. Yet such a company did not at the time exist anywhere on the continent and the British example, the Gas Council, was not one to encourage the DUC to begin production of natural gas. The impression that the government created the state company on general principles without being aware of the difficulties of the use of monopsonistic powers is strengthened by the events in 1978. It would not be until well into the 1978/9 natural gas negotiations that the government became fully aware of the difficulties of forcing a low monopsony price for the gas concerned.

9.3. The Background to Negotiations: II. The Incentive to Negotiate

Momentum for the development of the Danish natural gas fields was not due to the 1973/4 price rises alone, but originated in a move by the Danish Government either to terminate or improve the concessionary terms of 1962/3. As noted previously, the ten-year exploration period during which the DUC had to establish an 'economically defensible' production of oil or gas had been prolonged by two years to 1974. That this prolongation was granted did not remove the onus of an 'economically defensible' production from the DUC. In response to questions from the Folketing, the Ministry of Commerce for the first time called on the expertise of the American consultant firm, DeGolyer and MacNaughton. Six questions were addressed to this firm. The first four concerned the delineation of the Dan field reservoir and whether the Dan production could be considered 'a proper commercial extraction'. Of more interest were the questions about Cora and Bent. DeGolyer and MacNaughton were asked to judge the extent of these reservoirs. More importantly, the Ministry of Commerce noted that the DUC had done little to exploit Cora. Between its discovery in 1968 and 1974, only one additional delineation well had been drilled:

> Do circumstances exist or have existed which. . .from geological or engineering principles can justify that the concesssionaires did not until September 1974, carry through additional drillings in order to ascertain the possibilities of extraction?[5]

Although DeGolyer and MacNaughton neatly sidestepped this question (as well as that of 'proper commercial extraction' of the Dan field), the implications of their report would have far-reaching consequences for the development of Danish gas fields. The consultant firm differed notably from the DUC's judgements both as to the amounts of gas in Cora and Bent, and as to the investment required to develop these fields.

The DUC claimed that the results of their third delineation well had been disappointing, that there were only 8-14 billion cubic metres of gas in Cora, and that the capital costs were excessive for commercial production. A Gulf Development Corporation Report, the *Cora*

Evaluation Report was delivered to the government supporting this point of view. According to this report development of Cora would cost in the neighbourhood of $152 million without the adjoining pipeline to the coast. Peak production would be around 0.62 billion cubic metres *per annum.* With the adjoining pipeline, the Internal Rate of Return of the project would be less than three per cent at a gas price of $1.50 per thousand cubic feet.[6] Even assuming a one billion cubic metre production *per annum*, the IRR at the same gas price was only marginally better (eight per cent). Clearly these are unacceptable rates of return in the North Sea context.

Although DeGolyer and MacNaughton did not submit a sensitivity analysis to the government, their estimates differed substantially from those of the Gulf Development Corporation. First, they claimed the reserves of the fields were grossly understated. Their reserve estimates, however, were followed shortly by a DUC letter which also upgraded the reserves of these fields. The three sets of figures are illustrated in Table 9.1. Without even redrilling the Cora structure, the DUC in the course of 1975 revised their 1974 estimates upwards by about 80 per cent. Differences between the consultant firm and the DUC largely had to do with interpreting the Cora structure from seismic data. The discrepancy between the DeGolyer and MacNaughton and the DUC figures with regard to Bent were cryptically noted by the former:

> In their conclusions regarding reserves, DeGolyer and MacNaughton have not included possible seismic reserves in associated bi-structures which are seen on the seismic map. It is not clear if the DUC has taken account of these lesser structures.[7]

A major conclusion of the DeGolyer and MacNaughton assessment of the Cora structure was that the reservoir could produce over three times the minimum daily rate proposed by the DUC.

This conclusion, combined with the far lower cost of development for Cora as estimated by DeGolyer and MacNaughton, led automatically to the conclusion that the field was a very good investment. Not only was the daily rate of production three times that estimated by the DUC, but the overall investment was just slightly more than one-third of that claimed by the DUC (see Table 9.2).

Of the two discrepancies, in field production rates and in required capital investment, the first is the more understandable, since it lay in the interpretation of seismic data. In that the reservoir was enormous in size, estimated at some 48.8 square kilometres, differences in reserve

Table 9.1: Initial Estimates of Commercial Reserves, 1974/5
(Billions Cubic Metres)

	DUC 1974	DeGolyer & MacNaughton March 1975	DUC, September 1975
Cora	8.26-14.8	36.47	14.05-24.7
Bent	n.a.	4.5	8.24-14.06
Dan	n.a.	27.92	3.55- 7.27
Vern (Gorm)	n.a.	n.a.	0.96- 2.87

estimates could be expected. Until further delineation wells were drilled, either the DUC or DeGolyer and MacNaughton estimates could have been correct. More serious was the discrepancy between the investment figures. Included in the DUC estimates were a series of investments which would have improved the productivity of oil, more than that of the gas field. (This is especially true of the inter-field pipelines and storage systems.) Also hard to explain were the differences in estimated platform and flare tower costs.

To the degree that the DUC may have hoped to convince the Danish authorities that production of natural gas was uneconomical, the Consortium failed. Concessionary law on this point was clear and unambiguous. If one hydrocarbon under the concession was under production within ten years, concessionary rights to additional hydrocarbons would not elapse until an additional five years had passed. In as much as oil production had begun at the Dan field in July 1972, rights to natural gas should not be forfeit before 1977. The Danish Government in this case argued that since gas had been discovered well before 1974 (the expiration date of the exploratory period) and *had not been produced* by the end of the exploratory period, the additional five-year period did not obtain. The DUC argued that in any case the production of gas was not economically defensible in 1974 and that their judgement of what was economically defensible counted, not the government's.

Thus it was on a somewhat shaky legal foundation that the government undertook to press the DUC for modifying the concessionary terms of 1962/3. The nature and type of changes desired by the government were specified in a mandate from the Danish Folketing. This mandate contained a veritable 'rag-bag' of objectives. Production practices were to be changed: there was to be an end of

Table 9.2: Development of Cora (US $), 1975 Estimates

	DUC estimate	DeGolyer/ MacNaughton estimate
Cost of platform[a] (6-pile platform)	39,587,000	17,000,000
Condensate Storage		
1. DUC proposal		
Cora-Vern pipeline (8 miles, 12¾")	9,224,000	—
Vern-Dan field pipeline (17 miles, 12¾")	17,840,000	—
Storage facilities[b] (at Dan field)	30,276,000	—
2. DeGolyer & MacNaughton proposal		
Use of hulk for storage capacity		6,000,000
Drilling costs: 12 wells at $2,545,000 per well[c]	30,540,000	30,540,000
Demobilisation of drilling rig (removal from platform)	4,000,000	4,000,000
Flaring		
1. DUC proposal (and DeGolyer & MacNaughton estimates)		
3-pile flare structure	5,000,000	3,250,000
2. DeGolyer & MacNaughton alternative — use of flare booms[d]	—	44,000
Contingencies (10%)	13,646,700	6,079,000
Total cost (wi. flare platform)	150,113,700	66,869,000
(wi. flare booms)	—	63,342,400[e]

Notes:

a. Including processing equipment on the platform. DeGolyer and MacNaughton's estimates are costs of comparable contemporary platforms. 'We have utilized the most expensive of the comparisons. (The 14-well, self-contained, drilling production platform, standing in 390 feet of water in the Gulf of Mexico costing $11 million is most similar in design and purpose, but is not used due largely to industry arguments that more rugged designs are necessary for the tougher conditions in the North Sea. The $17 million figure is based on the costs of a $6 million 12-well self-contained platform plus a production platform for 150 million ft^3 per day costing $11 million. These specifications are for a development plan in the British North Sea and are considerably *over* those needed for the proposed Cora platform. The DUC platform is designed for 90 million ft^3 per day (60 million ft^3 proposed production + 50%) versus 150 million ft^3 per day, and stands in 135 feet of water versus 140 in the British case).'

b. Including storage for Dan and Vern fields.

c. Estimates are calculated as being the same for DeGolyer and MacNaughton in their report.

Table 9.2 *(contd.)*

d. DeGolyer and MacNaughton figure for flare platform based on estimates of an engineering contractor, but use of flares (figure is for four flares at 11,000 each plus — this figure is not included — burners rented at $650 per month).
e. Alternative total cost if flares and burners used includes $5,758,400 in contingencies.
Sources: DUC estimates: 'Cora Development Evaluation' (25 July 1975). DeGolyer & MacNaughton estimates: Correspondence in Appendices, Handelministeriets Tilsyn, *Rapport om Eneretsbevilling.*

flaring associated gas; all oil and gas was to be landed in Denmark. The question of access was addressed: the Danish Area was to be divided into blocks and a system of relinquishment was to be established. Finally, steps were to be taken to ensure that the Danish nation would share in the benefits of oil and gas; there was to be an increase in royalty and taxation rates; the Danish authorities also argued actively for a form of state participation. In the period January to July 1976, the concessionaires (the A.P. Moeller group) and the Ministry of Commerce discussed these issues. A.P. Moeller stood very strongly on their juridical rights. The Minister of Commerce, Mr Erling Jensen, was in a weak political position. His government was a minority government. His legal case was weak: the government was actually divided against itself in that the Ministry of Commerce and the Ministry of Justice disagreed about the juridical basis for negotiations. Finally the political problem of the North Sea resources had not yet attracted much public attention. None the less, negotiations were pushed through, resulting in a protocol, the Protocol of 15 July 1976. As revealed by the terms of this document, the combination of the weak negotiating position and of widespread public apathy meant that either the government objectives were not achieved (taxes, royalty, participation) or that they were watered down to such an extent as to be virtually meaningless (flaring, block system, relinquishment). The sole exception to this rule was natural gas.

9.4. The Basis for Negotiations

In this context, it is relevant to cite the 1976 protocol as it pertained to natural gas. The conditions of negotiations were summarised as follows:

The Concessionaires and their partners undertake to finalize the evaluation of the natural gas fields in the E-, M- (Dan), and the N-structures in accordance with generally accepted practice in the industry in order to obtain all necessary data to decide whether an economically and technologically feasible gas production can be established. . .

The Concessionaires and their partners will not later than May 1, 1978 — however subject to *force majeure*. . . — procure a final report concerning the possibilities of initiating a production from the finds mentioned. . .

In case the final report mentioned above indicates that a production seems economically feasible, Concessionaires and their partners will also prepare a report concerning the H-structure. This report will be ready not later than December 31, 1978.[8]

In return for this commitment, however, the state was to allow its claim on natural gas rights to lapse. Irrespective of the results of the assessment, the concessionary rights for natural gas would be maintained until 8 July 1984. This was a rather generous provision in that it guaranteed concessionary rights to natural gas for five years longer than allowed in the concessionary agreements of 1962/3.

The rights of the purchase were circumscribed. Upon finding that there were sufficient reserves to justify economic production from the gas structures, the DUC were to open negotiations with DONG as to the sale of the gas to Denmark. If these negotiations 'against expectations' should not be successful, the DUC could contract a deal with a third party. Upon completion of such a deal, DONG would have the right to purchase gas on the same terms as the third party, in fact 'stepping into the third party's shoes'. DONG therefore had the right of 'first refusal'. If a contract with a third party proved impossible, the DUC would re-enter negotiations with DONG. If these latter negotiations failed then the state could demand both Cora and Bent if it wished to establish a gas production from these fields.[9]

More interesting than the publicised agreement were the terms on which the government-owned company insisted for the purchase of gas. In public, it was noted that gas prices elsewhere on the European continent would be used as a basis for negotiation. It was not mentioned that the Danish state (and DONG) were to negotiate the purchase of natural gas *ab platform* alone. (The Protocol leaves open the sale of natural gas, purchased either on landing or *ab platform*.) Furthermore, governmental circles held privately that the price for natural gas would be such as to allow no more than a 20 per cent IRR for the DUC portion of any such project. The message was clear: through building a pipeline to the fields, the government could ignore most continental prices (which are landed prices), and pay a price so that the DUC's IRR would not exceed 20 per cent. 'Reference to continental prices' meant just that. The price paid *ab platform* might refer to landed prices elsewhere in the Netherlands and Germany, but it would be a price *ab platform* and hence considerably lower than other prices. DONG with the blessing of the Danish Government would be attempting to capture most of the rent involved in the Danish gas production. That these views were unacceptable to A.P. Moeller and the other DUC partners is no doubt why they were never entered into the text of the protocol.

A subsequent well (E-4) at the Cora field in 1977 tended to confirm the DeGolyer and MacNaughton interpretation of this structure. Further work on the Vern structure increased DUC enthusiasm for commencing production of oil from that field. The results of the DUC evaluation were presented to the government considerably before the 1 May 1978 deadline. On 17 March 1978, the four-volume *DUC Gas Report, 1978*, was presented to the Ministry of Commerce. Its conclusions, based on the assumptions in Table 9.3, were that the production of natural gas from Cora and the other fields was economically defensible.

While hardly disappointing, the DUC estimates were ill-fitted to the objectives of Danish energy planning, particularly those of the purchaser DONG. In the two-year gap between the 1976 Protocol and the 1978 report, both DONG and the Danish Government had been kept apprised of developments in the North Sea. DONG in particular had developed an extensive marketing plan for Danish gas which could hardly fit with the facts as the DUC saw them in its 1978 report.

Table 9.3: Danish Gas Production — DUC Gas Report, 1978, Assumptions

Field name	Cora	Bent	Vern (Gorm)	Dan
Investment (US $ millions)	265	70	10	65
Production rate (10^6 m³/year)	2,300	700	500	c. 600
Reserves (10^6 m³)	34-41,000	9,000	up to 10,000	10-15,000

Source: Dansk Boreselskab, *DUC Gas Report 1978*, 1, Table 1.

To begin with, plans for marketing gas necessarily had to begin with a low load factor. The DUC plans implicitly assumed at the beginning a load factor of 85 per cent. DONG's optimal load factor was around 40 per cent, 70 per cent at the most.

Secondly, DONG had planned to sell a maximum of 4 billion cubic metres *per annum*. Although the DUC figures could if added together mean a peak of 4.1 billion cubic metres, production from Dan and Vern was clearly not envisaged until the distant future. The DUC production figures were for Cora alone, 2.3 billion cubic metres *per annum*, about 57 or 58 per cent of the figure envisaged by the purchasers.

Thirdly, the production profiles of the seller and the purchaser varied widely, as is shown in Table 9.4. Implicit in the DONG figures was a far slower start-up and DUC investment in all four fields. The DUC intended a much lower capital investment and a quicker start-up. Nor were these differences insignificant. The DONG profile would have limited the DUC IRR to about 23-5 per cent.[10] The DUC profile would have yielded an IRR of over 30 per cent.[11]

Finally, there remained the unresolved question of reserves. The *DUC Gas Report, 1978*, was submitted to DeGolyer and MacNaughton for critical comment. The consultant firm also had access to much of the DUC's raw data. Although not disagreeing overly much with the DUC investments, the Dallas firm differed notably on the extent of the fields' reserves. Yet these differences were not as great as they once had been.

Table 9.4: Different Production Profiles (10^6 m^3 *Per Annum*), DUC and DONG

Year[a]	DONG Profile	DUC Profile (Cora only)[b]
1982/3	625	750
1984/5	1,250	1,600
1985-9	2,500	2,300
1989-92	3,000	2,300
1992-5	3,500	2,300
1996-?	4,000	2,100 and declining

Notes:
a. October 1982 to October 1983 etc. for DONG figures. Unspecified months for the DUC profile.
b. As calculated from the *DUC Gas Report 1978*. Source: Jerome D. Davis, Bo Anker Svendsen with Tommy S.F. Knudsen and Knud Lindholm Lau, *Dansk Naturgas — Problemer og Muligheder i 80'erne* (Åarhus, Denmark: Forlaget Politica, 1978), pp. 154-6.

Table 9.5: Differing Estimates of Recoverable Reserves (10^6 m^3), DUC and DeGolyer and MacNaughton, June 1974, 85 Per Cent Load Factor

Field	DUC estimate	DeGolyer and MacNaughton estimate
Cora	34,000-41,000	43,635-56,906
Bent	9,000	8,866-12,116
Dan	10,000-15,000	4,080- 8,576
Vern (Gorm)	up to 10,000	n.a.

Sources: Davis *et al., Dansk Naturgas*, p. 78. DeGolyer and MacNaughton, *Rapport om Tilvejebringelsen af et Beslutningsgrundlag Angående Produktion af Naturgas fra Cora, Dan, Vern, og Bent Felterne i den Danske Nordsø Sektor* (1 May 1978), p. 18, Table 1.

Nevertheless, the Danish Government was confident of a successful negotiated result. A brief flurry of publicity as to the anticipated profits of any gas deal was brought to an abrupt halt by the then Minister of Commerce, Ivar Nørgaard, who publicly declared that the Ministry expected to capture all the rent through enforcing a low-price monopsony position. 'The DUC have not recently contested our right to build a pipeline to the platform. They are aware that we are going to offer a price substantially lower than that on the continent. They have apparently accepted this arrangement', added Mr Noergaard in a private conversation with the author in May 1978. Events were to prove otherwise.

9.5. The Negotiations

The Danish natural gas negotiations went on for eight months and consisted of three phases. The government negotiating team encountered abrupt resistance in the first phase of the negotiations. The DUC insisted that only one field, Cora, was the topic of discussion. The government argued that all four fields should be considered. This impasse lasted about two months, and abruptly ended when the DUC agreed that all four fields could be the basis for negotiation. Shortly thereafter, on 13 July 1978, the highly favourable production permit for Gorm oil (see p. 176) was awarded. The connection if any, of this award to the DUC change of position is not known. No prices were discussed during this period.

The second phase began inauspiciously. The two negotiating teams exchanged draft contracts. That of DONG had been carefully prepared with help from DeGolyer and MacNaughton, Walter Levy and Associates, and legal experts from Trans-Canada Pipeline. It reportedly was much as previously indicated, based on a load factor of 70 per cent and a peak production rate of four billion cubic metres *per annum.* The price escalation clause reflected the DONG opinion that *ab platform* prices and a DONG offshore pipeline justified a low rate of escalation. The terms of the DUC draft contract are of course a secret, but it is clear that the DUC offered to sell natural gas on totally unrealistic terms. It was rumoured, for example, that the bottom price should escalate either at the rate of six per cent compounded *per annum*, or at the same rate as the Danish consumer price index (normally 9-11 per cent *per annum*), whichever was highest.

Negotiations during the second phase were, if anything, more difficult than during the first round. Despite apparent agreement earlier, the DUC refused to negotiate a quantity of more than 50 billion cubic metres. Everything else, however, was subject to negotiation and debate, particularly load factors, the pipeline, and escalation clauses. Negotiations were rendered all the more difficult by disagreement within the DUC. Each new suggestion had to be negotiated within the group before any agreement could be reached. Also problematic was the company negotiators' practice of disavowing previous agreements. A compromise agreement on a particular topic would be reached in one week, only to be rejected by the company negotiators the following week. This led to considerable strain on both sides. Eventually, it was insisted that every compromise result be typed out and signed by the negotiators at the end of a negotiation round.

If terms were difficult to agree upon, the issue of price further complicated matters. The initial price offered by the companies was reportedly of the order of 60 øre per cubic metre (about $3.26 per thousand cubic feet at the then existing exchange rates) and that of DONG around 33 øre per cubic metre ($1.80 per thousand cubic feet). The two sides negotiated themselves to offers of 45 øre per cubic metre (about $2.45 per thousand cubic feet) and of 37 øre per cubic metre ($2.02 per thousand cubic feet), respectively. Negotiations then became deadlocked.

At this point it was clear a political decision was necessary. The negotiators on the Danish side had gone as far as they could. Their position was difficult. First, there was no certainty that if the negotiations failed, the DUC could not sell the natural gas to another buyer. One of the DUC negotiators had close contacts with another potential buyer, the German firm Ruhrgas. It was also rumoured that the Dutch Gasunie was interested in the gas. Secondly, DONG could not afford a high price even if it had wanted to. An additional six billion kroner investment would be necessary to finance the transmission lines, pump stations, and distribution lines to sell the gas in Denmark. If DONG were to have a positive cash flow at all, it could not very well accept the terms of the DUC offer. Most importantly, the concessionaires wielded immense political influence. The A.P. Moeller firms have an enormous reputation in Denmark, a reputation which many outsiders find hard to conceive. The low point in the negotiations was when the government delegation postponed the date of the meeting scheduled for the week before Christmas to allow the Shell delegate time to travel home to his family for Christmas!

The period around Christmas 1978, was critical for the negotiations. It was at this time that the highly influential Cabinet Planning Committee, reportedly reviewed the case. The contrast between the Internal Rates of Return for the DUC and for DONG were absurd. While DONG was threatened with an overall negative cash flow, the DUC would have an Internal Rate of Return in excess of 30 per cent. It was decided to place the Minister of Commerce, Arne Christiansen, in charge of the negotiations.

With this, the third phase in negotiations began. Mr Christiansen spoke with the authority of the government and had none of the patience of his predecessor, the Solicitor General. The DUC negotiators threatened, stormed, and cajoled, but to no avail. They were told to come up with a sensible offer and were given specific deadlines within which to work. In six weeks, the DUC and the government could announce an agreement. Shell, which had previously taken the lead in obstructing progress towards an agreement while the A.P. Moeller group and Chevron and Texaco stood passively by, now strove to clinch matters in the final stages, pulling its reluctant partners fighting into the contract.

9.6. The Negotiation Issues

According to press reports, the final contract envisaged the delivery of 53.5 billion cubic metres of gas between 1984 and 2005. An additional contracted amount from the same structures could be forthcoming, depending on the results of an evaluation to be completed by the DUC by 1990. The average contracted price was 39 kroner per Gcal, about 42 øre per cubic metre. The initial price was to be higher, reflecting a 0.6 load factor, but would fall as the load factor increased in steps to 0.85. The bottom price was 33 kroner per Gcal, about 35 øre per cubic metre.[12] Remarkably, the bottom price was to rise by only three per cent *per annum* (at an arithmetic rate). The question of taxing the corporate income was highly complex. The results here were two ambiguously worded paragraphs which left taxation of windfall profits to conflicting interpretations. To the degree that the price of gas rises at a rate higher than that of an industrial commodity index (undefined) the difference between the two rates could be captured by a windfall tax, which however, could not impinge on the 'bottom price'. Very importantly, control of the offshore pipeline was left in the hands of the DONG, and the DUC pledged to utilise this pipeline's excess capacity should additional gas be discovered and exploited offshore.

The final result, as anticipated, was a compromise. Neither the DUC nor DONG received all they wanted. With the exception of price, however, the deal was not unfavourable to DONG. While the actual facts are highly secret, it is not too difficult to discern the elements of at least three package deals. The first of these was a trade-off between a high Internal Rate of Return and a lower price for natural gas; the second was a trade-off in the matter of taxes; and the third concerned control of the field-to-shore pipeline.

The first trade-off was natural. DONG wished for a low load factor, the DUC a high one. A high load factor would enable only the gradual introduction of natural gas into Denmark and rule out a fast start-up with a negative impact on DUC Internal Rate of Return. A low load factor allowed for increased flexibility in DONG's gas marketing and meant that DONG could afford to purchase a higher amount of gas in the early stages of the project. This would increase the positive cash flow of both parties early in the project. A low load factor had an additional advantage: the load factor was reflected in a higher price. This further enhanced the profitability of the project seen through the eyes of the DUC.[13]

The second trade-off was with regard to taxes. The DUC wished to have its earnings free of any special petroleum or natural gas 'rent-capture' tax. The government negotiators were somewhat undecided on this point. Initially, they were in favour of an unadulterated low price strategy, one which should have rendered additional rent-capture mechanisms undesirable. When it became apparent that the low price strategy would fail, the Danish negotiators became more convinced of the need for a 'windfall profit tax'. They therefore introduced the idea of a tax which might be levied on the difference between the gas oil/ heating oil-related gas price and the bottom price. A tax on this difference (of originally seven øre per cubic metre) was clearly unacceptable to the DUC. This inability to compromise threatened the outcome of the negotiations. A somewhat blurred reference to windfall profits, defined as the difference between a possible rise in natural gas prices and a general rise of various industrial indices, enabled the taxation issue to be amicably shelved. The two paragraphs are liable to many different interpretations and it is unlikely that either party will wish to return to the task of defining windfall profits and the amount which might be levied on these profits. The Danish state had *de facto* abandoned the issues of capturing any 'windfall profits' which might occur.

The third trade-off was between the number of fields from which the DUC would be committed to produce and the ownership and control of the platform-to-shore gas pipeline. This pipeline was deliberately designed with an eye to the future, having about twice the capacity necessary for the contracted quantities of gas. There were two reasons for this: the pipeline might be used as a general gas-gathering line for other fields in the mid-North Sea areas of Great Britain, Holland or Norway. More importantly, it could be used to assure the landing of natural gas from other Danish fields in Denmark and confer a right of purchase on DONG. Both parties in the negotiations recognised that there were considerable additional Danish reserves beyond those presently at issue. (DONG at one time estimated that there could be as much as 100 billion cubic metres of natural gas in Cora field alone.) The DONG/government side recognised this explicitly, the DUC implicitly. Thus while the DUC were arguing in one context that there were no more than 50-60 billion cubic metres, in another context, the negotiations over the pipeline, they were insistent on being granted the disposal of all excess capacity beyond the 50-60 billion cubic metres. The negotiations over control of the pipeline and over what it should ultimately carry were at the same time a part of the price negotiations, and a negotiation issue in and of itself.

The DUC's (in particular Shell's) final acceptance of DONG control of the offshore line relaxed contentions over the number of fields to be brought into production. As noted, the DUC were highly reluctant to commit themselves in the first instance to develop the Bent structure. The DUC surrender on the pipeline enabled the Danish negotiators to give in on this issue. If DONG has sole control of the gasline, and if the

DUC is pledged to use no other line in landing Danish gas, then whether or not Bent is one of the fields from which production is initiated becomes academic. Sooner or later DONG will have rights to Bent gas. From the DUC's perspective, however, whatever future control over the offshore line was surrendered, the elimination of the additional $70 million investment represented by Bent further enhances the overall project's Internal Rate of Return.

Although many other compromises were made, their exact form remains obscure. Other areas of compromise definitely included price escalation formulae, the nature of the linkage between the price of natural gas and gas oil and various heavy fuel oils, the manner of disposal of the condensate and sulphur produced with the gas, and various other administrative matters.

9.7. Conclusion

The Danish natural gas negotiations provide an interesting contrast to those of the UK. Both the Gas Council in 1968 and DONG ten years later had *de facto* monopsony powers. But whereas the powers of the Gas Council were juridical, those of DONG rested in the right to build an offshore pipeline to the Danish fields. There were additional weaknesses in DONG's position. Europe in 1978 was a far cry from Europe ten years earlier. Demand for natural gas had risen. Furthermore, any legal monopsony powers in the Danish case would be an obvious contradiction of EEC regulations on the free movement of goods and services. The Danish monopsony rested on the expense an offshore line would have incurred for the DUC. At least two of the DUC partners, perhaps three, were uninterested in their own line to Germany, Sweden, or Denmark, reportedly on the grounds of expense. This would not prevent their using the threat of such a pipeline, however, should DONG prices be perceived as being too low.

The position of DONG originally was that they and the DUC would share in the pipeline financing; this was seen as a form of state 'participation'. *Ab platform* prices would be very low, and profits would be collected in transit fees and split. Critical to this plan was DUC acceptance of DONG control over the pipeline. This acceptance was not forthcoming. In its absence, there was a floor to what DONG could pay *ab platform*. This floor was, of course, the profitability of a combined DUC gas project and DUC pipeline to alternative markets. Whether this was the case from the DUC side or not is not the issue. The point is that it was in the opinion of the government negotiators. Given this perception, the price which was finally obtained was not unreasonable. The reported price of Ekofisk gas landed in Emden in mid-1978 was around 57 øre per cubic metre (about $3.10 per thousand cubic feet). By January 1979, these prices had increased by at least ten per cent to around 62-3 øre per cubic metre ($3.41 per thousand cubic feet). Given this sort of price development, the pipeline monopsony strategy probably netted DONG a premium of 20 øre per cubic metre, or around 10.7 billion kroner for the period of the contract, and this figure, low in 1978 terms,[14] is several times that size given today's higher prices.

Another interesting similarity with the British case is the institutional context. DONG, not unlike the Gas Council, tended to take the leadership in the negotiations. To begin with, the personnel at DONG had a very high degree of engineering expertise. Many of them, including the manager, Gerhard Jensen, had also been employed with the oil industry. When it came to such issues as load factor, pipe dimensions, and marketing, it was DONG's view that ultimately prevailed. That the Danish state opted for a low price strategy may also be due to the influence of DONG. Such a low price strategy benefited DONG commercially while at the same time penalising the state, depriving it of tax revenues which it might otherwise have had.

Unlike the British, the Danes had to contend with 'marginal' fields right from the start. The discovery of Cora did not, as in the British case, lead to an incredible upturn in offshore activities. This is largely, as we have noted, as a result of the problem of access in the Danish case. That Danish gas was produced at all was not a result of a DUC initiative. Rather it was due to the state, which through its consultant firm, DeGolyer and MacNaughton, first differed with the DUC over the economic possibility of gas production, then by threatening concessionary rights to gas forced the DUC to re-examine the structures involved, and finally forced the DUC to swallow a natural gas contract. Oil companies have been known to complain at the manner in which they are treated by governments. This is not the least true of oil companies involved in British gas production. Unfortunately, if the Danish example is anything to go by, the oil companies may have only themselves to blame for this 'discriminatory treatment'. Nowhere in Europe can one find a better example of what oil companies do with marginal resources in the absence of governmental policy than in Denmark. When queried about the status of the Danish North Sea, oil executives themselves are somewhat evasive: 'the Government of Denmark gets what the Government of Denmark deserves' syndrome is perhaps the most consistent theme in oil company circles. This is a not uninteresting transfer of responsibility.

Yet Danish natural gas is not only an excellent case of oil company preferences leading to non-development of otherwise commercial resources, it is also a prime illustration of how governments, when supplied with proper technical expertise, can exercise control over their resources. The Danish authorities began cautiously by employing DeGolyer and MacNaughton in 1974, largely on the recommendation of the Norwegian officials. The initial DeGolyer and MacNaughton report formed the basis of concession reconsideration in 1976. It also, in indicating enormous discrepancies in the DUC's own work, led to DUC re-evaluation of the gas structures. The DeGolyer and MacNaughton Report of 1 May 1978, provided a sound technical basis for the Danish negotiation team during the eight-months-long natural gas negotiations. Finally, the DeGolyer and MacNaughton report of 30 March 1979 has led to a reappraisal of the entire Danish offshore area, as mentioned in the previous chapter.

Evidence from the natural gas dispute seems to confirm overwhelmingly the argument that 'marginal' resources, truly high-cost resources, can only be developed in the presence of a conscious government policy. The implications are not only unflattering for the oil industry, but are of some significance within and without the North Sea wherever high-cost resources are a focus of controversy.

Notes

1. Dansk Undergrounds Consortium, *Pressemeddelelse 36* (2 October 1968).
2. DUC, *Pressemeddelelse 39* (31 January 1969).
3. Dansk Naturgas A/S, later DONG, is a private corporation established in conformance with general corporate law in which the Danish Government owns 100 per cent of the shares. The name change to Dansk Olie og Naturgas A/S was in accordance with new powers granted the corporation to purchase oil on behalf of the Danish state.
4. J.D. Davis and Ib Faurby, 'The Paradox of Danish Offshore Policy: A Deviant Case in North Sea Oil and Gas Exploitation', in Martin Heisler and Robert Lawrence (eds.), *International Energy Policy* (Lexington, Mass.: D.C. Heath, 1980), p. 99.
5. DeGolyer and MacNaughton, *Report on the Results of the Dan Field, 'E' Structure, and 'H' Structure North Sea Continental Shelf, Denmark* (March 1975), pp. 1-8.
6. Ibid., p. 69.
7. 'Tilsynets Vurdering', *Rapport om Eneretsbevilling*, p. 153.
8. Protocol of 15 July 1976, as quoted in *Danshore* (September-October 1975), p. 35.

9. See Article 2 of the Protocol of 1976 for further specifics: *Danshore* (September-October 1976), p. 36.

10. See Jerome D. Davis, Bo Anker Svendsen, Tommy S.F. Knudsen and Knud Lindholm Lau, *Dansk Naturgas – Problemer og Muligheder i 80'erne* (Åarhus, Denmark: Forlaget Politica, 1978), pp. 154-6.

11. Ibid., pp. 89-90.

12. The base price expressed in terms of US dollars (5.2 Dkr per dollar) would be $2.28 per 1,000 cubic feet. The bottom price would be in the region of $1.91 per 1,000 cubic feet.

13. It should be noted that the only measure of investment profitability employment by the DUC throughout the negotiations was Internal Rate of Return.

14. This is about $2.057 billion and does not include additional benefits such as the reduced load factor. (Ekofisk gas is supplied at a 90 per cent load factor.) It does not include escalation factors either.

PART FIVE

CONCLUSION

10 HIGH-COST FIELDS — SOME INSTITUTIONAL IMPLICATIONS OF THE NORTH SEA CONTRACT

10.1. Current Policy Options Reconsidered

The *Economist* was unusually caustic in its commentary on the UK offshore industry:

> North Sea drilling is down to seven wells even though the companies hold rights to a bundle of offshore blocks that are still undrilled. Rather than drill these, the oil companies like to acquire new blocks and flit from one hot oil play to another as they are doing now in Mexico and Brazil. . .The companies claim future finds will be small and costly and that they will have to be persuaded by tax breaks and allowances. Then they will search for Britain's oil — but over the next five or six years, not now.[1]

This passage is striking for two reasons. First, as the companies see it, many North Sea projects can be left undrilled at present because in their eyes, better prospects exist elsewhere. Secondly for them actually to develop high-cost North Sea projects, the companies must receive discretionary economic incentives. Both points will be elaborated in our conclusion. What is particularly interesting about these company attitudes is that they have persisted, even despite the enormous OPEC price increases of 1979/80.

The questions to which we address ourselves, it is important to emphasise, are not of relevance just to Denmark and the UK. Although our attention has concentrated on these countries (and their widely divergent concessionary/licensing practices), the pattern of firm behaviour is not dissimilar elsewhere in the North Sea. Nor are the contractual contexts unlike those of Holland and Norway (and West Germany).

10.2. 'Bounded Rationality' and the Development Decision

The concern of the *Economist* over the oil multinationals 'flitting' from one 'hot oil play' to another world-wide implies a desire that a high rate of exploration and development activity be maintained in the North Sea.

In Part One, it was argued that pure economic criteria were in reality modified by organisational behaviour within the oil industry, by the oligopolistic nature of international oil markets, and by the political role which many oil multinationals are capable of exerting. Chapter 2 deepened this perspective further, indicating that corporate commitment to the North Sea does differ within the industry, and that project decision-making is a complex organisational process which is as subject to non-economic criteria as to economic criteria. The two case studies on Denmark and the United Kingdom lent further support to this contention. To what degree should the state not interfere in the development decision process in the light of the evidence?

A too-frequent answer to this question has been based on inter-temporal Pareto efficiencies, normally expressed in terms of net present values. Let us assume two projects, P_1 and P_2. The present values of such projects have already in this book been expressed as variations on the following pattern:

$$(10.1) \ PV(P_1) \ = \ \frac{NCF_{1,0}}{(1+i)^0} + \frac{NCF_{1,1}}{(1+i)^1} + \frac{NCF_{1,2}}{(1+i)^2} + \ldots + \frac{NCF_{1,N}}{(1+i)^N}$$

$$(10.2) \ PV(P_2) \ = \ \frac{NCF_{2,0}}{(1+i)^0} + \frac{NCF_{2,1}}{(1+i)^1} + \frac{NCF_{2,2}}{(1+i)^2} + \ldots + \frac{NCF_{2,N}}{(1+i)^N}$$

in which NCF_1 and NCF_2 represent the anticipated net cash flows of P_1 and P_2 respectively, i the rate of discount. P_1 and P_2 could either represent either different projects in different parts of the world or they could represent the same project undertaken at different points in time under differing conditions. In either case the higher present value would indicate the preferred alternative. Clearly such calculation relies heavily on the discount rate chosen, future price developments, anticipated appreciation of undeveloped reserves and the like.[2]

Critical to such inter-temporal calculations is the choice of i, the discount rate. What general discount rate should be used to indicate that a project is worth developing? Generally it is argued that a market interest rate is appropriate, plus an adjustment to account for risk and uncertainty. There are serious problems with even such a choice. First, such market rates of interest differ widely even within the same national market, let alone in terms of international markets. Secondly, the typical oil company has so many different rates of return measures and so many borrowing and lending rates that it is difficult for the decision-maker to know which rates should be utilised in the concrete example of a given North Sea oil or gas project. The problem is further complicated if a premium is to be added for risk or uncertainty in certain cases and not in others. As a result such discount rates can and do differ by a factor of as much as ten.

Another critical assumption to the inter-temporal Pareto efficiency approach is its assumption that all relevant costs and revenues are known at each point in time throughout the future. Normally these assumptions are based on extrapolated trends. In the North Sea such a calculation has been virtually impossible to make with any degree of precision. One future price scenario after another has been undermined by rapidly rising oil prices. Each cost estimate has been similarly sabotaged by unexpected increases in the rate of cost escalation. In such a situation the assumptions become little more than educated guesswork.

When seen in terms of 'bounded rationality', these calculations become even less precise. If the criterion is organisational dynamics (Cyert and March), the choice of interest rate is based on economics plus the behaviour of coalitions and sub-coalitions within the firm. Similarly, North Sea cost and price scenarios are negotiable within management in the individual firm and among firms within the North Sea group.

If the modifying criterion is oligopoly behaviour, then control of resources becomes of paramount import. Discount rate determination and price scenarios will be based on calculations of crude self-sufficiency and market proximity as well as on downstream profits.

Political conditions can modify economic behaviour both directly, in terms of calculation of the inter-temporal Pareto efficiencies of one or more project, and indirectly in terms of attempts to improve the political-economic context within which the development is undertaken. The choice of discount rate should vary widely among firms due to different calculations of political uncertainty and risk. One authority cited that for the same firm, acceptable discount rates varied from six per cent in the US to 80 per cent in Indonesia. Given that the market interest rates utilised by the firm in making this calculation were within the same range, it is clear that political uncertainty has an impact. Political conditions can also affect assumptions regarding future costs and prices. This is particularly the case with judgements as to OPEC pricing strategy — a strategy which in some respects has an overt political motivation. Assessment of future scenarios in today's oil world will continue to require a degree of political judgement and sophistication.

Indirectly, political strategy can affect the rate of development as well. This was particularly evident in the Danish case. Here the DUC has postponed the development of both the Ruth (Skjold) and Vern (Gorm) fields due to political considerations. Such action has been threatened in the British case as well but not carried out. Clearly political considerations can modify economic calculations considerably.

How do organisational dynamics, oligopoly behaviour and political calculation affect the use of the inter-temporal Pareto efficiency criterion? The answer to this question is uncertain. Clearly, such considerations as mentioned above can work in favour of the rapid development of the North Sea as well as in opposition to such rapid development. One thing is certain, however: the inter-temporal calculations of national policy-makers are considerably different from those of the oil industry. This is as true of Holland, Norway and Germany as it is of the two countries with which we have dealt in this book.

Here it might be said, the 'bounded' rationality of the firm is further modified by the contractual context within which that firm explores for and develops North Sea resources. The North Sea licence has in this regard been likened to a limited property rights contract – the nature of which further modifies corporate North Sea behaviour. The nature of this contract is critical for state policy – in particular, development policy.

Development policy is a function of both state responsibility for the future of North Sea resources and current demands for the rapid development of these resources. To date, state policy can be described as a balancing act between concern for the future and *ad hoc* policy considerations of the present: a desire for national self-sufficiency, a strategy of maximising onshore effects of offshore activity, a concern for the balance of payments effect of diminished oil production, and a means for riding out the current world economic slump. Given that these considerations are at present predominant in virtually every North Sea nation possessing hydrocarbon resources, how can these resources be more effectively exploited in the near future? How should contract provisions be altered to obtain the desired effect?

The *Economist*'s reference to persuasion by 'tax breaks' and 'allowances' alludes to one class of contractual provision – the discretionary provision. The nature of this provision was reviewed in the analysis of British policies in the North Sea. Here the emphasis was on the political activity of the UKOOA *vis-a-vis* 'marginal' fields and the

PRT. Focus was also directed to the *de facto* monopsony nature of contracts with British Gas — a factor which has led to corporate demands for higher gas prices as a *quid pro quo* for developing future fields. The granting of further discretionary economic incentives remains a future policy possibility, one with both advantages and disadvantages.

The value of the other set of contract provisions — access provisions — was highlighted in the analysis of Danish policies. In this case, access provisions did not consist of the more normal block relinquishment schemes, but of the imminent loss of the entire concession if development did not occur. Both the Danish oil and natural gas were developed under pressure. Despite the low priority of the Danish Area to the companies concerned, this pressure worked. Thus the policy ends toward which the British strived in their discretionary incentive system — to put high-cost projects in operation — where secured in Denmark not by exemptions from royalty payments, but through the threat of relinquishment. Clearly, modification of access provisions is a workable alternative policy to discretionary economic incentives.

10.3. The Development Decision and National Policy

What form should concern for the future take? Policy answers to this question will differ according to the context of national policy. To date it would appear that states have not reverted to the inter-temporal Pareto efficiency calculations previously described; policy appears instead to be prompted by *ad hoc* considerations, in particular shorter-term perspectives. This is for obvious reasons. Not only are such calculations difficult, but for the purposes of national policy, it can be contended that they do not give adequate attention to the wider context. This can be expressed in terms of the 'social discount rate'.

First, a social discount rate suitable to state North Sea policy, if at all forthcoming, would probably differ considerably from the private discount rates utilised by industry. Not only must the choice of a discount rate be based on its broader impact on the national economy, but the time frames of firm and state can be widely different. This has been the case most obviously with Danish policy for the last 18 years, but is of concern to other countries as well. Further, a social discount rate would put less emphasis on project risk and uncertainty than any industry discount rate. Not only can the state ignore certain aspects of uncertainty (it is itself a source of uncertainty in corporate calculations), but through 'spreading' and 'pooling' strategies, the state has a legitimate reason for minimising risk avoidance in its choice of discount rate.[3]

10.4. Discretionary Economic Incentives

The evidence presented in this book has indicated a number of disadvantages in the use of discretionary economic incentives. These are reinforced by the existence of other more general problems with this approach.

First, despite the designation 'high-cost', it is clear that many of the fields yielding rates of return of 20 per cent or less, actually yield considerably more than that depending on the method of measuring profits. Thus far, high-cost fields have been discussed in terms of investment measures, not measures of profit. The two concepts are fundamentally different, however, and this can be of critical importance. An investment measure (or yardstick) such as the IRR, payout period, or net income ratio is utilised to compare the costs of alternative projects. It says nothing of the profits involved in the project itself. These will depend on the amount of equity capital invested in the project, the amount of loan capital, the terms on which the loan capital is secured, and the like. The two concepts are constantly confused in the context of North Sea activities. Thus, in discussions of the 12.1 per cent IRR (investment measure) of Frigg, comments have been made that the CFP could better place its money in government securities (profitability of equity capital).

This distinction is crucial in that in profit terms, high-cost fields are by no means unattractive. Depending on loan financing — interest rates, royalties, if any — and timing, a high-cost field yielding an IRR measure of 15-20 per cent can well earn 30-45 per cent in terms of Internal Rate of Return to corporate equity.

There are other types of investment yardsticks than the IRR. One of them, 'Booked Rate of Return', relates the net cash flow to the total average value of the assets (equity) involved, allowing for depreciation. The Internal Rate of Return, by contrast, is that unique discount rate which balances the negative and positive cash flows of a project over time. The two measures are not entirely comparable. Notably, the difference between the two rates of return measures widens considerably for projects promising a relatively high Internal Rate of Return. In such cases the Booked Rate of Return, depending on the timing of equity capital can be up to two or three times higher for the same project.

Bearing these distinctions in mind, how do North Sea fields compare with similar investments? Given the political stability of the North Sea, about the only truly comparable province is in North America. W. Meade, in an analysis of oil company Internal Rates of Return from US offshore leases, estimated these to be between seven and eight per cent *before* taxes in the period 1954/5, and six to ten per cent before taxes in 1968.[4] Although rates of return are higher for the US offshore today — and although these figures are probably biased due to the system of bonus bidding for offshore acreage — the discrepancy between the 12.1 per cent earned by CFP after taxes and the average for the US offshore before taxes would appear significant. An IRR of below 12 per cent *after* taxes should hardly be interpreted as a disaster in a North Sea context.

In terms of booked rate of return to equity capital, the North Sea seems hardly unattractive. World-wide, the average return to equity in exploration and production ranged from 15 to 17.4 per cent in 1975, and 9 to 10.1 per cent in 1971.[5] Average return to equity for operations outside the US was 17.8 per cent in 1975, all activities included.[6] A high-cost field in the North Sea can well return over 50 per cent by this measure, assuming that all taxes and royalties are paid. This certainly compares favourably with overall industrial averages, even allowing for accounting differences among firms in calculating Booked Rates of Return.[7]

In this light, discretionary economic incentives would appear to be essentially unnecessary for profits, except in the most extreme cases. It is also by no means certain that they would have more than a very minimal impact on perhaps the major discentive to develop truly high-cost fields — the element of risk. The best example of development risk in this book is that of the Dan field. The Dan's profitability could not have been bettered through tax breaks or in 1978 by the granting of royalty refunds. In both instances it would not have broken even by the end of 1979.

Most of the fields discussed in the preceding chapters are highly sensitive to changes in their environment. As with the Dan, the worst development risks will remain to plague the groups owning these fields whether or not the British Government should refund royalties or forego PRT revenues. The best hypothetical example of the sort of risk discussed here is undoubtedly the somewhat crude 'sensitivity' test taken of the Auk, Forties and Heather fields in Chapter 2. Here Heather was contrasted with the other two fields — in the absence of any taxes or royalties at all. In Table 2.5, when production rates were halved and

capital costs doubled, Heather proved the only one of the three fields
where the IRR fell below 15 per cent, to 2.04 per cent (at a $12.00/bbl.
price). It is this sort of sensitivity which makes Heather an especially
high-cost field. Tax breaks, royalty refunds and the like will not make
Heather any better a prospect under the conditions above. It is doubtful
that they will tip the scales on any but a handful of the high-cost fields
currently under consideration. Financial incentives are no palliative to
risk in this area — and it is development risk which makes these fields
high-cost.

A third problem is one of definition. What is a high-cost or 'marginal'
field? How does one design financial incentives to apply to one
'marginal' field but not to other fields which do not need such
incentives to induce corporate investment? Arguments regarding
discretionary economic incentives all founder on such problems of
administration. Chapter 5 dwelt on this aspect of financial incentives
with respect to the 1975 Oil Tax Act. If anything, given the pressure for
additional financial incentives today, the problem of their administration
is more important than it was in 1975. In countless interviews with
British bureaucrats during the autumn of 1977, the problems of
simplicity and administrative enforcement were raised. To be effective,
incentives must be highly complex and complexity can lead to problems
of interpretation; problems of interpretation can open loopholes in the
present rent-capture system and such loopholes could be inordinately
costly to the British Exchequer. These companies, for their part, have
little to lose and everything to gain through asking for the whole cake
rather than a slice.

A good example of the difficulties involved can be seen in the
politics surrounding the question of royalty rebates for high-cost fields.
Exemption from royalties is made at the discretion of the Minister of
Energy — but what guidelines are to be used? Suppose the Minister at
his discretion exempts a high-cost field from paying royalties. How is he
to justify his decision? What loopholes would be left open through such
a justification? It is fruitless to expect that other non-benefiting
companies will accept 'favouritism' for one field without any
justification. This reasoning would have to be well-thought out in
advance to cover all possible contingencies. Nor can the government
expect much co-operation from the industry. When the British
authorities in late 1978/9 were rethinking royalty exemption policies,
the oil companies were asked for comments. One company reportedly
stated that since it regarded the entire British sector as a single province,
should it decide to invest in a high-cost field, it would expect exemption

from royalties to apply to its more economic fields as well.[8]

Thus if such a system were to work, a company like BP (not the party described above) could, for example, expect a royalty exemption on its Forties field as well as on a high-cost prospect such as Buchan. The cost in loss revenues to the Exchequer would be enormous — as would be the profits to BP.

Thus to sum up, financial incentives do not enable high-cost fields to overcome development risk. They do increase corporate profits, however, at the expense of state revenues, and given problems of administration, the cost of such financial incentives could well outweigh the benefits of the marginal amounts of oil involved. Under these circumstances, one can understand why the 1978 60 per cent PRT reform did not contain special provisions for high-cost fields. The increased government take — the decreased profitability of such fields — has been made up substantially through past and future price increases. And a small miscalculation on the part of the state could in fact lead to 'windfall' corporate profits.

Moreover, even if field profitability and 'sensitivity' could be improved through the granting of discretionary incentives, it is not wholly obvious that this strengthens the will to develop a high-cost reservoir. In Chapter 2, the barriers to concerted action in the corporate decision-making process were described. Whether a North Sea group can overcome all the obstacles to decision — even with a prospect which some think promising — may in the last instance not depend on incentives at all.

The experience provided by the Danish case underlines the cogency of these arguments. The Danish concession was (and is) the most favourable in the North Sea. Without exaggerating, it can rightly be labelled one enormous discretionary economic incentive (to A.P. Moeller in the early 1960s). Here firms have largely been able to follow their own preferences, exploring and developing of their own pace, save only for the ultimate need to start an 'economically defensible' production of oil and gas by a certain time. Yet of all the areas in the North Sea, it was the Danish sector that remained a backwater. When there was finally progress in the area, this was not due to the favourable concessionary terms, but to government pressure. Even then, discretionary preferences did not mollify the DUC, which pre-conditioned much of its development plans on government compliance with its wishes (as with the Gorm and Skjold projects). There is little reason to believe that discretionary economic incentives will work any better elsewhere.

The experiences learned from the Danish concession are also important for another reason. While government policy there has revolved around the question of access, it has been defined very broadly: the DUC faced the loss of the entire concession if a certain development was not initiated. Yet this policy has not been instrumental in encouraging development beyond this particular minimum. Both the British and the Danish cases thus would seem to indicate the need for a new approach.

10.5. Policy Alternatives

If discretionary economic incentives are both costly and work imperfectly and if the 'access' provisions in the Danish Area have had only a limited value, what are the alternatives? One possible solution is more and better licensing rounds. These rounds serve two purposes: they enable the continuation of a high rate of exploration in the more attractive prospects, and they increase information. Such rounds do not, however, encourage investigation of high-cost structures remaining on old licensing acreage. Rather, like the Danish fields, these are kept for better times while the companies press for more promising acreage elsewhere in the North Sea.

For the nations involved, moreover, additional rounds pose a problem: round succeeds round. If the block offerings are not good enough — or if there are too many conditions attached to applications (i.e. BNOC participation) — the exploration rate falls. And the high-cost structures on old acreage remain untouched.

The evidence presented in this book has suggested that the key to the development of high-cost fields which, for one reason or another, are not developed, lies in the construction of a more effective policy regarding access provisions. The advantages of a freer assignment policy, or relinquishment, of escalating area payments have been stressed in this volume. Not only do these measures encourage rapid exploration and development, but they can reward the more efficient and committed oil firms and penalise the less efficient and committed. In short, these are rules which establish the 'market' in offshore real estate. The more clear-cut and efficient these rules are, the better the chance that those structures which have a chance of being developed can in fact be developed.

There is latitude for such policy in most North Sea countries. Britain and Norway have yet to award all their promising acreage. Holland has a goodly chunk of relinquished acreage and can await more such acreage when the initial 15-year exploration period runs out for the licence round of 1968 (in 1983). Denmark is examining the possibility of repossessing a vast amount of acreage with a view to establishing a licensing policy based largely on the Norwegian model. What can these nations do in future licensing rounds? The thrust of our analysis is that licensing rules governing the extent and timing of contractual access rights should be tightened in the future. To this end, we will briefly examine in turn the following policy changes: the potential for a liberalised assignment policy, the possibility of a further separation of exploration and production licences, the question of changing relinquishment rules, and the issues of revising area rental rates.

(i) A Liberalised Assignment Policy

Assignments, farm-ins, and farm-outs, can be more actively encouraged in the majority of North Sea licensing regimes. Controls on licence assignments are costly in more than one manner. First, they are expensive to administer. Ministerial approval of an assignment can involve considerable bureaucratic leg work. More importantly, government-imposed conditions on the newly reconstituted group can work as an active disincentive to change partners in cases where such changes may be necessary to procure the development of a North Sea field.

British government policy regarding the BNOC is a case in point. Whatever the marginal benefit to the BNOC of being included in a reassignment of licence interests this can be more than outweighed by a consequent reluctance of many groups to allow a farm-in for fear of getting the BNOC as a partner. This policy reached a high point in 1978/9 when for a period it was agreed that the BNOC as a third party would get 'right of first refusal' in any transfer of group licence interests. Assignments during this period of 'first refusal' reportedly dropped significantly. Fortunately, the proposal has since been dropped. The BNOC has more than enough diversified interests elsewhere on the British North Sea shelf and has no real need of yet further commitments.

Encouragement could go so far as to promote active speculation in North Sea territory, as is the case in Holland. The overall amounts of money to be made through such speculation are relatively small when compared to the costs of exploration and development. And the increased flexibility of the groups resulting from this freer policy could allow for more latitude in deciding for or against a high-cost project.

(ii) The Further Separation of Exploration and Production Periods

Exploration and production periods mean different things in different
North Sea regimes. With the exception of the Dutch, there are normally
two separate periods. In Denmark 'exploration' covers both the
preliminary survey work and actual exploration drilling on the
concessionary area. The establishment of the production of oil
(eventually gas) were prerequisites to continued concession ownership.
In contrast, the 'exploration licence' in the Norwegian and British
systems covers the preliminary general geological and geophysical
surveys alone. Only on award of 'production licences' covering allocated
blocks can firms eventually begin to drill and see what resources can be
found. The definition of 'exploration' and 'production' periods in
Norwegian and British legislation has led to inflexibility. In return for a
pledge to drill a specified programme, firms acquire rights to 50 per cent
of a licensed area for 46 years in both systems, irrespective of whether
they drill adequately beyond the original specification or not. In as
much as the period is defined as a production period, but includes the
drilling of exploration wells, it is impossible to place further
requirements as to exploration drilling in an undrilled area without the
counter-argument being made that such drilling as was originally
required in 1964 has already been fulfilled and that legally no more
drilling is necessary. Forty-six years of extended exploration is surely a
very generous span of years — particularly when compared to similar
terms available 15-20 years ago in the Middle East.[9] It is true that the
North Sea is a high-cost area. On the other hand, the North Sea is a
politically stable area and exploration today involves considerably less
risk than it did when the first British and Norwegian licences were
issued, 15-16 years ago.

Denmark, for political and legal reasons, has thus far been
unsuccessful in adopting a new licensing scheme; but what might be
considered for the British (and the Norwegian) system is a three-step
licensing process, perhaps patterned after the Dutch model. Such a
hypothetical system would consist of several steps: first, the issue of a
general exploration (reconnaissance) licence; secondly, the grant of a
licence to undertake exploration drilling for a period (12-15 years); the
third step, a production licence, would be issued only for hydrocarbons
found in the preceding 12-15-year period. Failure to find hydrocarbons
which qualify for a production licence in the first two periods would
cause the relinquishment of the entire licensed area. Such a three-step
regime could encourage exploratory drilling. A greater amount of

acreage would also be relinquished. This would encourage outside groups to try their luck (and their geological concepts) on areas which might otherwise be 'locked up' for up to 46 years.

(iii) The Case for Per Block Relinquishment

With the exception of the Danish Area (post-1976), relinquishment is defined in terms of the per licence acreage allotted to various groups. In such systems, the provisions governing shape and size of the relinquished areas vary. At one extreme, the Norwegians have a rather strict definition of the boundaries of the retained area, at the other extreme, the Dutch have much looser provisions. A per licence relinquishment scheme is not perfect. A group willing to invest in an extensive drilling programme can acquire a considerable number of blocks, including many in which it is not interested. With relinquishment, the uninteresting area can be abandoned, and the more valuable acreage simultaneously retained. In many cases these can be full blocks on which no exploration wells have been drilled for up to 15 years (see Table 3.2 in Chapter 3).

Relinquishment on a per block basis — in which 50 per cent of each block was abandoned after six years — would therefore increase the incentive to drill actively on all blocks possessed by our hypothetical group. Such a change would have some desirable results. First, per block relinquishment will increase the rate of exploration on already awarded blocks. Lack of precisely such activity has already been criticised in Great Britain. Wells would be drilled in areas previously unexplored. There would be a greater geographical spread of exploration activity as well. Thus, such a per block relinquishment system could enable greater information as to potential reserves on already allocated acreage, a result of wider, more active exploration. This would be of benefit in the planning of future licensing rounds. Increased knowledge of what these blocks contain will also benefit those groups which do not hold the blocks concerned — and may stimulate group interests in adjoining blocks. Thus both the state and the industry would benefit from the increased information in such a system. Thirdly, depending on the extent and location of those resources discovered, such a requirement may force development of resources which might otherwise not have been developed — particularly if a block area of greater than 50 per cent could only be retained upon development.

There are disadvantages to the system. In Canada, for example, it has led to a patchwork quilt of retained and relinquished areas,[10] with consequent administrative difficulties. Yet the benefits of a per block relinquishment are considerable, and merit more serious attention, at least on a trial basis.

(iv) The Revision of Area Rental Schedules

At present, rental schedules are low for the reason that their purpose is to expedite exploration, not relinquishment, and definitely not the development of fields. The British schedule is not atypical (see Table 10.1). As it now exists, an oil structure of 116 million barrels and covering 50 square kilometres will carry a maximum annual area rental charge of £17,500 *per annum* after 17 years, the top of the current sliding scale. Assuming the field was found in a block issued in 1972, this rental rate will not be achieved until 1989! By contrast if we assume a real increase in the hydrocarbon values of the field of around two per cent *per annum* in the next ten years, the 116 million barrels will increase in value at an average *per annum* rate of $56 million, or roughly £28 million. Rental rates, then, do not provide an incentive for developing a 'marginal' field.

Two proposals can be made for revision of area rentals: the manner in which the current rates are levied can be changed; or the schedules themselves can be updated to coincide with the higher prices currently obtained for oil.

To date, area rentals are deductible from taxes in both the British and Norwegian sectors, not only from royalties and corporate taxes, but often from oil revenue taxes as well. This provision implicitly favours those groups which have commenced development of one or more fields on a given licence. In other words, unlucky firms which must pay the full rates are discriminated against. Denying such deductions should remove this inequity and additionally sharply increase state revenues from rental rates. This should decrease the incentive to hang on to the less promising areas in the North Sea. While such a change might be introduced administratively on a licence by licence basis, an alternative to this practice could be to charge rental rates on a block-by-block, rather than licence-by-licence, basis. In this manner unless the production of hydrocarbons is from the block concerned, rental payments could not be deducted from royalties or taxes.

More effective could be to index area rental payment to the price of crude, a method already adopted by one North Sea nation. In the Netherlands, the calculation of area rental rate can be expressed by a/b where a is the wage index on the first day of the year concerned and b is defined as the same index on the date in which the Dutch Continental Shelf Act was enacted.[11] A similar formula could be easily

Table 10.1: UK Area Rental Rates — Rounds One to Four

Round	Application fee per block	Annual rental			
		Years 1-6 (initial payment)	7th year	Increase per annum	Maximum per annum
First	£200+£5 for every block over ten	£6,250 or £25/km²	£10,000 £40/km²	£6,250 £40/km²	£72,000 £290/km²
Second	"	"	"	"	"
Third	"	£7,500 £30/km²	£12,500 £50/km²	£7,500 £30/km²	£87,000 £350/km²
Fourth	"	£11,250 £45/km²	"	"	"

Source: *First Report*, Select Committee on Nationalised Industries, Session 1974/5, p. 191.

adopted for British, Danish or Norwegian leasing schedules. Perhaps more appropriately, these could be based on crude or crude product prices of 1964/5 versus such prices today — or some similar basis.

Still more effective would be a two-tiered structure of rental rates. The first tier would provide incentives for exploration, the second incentives for developing 'marginal' fields. Rental rates should not be structured to deprive prospects of all economic rent. Rather, rates could be geared to a certain percentage of the real appreciation of undeveloped reserves, perhaps 25 per cent. In our example of the field containing 116 million barrels, the group would then be faced with an average annual rent of £7 million, not £17,500 as is currently the case. (Should the field be developed, this second tier of rental rates would not apply.)

Such penalties would either spur the group to develop the field itself or to relinquish the field. In either circumstance an optimum result is achieved. If the field is developed, the state benefits by an additional supply of oil or gas. If the field is relinquished, the government could offer the field to a group more committed to the development of high-cost resources.

This scheme would involve costs. There would be a strong incentive among firms either not to drill a licensed prospect at all or to underestimate the recoverable reserves of any field discovered — thereby decreasing its rental rates. There would consequently be a need for expanded bureaucratic supervision. Still the increased income could defray some, if not all of the additional expenses involved.

10.6. A Market Solution?

The impact of these proposals — adopted either singly or in combination
with one another — would be to create a supply of blocks or more
specifically a supply of high-cost resources. But for such a supply there
would have to be a demand. From where should this demand come?

Demand for North Sea real estate in general exists already. One good
indication of this demand is the increasingly high number of offers, in
terms of blocks per sale, in each succeeding UK licensing round. This
trend has held true recently despite the harsher terms of the Fifth and
Sixth Rounds, and can be expected as Table 10.2 shows, to continue to
do so in the future as oil prices shoot further upwards. There were 31
group bids for 960 blocks in 1964, 21 bids for 1,102 blocks in 1965,
and 34 bids for 157 blocks in 1970. In 1972 no fewer than 123 group
bids were made for 421 blocks, and, although the number of blocks on
offer in 1977 and 1978 diminished to 71 and 40 respectively, the group
bids numbered 53 and 55 for these two respective rounds. There were
about 52.5 blocks on offer for every bid received in 1965. By 1978/9,
the ratio had declined to around 0.8 blocks available for every offer,
and this is demand for areas in which it is not certain that resources
exist. These figures are clearly not fully comparable, as concessionary
terms and oil prices have varied for each of them. But they do lead one
to pose the critical question: 'How much more demand would be
created should areas *known* to have resources "come on the blocks?"'

Demand for high-cost undeveloped resources will be a function of a
corporation's calculation of present development costs *vis-a-vis* future
cash revenues appropriately discounted to reflect present values as
explained in Chapter 1. Present versus future development costs will
also enter the picture.

Development groups approach the North Sea differently as stressed

Table 10.2: Demand for North Sea Blocks — UK Sector 1964-79

Licensing	Year	Blocks on offer	Group bids	Ratio: blocks per group bid
1st	1964	960	31	30.9:1
2nd	1965	1,102	21	52.5:1
3rd	1970	157	34	4.6:1
4th	1972	421	123	3.4:1
5th	1977	71	53	1.3:1
6th	1978/9	46	55	0.8:1

in Chapter 2. The calculation of present development costs and future cash revenues will also be a function of the composition of particular groups. That one North Sea consortium will not touch a field which it believes to be high-cost is not a *prima facie* case that the field will not be attractive to another. The desirability of resources is also a function of the exploration and delineation efforts, the Danish Gorm field and natural gas projects being prime examples. Both projects improved in economic terms, not due to price increases (although these undoubtedly helped) but to delineation drillings — and some well-founded criticism from DeGolyer and MacNaughton. What is true of such projects in the Danish area is true of prospects elsewhere in the British, Dutch or Norwegian sectors of the North Sea.

Present versus future development costs will also change, reflecting newer technology. Some fields which are exceptionally costly for a particular reason can be rendered more attractive through technological means. Lack of permeability, for example, has long plagued Danish fields. Yet recently, due to a new Shell process of horizontal drilling, fields previously uneconomical are being reconsidered. Much of this new technology is proprietary to the firms involved. These firms and no others can make money out of fields which would otherwise be uneconomic, and undeveloped.

Furthermore, not all technological innovations available are used. Many of the more prominent firms in the North Sea, including those with many undrilled blocks, have resisted new development concepts. Engineering consultants have often stressed the 'money-wasting' conservatism of the majors. To date the major North Sea innovation, the use of a semi-submersible platform as a production platform on the Argyll field, was made by a small American independent, Hamilton Brothers. In spite of Argyll's early start-up date — it was the first field in production in the British sector — other companies have been slow to adopt the concept. 'The majors would never have risked it themselves', confided one highly-placed consultant to the author in a private interview. Different firms will approach a prospect in different engineering terms. Some will pass the prospect up. Others will invest in it.

Demand for North Sea real estate in general and high-cost resources in particular varies not only in accordance with opportunity cost and with technology, but also comes from various sources. State-owned firms might be interested in expanding their holdings for instance. Less well-known but nonetheless increasingly important, a group of non-oil companies 'new' to the North Sea have recently begun to invest in it:

Seagram Distillers, Thomson Newspapers, the P and O Line, National
Westminster Bank, Century Power and Light, and British Electric
Traction to name a few in the British Area. Some of these 'non-oil'
companies have already developed a considerable expertise.

A.P. Moeller, a shipping firm, is now an operator on the Dan field and
in all Danish land exploration — although what is involved in these areas
is a far cry from shipping. Nor do non-oil companies need to get
involved directly. A growing number of small firms such as Tricentrol,
GAO and Ultramar, are acquiring expertise and are willing to undertake
ventures which the majors have been reluctant to begin. The problem
with these firms is that they lack capital. Such capital can (and has)
come from outsiders. A good example is the recent deal between Dow
Chemical, an outsider, and Siebens Exploration, a small firm in this
context. In return for 25 per cent of Siebens's future revenues from the
latter's four per cent holding in the Brae field, Dow Chemical advanced
Siebens Exploration $15 million — a sum which Siebens will utilise in
the British Seventh Round and in future exploration wells.[12] In that
such 'non-oil' firms have different priorities and interests from the oil
companies they could well be more committed to the development of
hitherto undeveloped high-cost resources in the North Sea.

Demand will arguably not only come from sources previously foreign
to the North Sea, but also be stimulated via the technical aspects of
rent-capture legislation. A good example of this was BP's decision to
proceed with the Buchan project, a field with an eleven per cent IRR in
1979 prices. Many thought at the time that the field would yield an
insufficient return to justify investment. But in BP's eyes, investment
in Buchan reduced the corporate taxes due on profits from the Forties
field. Nor will the BP situation remain unique. As field after field comes
'on stream' and as corporate taxes fall due, many previously
unappetising prospects may become relatively desirable.

Demand can also be stimulated. This should be done through wide
distribution of information on various high-cost prospects as these come
'on the market'. Such information, widely considered proprietary by
companies today, would become available. This is because the
companies themselves would perceive it to be in their interests to reveal
this information, thereby enhancing the attractiveness of what they
have on offer to prospective buyers. The more information provided,
the more the companies can hope to get the price demanded.

For those prospects for which there is no demand, and thus no
market value, the companies offering the real estate lose nothing. It was
worth precious little to them in the first place. Here, the state might

step in as a purchaser of last resort if circumstances justify such a move. As oil prices rise and knowledge and technology improve, it may well turn out to be valuable to give the state access to appreciating assets. The state will also be better able to co-ordinate field development in the North Sea to perceive needs of national self-sufficiency and the like. State purchasing could additionally act as a floor to demand. It could provide the groups abandoning the high-cost prospect with compensation for out-of-pocket expenses incurred to the point of abandonment. Such a floor would encourage groups to unload acreage kept 'on spec' while at the same time giving the state control over acreage which might be of considerable future value.

10.7. The State and Market Regulation

In encouraging such a 'market' in North Sea real estate, the state has considerable leeway in establishing the rules by which this 'market' is regulated. The state may prefer to work through a liberalised assignment policy as described earlier. In this case, the pressure created by accelerated relinquishment rates, higher area rents, and so forth, would accelerate the passage of firms in and out of groups holding various licences. Groups would be left alone to determine their own terms for farming-in and out. Assignment and reassignment would be seen in terms of providing exploration and development stimulus.

The state could also intervene more actively on the market. Most probably a good deal of real estate will revert to state ownership over time. The state could then actively shop around for alternative takers. In a real sense, such areas could be regarded as 'marginal'. It might even make sense to sweeten the reawarding of such areas with incentives.

State companies could be utilised in several respects. They could receive all acreage relinquished, for example. This would leave these companies with increasingly direct access to higher-cost resources. Such a situation has its disadvantages. It is uncertain, for example, that state companies possess the required variety of ideas and expertise to explore for or develop these high-cost resources alone. By relegating all relinquished acreage to state company ownership, one might actually have an effect opposite to that intended — the state monopoly of such acreage could actually delay the discovery/development of high-cost resources. In other words a situation not unlike that of Denmark might occur. It is not a given fact that a state company with a monopoly to such resources will automatically be more active than the DUC has been.

Alternatively, state companies could figure in any state effort to 'shop around' for other takers. Here too, there are disadvantages. Such a state company role would essentially be a 'balancing act' — neither too much state control nor too much state company subsidy could be allowed. One extreme would act as a disincentive, the other as a considerable drain on the state company (ultimately the taxpayers') budget.

Perhaps the most intriguing possibility in so far as state regulation of such a market is concerned could be that of auctioneer. The fundamental concepts behind this idea are simple. Groups holding high-cost fields for which they have no immediate plans would be induced to part with these prospects due to increased area rentals or changed relinquishment provisions. Groups and companies without access to such acreage would be encouraged to consider investing in what becomes available. The two sets of interested parties could arrange an auction in which the assets concerned would be transferred to the highest bidder.

Such auctions or bidding systems are in fact characteristic of the oil industry elsewhere. In the United States, in particular, bidding for Federal leases is a noted feature of that country's petroleum policies, and the focus of a considerable literature.[13] In the US such bidding is the primary means of rent capture; in the North Sea by contrast, bidding would serve instead to transfer already known resources.[14] (It is unlikely that bidding will ever be an accepted manner of rent capture in the Dutch, British, Norwegian, or Danish offshore areas.)

The procedure in such a bidding system could follow the North American practice with few changes. The state could undertake to police proceedings. Upon relinquishment of a high-cost field, the group concerned, in co-operation with the authorities, would place all the pertinent information about the particular structure in the public domain. Potential bidders might have time to investigate the structure on their own — perhaps (with ministerial permission) even going so far as to drill a step-out well or two. Such additional information would be proprietary. Then interested parties would bid for the resources concerned. Such an auctioning system would have to recompense the original groups that laid out money for exploration and evaluation. And, as noted, it would give other groups, with different preference structures and opportunity cost perspectives, access to acreage they might wish to develop, *ceteris paribus.*

In the British sector, there have already been one actual and one proposed transfer of ownership on high-cost fields in which an auction system might conceivably have been used. The first concerned the sale of the Rough field by Gulf in 1973, a field which lay half in the Gulf block 47/8, but which Gulf did not wish to develop. A British firm, Berry Wiggins, attempted to take over Gulf's interests, but was prevented from doing so by the Gas Council, which entered the field in its partnership with the Amoco group and purchased it for $2 million plus an 'overriding interest of seven per cent'.[15] The proposed transfer of ownership concerned natural gas in the South-east Indefatigable field. Here, Shell/Esso, the National Coal Board and others offered the one-half trillion cubic feet concerned to the BGC and were told that the natural gas was unwanted, but that the BGC would be interested in buying the gas in the ground in order to develop it later themselves. Negotiations ensued about such a purchase, but no result apparently was forthcoming.[16]

In both the Rough and the South-east Indefatigable cases, auctioning of the resources concerned might have been a fairer manner of transferring ownership. In such an auctioning system, there would be room for bidders other than the BNOC or the BGC. Government firms would therefore be reduced to one set of bidders among others. But in terms of high-cost resource development *per se* this is immaterial. Such auctions would allow high-cost resources to be transferred as close to their market value as possible and prevent state firms from foreclosing a sale that, in the eyes of the previous owners, might constitute a loss. A veritable market in high-cost resources might be created. This could remove company opposition to proposed licensing changes whether in the form of higher rental payments or accelerated relinquishment provisions. More importantly, such a system of auctions would also transfer high-cost resources into the hands of groups willing to develop them.

10.8. The 'Market' and Discretionary Economic Incentives: A Combined System

Once such a 'market' in high-cost fields was established, the use of discretionary economic incentives — which we have argued do not work in the North Sea systems as structured today — could become an extremely valuable tool in promoting the development of particular fields. Outside the question of administrative costs and the like, the biggest problem with discretionary incentives is that of definition as mentioned earlier! How is a 'marginal' or high-cost field defined in the

first place? How can a system be devised which benefits precisely these
fields more than others? How does one treat the oil company argument
as to royalty refunds cited earlier in this chapter?

The use of a 'market' system would specify the definition of such
high-cost fields. A 'marginal' field would be any field not successfully
auctioned off. A pool of such fields, now ownerless, could be created.
In such a context, financial incentives could be discussed. These would
be granted at ministerial discretion, and fields could be offered up
again under varying circumstances. Such a process will avoid the 'special
pleading' now so characteristic of the industry. If the only manner in
which financial incentives are granted is through giving up title, there
is little reason for firms to argue for royalty exemptions in the hope
that they themselves will benefit from the said exemptions. Such a pool
of fields would clearly also be in a different legal and economic category
from fields retained by various groups for various reasons. Preferences
offered fields in the pool need not be justified in terms of fields which
have not been offered up for auction. In this manner one could forego
unnecessary loss to the Exchequer, control the rate of development of
such fields, and reward or penalise development groups solely on the
criterion of their commitment to development of the fields concerned.

This solution is not free of problems. The redistribution of acreage
in this manner is liable to abuse. Governments can in fact prefer one
firm or group to another. By individually parcelling out high-cost fields
with individual sets of discretionary incentives, the result could be
highly inequitable — and highly expensive. This could be solved,
however, by the government announcing a particular discretionary
incentive, such as the non-collection of royalties, and then offering a
selected number of blocks up for competitive bidding under this
condition. Such a system would be fair and equitable. It would further
reward the more efficient groups in the North Sea and provide the
government with a form of rent capture, in this case through the money
received in bidding.

10.9. The 'Market' and Natural Gas Fields

An objection to any system of 'marketing' high-cost resources can be
found in the special circumstances of natural gas fields. This is
particularly true in that 'cost' in this case is a function of the terms of
delivery. As long as these terms are dictated by a *de facto* monopsony
buyer (the British Gas Corporation) or a monopsony buyer with limited

powers (DONG), what is to prevent these state corporations from refusing to strike a 'deal' with the owners of high-cost gas fields well knowing that the owners will be forced to part with their fields eventually? The state companies can then hope to come in and pick up the fields on their own terms.

Due to the essentially bilateral nature of North Sea natural gas markets (as covered in Chapters 6 and 9), a slight variation of the proposed auction system will be necessary. For example, if a group discovering a field, for whatever reason is incapable of reaching an acceptable contract with the national gas company concerned and eventually has to relinquish a field, due either to sharpened relinquishment terms or to increased area rental rates, the area relinquished would be held in reserve by the state.

The future auctioning of the field would exclude national gas companies from the competitive bidding. Rather, these companies would help set bidding conditions – anticipated price and terms of delivery. Bidding would be on the basis of the proposed contract and the real estate involved. Included in the bidding provisions would be some form of recompense for the original discovering group. Expenses incurred in exploring the area plus a margin could be obtained through the inclusion of a fast royalty payable by the developers to the discovering group. (Such a system was used to great effect with regard to Gulf Oil in the transfer of Rough field to Amoco/British Gas.) If there are no bidders, then the national company has a choice of either foregoing eventual development of the resources concerned or of re-offering it on improved terms. The end result would be a reiterative bidding process which would procure the development of the resources concerned – if these resources are at all worthwhile.

This solution – a form of cutting the Gordian knot – is by no means a universal palliative. It is one thing to propose changes, quite another to implement them. There are several possible objections to such a scheme. The first is that the national company will not be able to participate in the development of such resources. In an ideal auction system this would be true. In contrast it should be pointed out that national companies such as British Gas already have their hands full with structures like the Morecombe field. They can additionally bid for blocks and operate them on equal terms with other companies. The degree to which they are excluded from actual ownership of high-cost resources could be more than made up by the fact that ultimately they could receive their desired prices and terms of delivery without any expenditure on their part.

The second objection could be that the inclusion of a form of compensation to the discovery group (probably a form of royalty) would place that group in a favoured competitive situation in any bidding round. Other groups would have to reckon with the royalty as a cost. This is also true. But one could argue that the discovery group should also be placed at some sort of competitive advantage should bidding take place. On the one hand the advantage conferred by royalties would constitute a 'reward' for the relinquishment of the resources involved, while on the other hand, should the group refuse to meet reasonable terms, they can well be outbid by a more enterprising group. In either case, the price and terms of delivery would be more attractive than those which might ultimately be procured through stalemates such as that over South-east Indefatigable.

More serious perhaps is the objection that such a system confirms a monopsony role for a corporation like British Gas. It is hard to see the reasoning in this. Clearly the Minister concerned can rule that a contract is out of order whether that contract is reached in 1968/9 or whether it is written in 1980.

10.10. Conclusion

In Part One of this volume the issue of high-cost fields was introduced, and the central problem posed: how to procure their development. The policy means accomplishing this end were of two basic types: the use of direct economic incentives — generally waivers of rent-capture legislation; and the placing of stricter limits on the licensing of offshore blocks — tightening the basic North Sea 'contract'.

The analysis of British and Danish policies elaborated these views. In Britain, authorities have attempted to encourage the development of high-cost fields through granting waivers to rent-capture legislation. This has not quietened the oil companies. Rather it has had the opposite effect for the companies even today — in a period of remarkably higher prices — are still interested in obtaining special conditions for high-cost projects under consideration. The same can be said of Norway. Here, high-cost fields have not been a focal point in the debate, but oil companies have expected special considerations when an East Frigg or an Odin is to be developed.

In Denmark, there is no rent-capture legislation beyond an 8.5 per cent royalty charge. Yet it was clear from the beginning that the Danish concession was limited in time if no oil or gas field were developed. This condition has led to the development of the Dan; it will lead to the development of four additional gas fields as well. The limit on the North Sea contract in the Danish case did bear fruit.

The pros and cons of these various policies have been discussed. What is recommended is an abandonment of the type of discretionary incentives used now for stricter licensing policies, ultimately aiming at the establishment of a 'market solution' to the problem of developing high-cost reserves (with incentives reinstituted in this system as a last resort).

One final objection might be made to such a scheme. Given the great OPEC price increases of 1979/80 and an increase in North Sea activity, are such changes as proposed in this volume still necessary? Won't the companies go ahead and develop new high-cost fields without prodding? Corporate profits are higher everywhere. But the same arguments are still heard. The DUC in Denmark has suddenly discovered Jurassic prospects which it has previously ignored and is engaged in a furious debate with the Danish authorities as to whether any of the highly promising 10,000 square kilometre South-west area will be relinquished on this side of the year 2000. In Norway, companies have not ceased arguing for a relaxation of the recently increased oil revenue taxes on the one hand and for increased block awards on the other. In Great Britain, the UKOOA successfully argued the government into increasing from 70 to 90 the number of blocks offered in the Seventh Round. The UKOOA was far from satisfied however; its comments on the blocks offered having a familiar ring to them. Claiming that the 90-block round was insufficient the UKOOA called on the government to schedule regular rounds over the next ten years. Although claiming that 50-100 new fields would have to be discovered to keep the UK self-sufficient, the UKOOA pointed out that of some 40 existing undeveloped fields there were many which were 'too small' to be developed.[17]

What is advocated here is a system which established competitive bidding for undeveloped high-cost reserves which is fair and equitable for all concerned. Furthermore, given the rate and size of future licensing rounds, changes in the present system of licensing will become inevitable. Theoretically there can be a day when all that North Sea Governments can offer is 'whale pasture' for which there are no takers.

The development of all economically feasible North Sea resources could hardly be more important than it is today. They can make a critical contribution to national economic growth of the possessing North Sea nation, to European energy self-sufficiency, and to lessened political and economic dependence on OPEC. The recent turmoil in

Iran and the Middle East only underlines this urgency. Despite frequent disclaimers to the contrary, the interests of government and industry clearly do not always coincide in the decision as to whether or not to develop particular high-cost resources, as demonstrated by the evidence presented in this study. A revision of access provisions provides the key to the development of many fields which would otherwise not be developed. As a means of updating the North Sea contractual relationship, such revision is both moderate and necessary to continued efficient, orderly development of these highly important resources.

Notes

1. *Economist* (14 July 1979), pp. 80-1.
2. For an up-to-date economic analysis of these problems see Charles W. Howe, *Natural Resource Economics* (New York: John Wiley and Sons, 1979).
3. Risk spreading is the dispersion of risky net benefits of a public project over a large number of individuals. If the aggregate number of individuals is large enough the cost of bearing the risk declines. Risk pooling offsets the anticipated risks of one project against the anticipated benefits of another. The more risky projects are included in such a pool the greater the ratio of anticipated net benefits to anticipated costs. A sole project unacceptable on its own merits may be attractive in a sufficiently large pool (Howe, *Natural Resource Economics*, p. 163).
4. W. Meade, 'Rate of Return Analysis', *Study of OCS Lands of the United States* (Washington, D.C.: Public Land Law Review Commission, November 1969), III, pp. 526-30.
5. Shyam Sunder, *Oil Industry Profits* (Washington, D.C.: American Enterprise Institute for Public Policy Research, 1977), pp. 9-48. The figures used reflect the return to common equity owners.
6. Ibid., p. 48.
7. The calculation of the book yield can vary much more among firms than that of the IRR (true yield). Such diversities in accounting procedure make uncritical comparisons of accounting measures dubious.
8. 'Oil Firms: Higher Taxes but Easier Avoidance', *New Statesman* (9 March 1978), pp. 310-11.
9. Iran in 1957 entered a joint venture with ENI on the following relinquishment terms: one-half of the licensed area relinquished after ten years, the balance after two additional years if no commercial find is made. Iraq's ERAP licence required relinquishment of 50 per cent after three years, 25 per cent after the fifth year, and the balance after the sixth year.
10. See K. Dam, *Oil Resources: Who Gets What How?* (Chicago: The University of Chicago Press, 1976).
11. Jens Evensen, *Oversikt over Oljepolitiske Spørsmål* (Norway: Industridepartementet, January 1971), p. 52.
12. *Financial Times* (10 May 1980), p. 22.
13. The most noted of these is Dam, *Oil Resources*. Other treatments focusing particularly on US offshore leasing are: E. Dougherty and J. Lohrenz, 'Statistical Analysis of Solo and Joint Bids for Federal Offshore Oil and Gas Leases', SPE 6517, Society of Petroleum Engineers, Dallas, April 1977; Federal Trade

Commission, *Staff Report on Federal Energy Land Policy* (US Department of Commerce, 1975); D.W. Gaskins and T.J. Teisberg, 'An Economic Analysis of Presale Exploration in Oil and Gas Lease Sales' in R. Masson and P. Qualls (eds.), *Essays in Industrial Organization in Honor of J.S. Bain* (Cambridge, Mass.: Ballinger, 1976). See also E.C. Capen, R.V. Clapp and W.M. Campbell, 'Competitive Bidding in High Risk Situations', *Journal of Petroleum Technology* (June 1971), pp. 641-53, and Robert B. Wilson, 'Management and Financing of Exploration for Offshore Oil and Gas', *Public Policy*, 26:4 (1978), pp. 629-57.

14. This particular use of auction bidding is an elaboration of the ideas expressed in a slightly different context in Dam, *Oil Resources*, and Wilson, 'Management and Financing of Exploration'.

15. Adrian Hamilton, 'The Lessons of the Rough Field Affair', *The Financial Times* (6 April 1973), p. 9.

16. Testimony of National Coal Board before the Select Committee on Nationalised Industries, *First Report*, Session 1974/5, p. 82.

17. *Financial Times* (7 May 1980), p. 8.

TECHNICAL APPENDICES

TECHNICAL APPENDICES TO CHAPTER 1

Appendix 1A: Significant Oil and Gas Finds in the UK North Sea Sector (Up to End 1979)

Field name	Block number	Discovered by	Date discovered
Ann	49/6 (gas)	Phillips Group	May 1966
Dotty	48/30 (gas)	Phillips Group	May 1967
Scram	53/4a (gas)	BODL/Conoco	July 1967
—	48/21a (gas)	Placid	August 1967
Deborah	48/30 (gas)	Phillips Group	August 1968
—	48/28 (gas)	Arpet Group	March 1969
Sean	49/25a (gas)	Allied Chemical	April 1969
—	49/28 (gas)	Arpet Group	May 1969
—	41/24a (gas)	Total Group	June 1969
—	43/20a (gas)	Hamilton Group	June 1969
South Montrose	22/17, 22/18 (oil)	Amoco Group	December 1969
—	43/8a (gas)	Whitehall/Hamilton	January 1970
—	47/13a (gas)	Tricentrol/Conoco	April 1970
Broken Bank	49/21 (gas)	BODL/Conoco	July 1970
Josephine	30/13 (condensate)	Phillips Group	September 1970
—	49/16 (gas)	Conoco/BNOC	January 1971
—	30/2 (condensate)	BODL/Hamilton	June 1971
—	48/18b (gas)	Ranger/Berry Wiggins	April 1972
Lomond	23/21 (condensate)	Amoco Group	May 1972
—	49/22 (gas)	Mobil/Conoco	May 1972
Amethyst	47/14a (gas)	BODL	October 1972
—	3/15 (oil)	Total Group	July 1973
—	3/19 (gas)	Total Group	July 1973
Alwyn	3/14a (oil)	Total Group	November 1973
Andrew	16/28 (oil)	BP	June 1974
N. Beryl	9/13a (oil)	Mobil Group	June 1974
Bruce	9/8 (condensate)	Hamilton Group	July 1974
—	211/13 (condensate)	Shell/Esso	July 1974
—	211/18-6 (oil)	BODL	August 1974
—	110/2 (gas)	Hydrocarbons (GB)	September 1974
—	15/23 (oil)	Texaco	October 1974
—	3/11 (oil)	Amoco Group	December 1974
—	2/5 (oil)	Union Oil Group	December 1974
—	14/20 (oil)	Texaco	February 1975
—	9/12 (oil)	Union Oil Group	February 1975

Field name	Block number	Discovered by	Date discovered
Crawford	9/28 (oil)	Hamilton Group	February 1975
Mabel	16/28 (oil)	BP/Phillips	February 1975
—	3/4 (oil)	Texaco	March 1975
Tern	210/25 (oil)	Shell/Esso	April 1975
—	2/10 (oil)	Siebens Group	April 1975
—	21/2 (oil)	Zapata Group	June 1975
Lyell	3/2 (oil)	Conoco/BNOC/Gulf	June 1975
—	211/13 (oil)	Shell/Esso	July 1975
—	16/21 (oil)	Sun Oil Group	August 1975
—	3/4 (oil)	Texaco	August 1975
—	211/18 (oil)	BODL Group	September 1975
—	15/30 (condensate)	Conoco/BNOC/Gulf	September 1975
—	15/13 (oil)	BP Group	October 1975
—	3/9 (oil)	Total Group	October 1975
—	15/21 (oil)	Monsanto Group	October 1975
—	21/2 (condensate)	Zapata Group	December 1975
—	48/12 (gas)	Transocean Group	December 1975
—	211/13 (oil)	Shell/Esso	December 1975
—	23/27 (oil)	Ranger/Scot Group	March 1976
—	23/26a (oil)	BP	March 1976
Audrey	49/11a (gas)	Phillips Group	March 1976
Renee	15/27 (oil)	Phillips Group	April 1976
—	14/20 (oil)	Texaco	April 1976
—	211/27 (oil)	Amoco Group	May 1976
—	9/19 (oil)	Conoco/BNOC/Gulf	May 1976
—	211/16 (oil)	Shell/Esso	May 1976
—	3/7 (oil)	Chevron/Canada NW	June 1976
—	49/29b (gas)	Mobil	June 1976
Thelma	16/17 (oil)	Phillips Group	July 1976
—	211/18 (oil)	BODL Group	July 1976
Toni	16/17 (oil)	Phillips Group	August 1977
—	30/17b (oil)	BNOC/Shell/Esso	June 1978
Tiffany	16/17 (oil)	Phillips Group	July 1979

Source: *Development of the Oil and Gas Resources of the United Kingdom*
(London: HMSO, 1979). The number of fields has been adjusted to accord with
the situation at the end of 1979. Some of these fields are now probably under
development consideration. Neither is this list all-inclusive: there are fields in the
UK sector which are not listed here.

Appendix 1B: Undeveloped Oil and Gas Finds in the Danish North Sea Sector

Field name	Block number/well	Discovered by	Date discovered
Anne	7,3/A-1 (gas/oil)	DUC	1966
Cora	6,2; 6,3/E-1 (gas)	DUC	1968
Bent	6,2/H-1 (gas)	DUC	1969
Arne	5,2/I-1 (oil)	DUC	1969
Gorm/Vern	6,2/N-1 (oil/gas)	DUC	1971
Gwen	5,2/Q-1 (oil)	DUC	1973
North Arne	5,2/T-1 (oil)	DUC	1975
Ruth/Skjold	6,2/Ruth-1 (oil)	DUC	1977
Adda	6,3/Adda-1 (oil)	DUC	1977
Nils	/Nils-1 (oil)	DUC	1978

Source: Olaf Michelsen, 'Kortfattet Oversigt over de Geologiske Forhold i den Danske del af Nordsøen', *D.G.U. Årsbog* (1975), pp. 129-32. *Danshore* (1976 *et seq.*)

Appendix 1C: Undeveloped Norwegian Finds

Field name	Block number	Discovered by	Date discovered
Murphy	2/2 (gas)	Murphy Group	1969
—	25/8 (oil)	Esso	1970
Bream	17/12 (oil)	Phillips Group	1971
Heimdal	25/4 (gas)	Petronord Group	1972
S.E. Tor	2/5 (oil/gas)	Amoco/Noco Group	1972
Flounder	1/5 (oil)	Shell	1973
East Frigg	25/2 (gas)	Petronord Group	1973
Brisling	17/12 (oil)	Phillips Group	1973
Southeast Frigg	25/2 (gas)	Petronord Group	1974
Northeast Frigg	25/1 (gas)	Petronord Group	1974
Odin	30/10 (gas)	Esso	1974
Sleipner	15/6 (gas)	Esso	1974
Balder	25/11 (oil)	Esso	1974
25/2-4	25/2 (gas)	Petronord Group	1975
Hod	2/11 (oil)	Amoco/Noco Group	1975
Valhall	2/8 (oil)	Amoco/Noco Group	1975
—	15/3 (oil/gas)	Petronord	1975
—	30/7 (oil)	Statoil/Norsk Hydro	1975
33/9-Alfa	33/9 (oil)	Statoil/Mobil	1976
33/9-Beta	33/9 (oil)	Statoil/Mobil	1976

Field name	Block number	Discovered by	Date discovered
—	7/12 (oil)	BP/Conoco Group	1976
1/9-Alfa	1/9 (oil)	Statoil/Phillips	1976
1/9-Beta	1/9 (oil)	Statoil/Phillips	1977
34/10-Alfa	34/10 (oil)	Statoil Group	1978
34/10-Delta	34/10 (oil)	Statoil Group	1978

Source: *Oljedirektoratets Årsberetning 1978*, p. 32.

Appendix 1D: Undeveloped Fields in the Dutch Sector

There exists no real listing of all the gas and oil finds in the Dutch sector. What follows are a few of the more significant high-cost finds.

Field name	Block number	Discovered by	Date discovered
—	P/6 (gas)	Kewanee Group	1968
—	L/2 (gas)	NAM	1968
—	K/7 (gas)	NAM	1968/9
—	F/18 (oil)	BP Group	1970/1
—	K/17 (gas)	NAM	1971
—	K/6 (gas)	Petroland Group	1972
—	L/8 (gas)	Pennzoil Group	1972
—	F/3 (gas/oil)	NAM	1973/4
—	L/4 (gas)	Petroland Group	1974
—	K/4 (gas)	BP Group	1974
—	Q/1 (gas)	Unionoil Group	1974/5
—	L/14 (gas)	Placid Group	1975
—	K/12 (gas)	Placid Group	1975
—	F/2 (gas/oil)	Unionoil Group	1976
—	L/12 (N) (gas)	NAM Group	1976
—	Q/8 (gas)	BP/Gulf	1976
—	L/16 (gas)	City Services Group	1977
—	P/1 (gas)	NAM	1977
—	L/11 (E) (gas)	Unionoil Group	1978
—	L/15 (gas)	NAM Group	1978

Source: *European Continental Shelf Guide 1979* (London: Offshore Promotional Services Ltd., 1979).

Production, Operating Cost and Investment Profiles for Auk, Forties and Heather — the Examples Used in Chapter Two

Year	Auk			Forties		
	Production (1000 bbl./d)	Operating costs ($m)	Investment ($m)	Production (1000 bbl./d)	Operating costs ($m)	Investment ($m)
1972	—	—	—	—	—	150
1973	—	—	—	—	—	300
1974	—	—	45	—	—	600
1975	20	15	45	50	30	300
1976	40	25		200	75	150
1977	40	25		400	75	
1978	40	25		400	75	
1979	35	25		400	75	
1980	35	25		360	75	
1981	35	25		324	75	
1982	35	25		292	75	
1983				262	75	
1984				236	75	
1985				213	75	
1986				191	75	
1987				172	75	
1988				155	75	
1989				139	75	
1990				126	75	
1991				113	75	
1992				102	75	
1993				92	75	
1994				82	75	

Source: D.I. MacKay and G.A. Mackay, *The Political Economy of North Sea Oil* (London: Martin Robertson, 1975), pp. 46-7.

Year	Heather		
	Production (1000 bbl./d)	Operating costs ($m)	Capital expenditure ($m)
1975			20
1976			100
1977			145
1978	10	30	30
1979	30	40	65
1980	55	40	40
1981	60	40	
1982	60	40	
1983	60	40	
1984	54	40	
1985	49	40	
1986	44	40	
1987	40	40	
1988	36	40	
1989	32	40	

Source: A.G. Kemp, 'The Taxation of North Sea Oil', *North Sea Occasional Papers*, 11 (August 1976).

TECHNICAL APPENDICES TO CHAPTER 5

Appendix 5A: Assumptions behind the 1974/5 UKOOA Representations to the UK Government

The UKOOA arguments summarised in pp. 104-8 are based on the data given in this appendix. Table 1 shows the general capital cost allocations year-by-year for the fields representing four cases: case I (30 million tons oil reserves); case II (40 million tons oil reserves); case III (50 million tons oil reserves); and case IV (60 million tons oil reserves)

Table I: PRT Analysis Assumptions Data

Case	I		II		III		IV	
Recoverable reserves[a]								
Million tons	30		40		50		60	
Million bbls.	225		300		375		450	
Investment[b]	£MM	$MM	£MM	$MM	£MM	$MM	£MM	$MM
Year								
1	8.5	20	8.5	20	8.5	20	8.5	20
2	38.7	91	41.5	98	43.9	103	45.3	107
3	59.0	139	62.5	147	65.5	154	67.3	158
4	70.8	167	75.0	176	78.6	185	80.7	190
5	23.6	55	25.0	59	26.2	62	26.9	63
6	23.6	55	25.0	59	26.2	62	26.9	63
7	11.8	28	12.5	29	13.1	30	13.4	32
Termination cost	21.0	50	21.0	50	21.0	50	21.0	50
Total	257	605	271	638	283	666	290	683
£/peak daily barrel	3,480		3,000		2,760		2,610	
$/peak daily barrel	8,180		7,050		6,490		6,150	
£/ton reserves	8.57		6.78		5.66		4.83	
$/barrel reserves	2.69		2.13		1.78		1.52	
Annual cash operating costs								
1st year of production £ (million)	15.2		15.9		16.4		16.7	
1st year of production $ (million)	35.7		37.2		38.5		39.3	
Average £ per year (million)	20.7		24.2		24.9		25.4	
Average $ per year (million)	48.7		56.9		58.6		59.7	

Table II *(contd.)*

Case	I	II	III	IV
Average cash operating costs				
£/ton	8.98	9.07	8.48	7.20
$/barrel	2.81	2.84	2.66	2.26
Crude price range				
£/ton	28.72		38.30	47.87
$/bbl.	9.00		12.00	15.00

One platform development (incl. share of pipeline system)

Escalation Investment escalated from 1 January 1975 base: 10 per cent per year.
Operating costs escalated from 1 January 1975 base: 5 per cent per year.

Notes:
a. 1 long ton = 7.5 bbls.
b. 2 £1 = $2.35.

Table II summarises the production profiles for the various cases and additionally specifies the expected 'peak rate' of production for each case.

Table II: Assumptions on Reserves and Production

Case		I			II	
Recoverable reserves						
Million long tons		30			40	
Million barrels		225			300	
Annual production	% of reserves	MM tons	MM bbls.	% of reserves	MM tons	MM bbls.
Year of production						
1	6	1.8	13.5	6	2.4	18.0
2	12	3.6	27.0	11	4.4	33.0
3	12	3.6	27.0	11	4.4	33.0
4	12	3.6	27.0	11	4.4	33.0
5	11.5	3.5	25.9	11	4.4	33.0
6	9.8	2.9	22.0	9.4	3.8	28.2
7	8.3	2.5	18.7	7.9	3.2	23.7
8	7.1	2.1	16.0	6.8	2.7	20.4
9	6.0	1.8	13.5	5.8	2.3	17.4
10	5.1	1.5	11.5	4.9	2.0	14.7
11	4.4	1.3	9.9	4.2	1.7	12.6
12	3.7	1.1	8.3	3.6	1.4	10.8
13	2.1	0.7	4.7	3.0	1.2	9.0
14				2.6	1.0	7.8
15				1.8	0.7	5.4
Total	100	30	225	100	40	300
Peak Rate 000 B/D		74			90	

Table II *(contd.)*

Case		III			IV	
Recoverable reserves						
Million long tons		50			60	
Million barrels		375			450	
Annual production	% of reserves	MM tons	MM bbls.	% of reserves	MM tons	MM bbls.
Year of production						
1	6	3.0	22.5	5	3.0	22.5
2	10	5.0	37.5	9	5.4	40.5
3	10	5.0	37.5	9	5.4	40.5
4	10	5.0	37.5	9	5.4	40.5
5	10	5.0	37.5	9	5.4	40.5
6	9.4	4.7	35.3	9	5.4	40.5
7	7.9	4.0	29.6	9	5.4	40.5
8	6.8	3.4	25.5	7.7	4.6	34.7
9	5.8	2.9	21.8	6.5	3.9	29.3
10	4.9	2.5	18.4	5.5	3.3	24.7
11	4.2	2.1	15.8	4.7	2.8	21.2
12	3.6	1.8	13.5	4.0	2.4	18.0
13	3.0	1.5	11.2	3.4	2.0	15.3
14	2.6	1.3	9.8	2.9	1.7	13.1
15	2.0	1.0	7.5	2.5	1.5	11.3
16	2.0	0.9	7.5	2.2	1.4	9.9
17	1.8	0.9	6.6	1.6	1.0	7.0
Total	100	50	375	100	60	450
Peak Rate 000 B/D		103			111	

Source: *Noroil* (February 1975), pp. 21-2.

Appendix 5B: Assumptions behind the 'Marginal' Fields Used as a Comparison to the UKOOA Models

In the discussion of the PRT, reference is made to the following fields: Auk, Beryl, Claymore, Cormorant, Dunlin, Heather, Montrose, Thistle, and (although it is by no means 'marginal') the Forties. The tables in this appendix specify the estimated capital costs, operating costs and production rates from these fields. These figures are all from one source: Alexander G. Kemp, 'The Taxation of North Sea Oil', *North Sea Study Occasional Papers*, 11 (August 1976). For the purposes of comparability (the UKOOA representations assume real cost inflation rates of 10 per cent for capital expenditures and 5 per cent for operating expenditures), and to take account of the constantly rising costs since 1976, the figures in these tables are inflated by 10 per cent *per annum* (capital costs) and

5 per cent *per annum* (operating costs) when used or cited in the text of the chapter. Here all expenditures and costs are given in constant 1976 dollars.

Year	Thistle			Auk		
	Production (1000 bbl./d)	Operating costs ($m)	Capital expenditure ($m)	Production (1000 bbl./d)	Operating costs ($m)	Capital expenditure ($m)
1973						20
1974						35
1975			205			30
1976			305	30	25	25
1977	15	15	90	50	25	
1978	90	30	80	50	25	
1979	160	40	80	30	25	
1980	185	40	50	10	25	
1981	185	40				
1982	185	40				
1983	185	40				
1984	157	40				
1985	134	40				
1986	121	40				
1987	109	40				
1988	98	40				
1989	89	40				

Year	Claymore			Cormorant		
	Production (1000 bbl./d)	Operating costs ($m)	Capital expenditure ($m)	Production (1000 bbl./d)	Operating costs ($m)	Capital expenditure ($m)
1975			90			105
1976			250			125
1977	10	10	95			65
1978	50	20	55	25	10	60
1979	90	35		70	20	45
1980	110	35		90	35	
1981	110	35		90	35	
1982	99	35		90	35	
1983	89	35		81	35	
1984	80	35		73	35	
1985	72	35		66	35	
1986	63	35		59	35	
1987	57	35		53	35	
1988	51	35		48	35	
1989	46	35		43	35	
1990	41	35		39	35	
1991	37	35				

Year	Dunlin Production (1000 bbl./d)	Operating costs ($m)	Capital expenditure ($m)	Forties Production (1000 bbl./d)	Operating costs ($m)	Capital expenditure ($m)
1972						100
1973						245
1974						350
1975			220	15	25	540
1976			305	220	75	225
1977	25	10	85	400	80	135
1978	60	20	50	450	80	65
1979	95	35	40	450	80	
1980	120	35	30	450	80	
1981	120	35	25	450	80	
1982	120	35	25	405	80	
1983	108	35	20	365	80	
1984	97	35		328	80	
1985	87	35		295	80	
1986	78	35		266	80	
1987	70	35		239	80	
1988	63	35		215	80	
1989	57	35		194	80	
1990	51	35		174	80	
1991	46	35		157	80	
1992	41	35		141	80	

Year	Heather Production (1000 bbl./d)	Operating costs ($m)	Capital expenditure ($m)	Montrose Production (1000 bbl./d)	Operating costs ($m)	Capital expenditure ($m)
1974						40
1975			20			110
1976			100	5	15	75
1977			145	35	30	55
1978	10	30	30	50	30	
1979	30	40	65	50	30	
1980	55	40	40	50	30	
1981	60	40		50	30	
1982	60	40		50	30	
1983	60	40		45	30	
1984	54	40		40	30	
1985	49	40		37	30	
1986	44	40		33	30	
1987	40	40		30	30	
1988	36	40		27	30	
1989	32	40		24	30	
1990				22	30	
1991				20	30	

Year	Production (1000 bbl./d)	Beryl Operating costs ($m)	Capital expenditure ($m)
1974			90
1975			190
1976	40	25	90
1977	100	45	60
1978	100	45	20
1979	100	45	
1980	100	45	
1981	100	45	
1982	100	45	
1983	100	45	
1984	100	45	
1985	100	45	
1986	90	45	
1987	81	45	
1988	73	45	
1989	65	45	
1990	59	45	
1991	53	45	
1992	48	45	
1993	43	45	

TECHNICAL APPENDICES TO CHAPTER 6

Appendix 6A: Production Profiles and Investment Patterns — Model Gas Field. Gas Council Development Plan Versus Companies' Development Plans

In this appendix the specifics behind the model field, mentioned in Table 6.5 and utilised throughout the chapter, are spelled out in more detail, and the differences in production rates and capital investment flows are illustrated briefly.

	Companies' Plan		Gas Council Plan	
Operating expenditures	$6.2m/yr		$6.4m/yr	
Capital expenditures	$105.73m		$128.75m	
Year	Capital expenditures ($m)	Production (10^9 ft^3)	Capital expenditures ($m)	Production (10^9 ft^3)
0	15.39	0	15.39	0
1	21.1	0	21.1	0
2	25.5	0	26.65	0
3	6.75	57	9.75	22
4	—	115	3.37	38
5	—	173	7.25	60
6	2.25	173	11.0	88
7	6.0	173	6.75	120
8	6.75	173	—	120
9	2.62	173	—	125
10	7.0	173	—	125
11	7.87	173	—	125
12	—	173	—	125
13	—	173	1.25	125
14	4.5	173	2.5	125
15	—	143	2.5	120
16	—	120	—	120
17	—	99	5.0	120
18	—	81	1.68	100
19	—	67	9.5	89
20	—	55	5.0	80
21	—	0	—	72
22	—	0	—	64
23	—	0	—	58
24	—	0	—	52
25	—	0	—	46
26	—	0	—	42
27	—	0	—	39
28	—	0	—	0

Estimated expenditures are as follows:

All production platforms   — $7.5 million per copy incl. installation
All production wells   — $1.25 million per well
Treatment and separation   — $5.0 million for each plan
Field to shore pipeline (35 miles in length) — $1.0 million per mile
Compressor platforms   — $7.5 million per copy incl. installation
Compressors — $5.0 million per copy incl. installation

These expenditures are allocated so that all items installed on the field take three years from initial contracting to installation and commencement of operations. Wells are completed the same year as scheduled. Otherwise (with the exception of pipeline and treatment) capital expenditures are allocated as follows:

year 0 — 15 per cent of total investment (planning and design)
year 1 — 40 per cent of total investment (construction)
year 2 — 45 per cent of total investment (construction and installation).

The schedule for installation and start-up of these items is given below for both the corporations' and the Gas Council's respective plans:

Year	Companies' Plan	Gas Council Plan
0		
1		
2	Platform x 5 wells, pipeline and treatment installed	Platform x 5 wells, pipeline and treatment installed
3	Platform 2 x 6 wells installed pipeline completed	Platform 2 x 6 wells installed, pipeline completed
4		Platform 3 (compressor) installed
5		Compressor 1 installed
6		Compressor 2 installed
7		Platform 4 x 6 wells installed
8	Platform 3 x 6 wells installed	
9		
10		
11	Compressor platform, 2 compressors installed	
12		
13		Additional well drilled from first platform
14	3 additional wells drilled + 1 recompletion	2 additional wells from platform 2

Year	Companies' Plan	Gas Council Plan
15		2 additional wells from platform 3
16		
17		4 additional wells
18		
19		Compressor 3 installed
20		Platform 5 x 3 wells installed
21		
22		
23		
24		
25		
26		
27		
28		

Appendix 6B: High-cost Natural Gas Fields — Southern British Basin

This list is most likely not entirely complete. For some fields listed, development plans are in progress. But, for the majority, development will have to await the offering of better prices by the BGC.

Fields which will shortly be developed	Fields which will probably be developed	Fields which will possibly be developed
Little Dotty (Deborah)	Amethyst	Amoseas 48/7-1,2
Viking (Broken Bank)	Amoco 49/23-2	Arpet 48/11A
Viking S (49/22-2)	Ann	Arpet 49/28-5,6
	Arpet 49/28-2,3,4	BP 42/30
	Audrey	Conoco 47/13-1
	BP 48/7B-3	Conoco 49/16-4
	Conoco 49/12-6	Conoco 49/16-6
	Conoco 49/17-4	Conoco 49/22-3
	Indefatigable D,E,M	Hamilton 43/8
	Leman E,F,G,H	Hamilton 43/20
	Placid 48/21	Mobil 49/29-2
	Ranger 48/18B	Mobil 53/2-2
	S.E. Inde	Phillips 48/30-3
	Shell/Allied 53/4	Shell 48/13-1
	Shell 49/24-2	Total 41/21A
	Shell 49/24-12	
	Shell 48/19A	
	Shell 48/20A	
	Transocean 48/12	

Source: Cliff Browne, *Status Report on the North Sea Development Drilling Market* (Washington, D.C.: Riggs National Bank, September 1977), p. 5 (Table I).

TECHNICAL APPENDIX TO CHAPTER 7

Comparative Table: Danish Concessionary Conditions 1950 and 1962/3

The table here illustrates the differences between the concessionary terms of 1950 with those awarded to A.P. Moeller. Of particular import are the items under heading 'IV. Conditions of Concession', in particular a.1 and a.2, b.1 and b.2.

Danish Concessionary Law: 1950, 1963

		Dapco concession of 1950	A.P. Moeller concession of 1962 (as amended in 1963)
I.	Geographical area	Jutland and the Danish Islands (not including Greenland, Faroe Islands or the Shelf)	Jutland and the Danish Islands (not including Faroes and Greenland), but including after 7 November 1963 the Continental Shelf
II.	Raw materials covered	All hydrocarbons, materials associated with rock salt (calcium, magnesium, anhydrate etc.); sulphur, helium. Excluding coal, diamonds, potash etc.	All hydrocarbons whether solid (asphalt), fluid (oil) or gaseous (gas), sulphur, and helium. Protocol to concession pledges government aid to procure concessionaire the monopoly concession to other resources if found
III.	Terms of concession	Monopoly rights for 10-year exploration period (can be prolonged through *force majeure*); upon successful discoveries, additional 40 years exploration rights	Same as in 1950
IV.	Conditions of concession		
	a. Exploration/ exploitation	1. Concessionaire may upon successful discovery, for those materials which he estimates can be produced in 'an economically defensible manner' begin to produce. Concession will be continued to 50 years for the raw material concerned if 'commercial production' is in progress	1. Operative paragraphs substantially the same, except the term 'commercial production' is reduced merely to 'production' with the consequence that it is the concessionaire who decides what is in effect commercial (Danish Concessionary (Law, 1950-63)

Dapco concession of 1950	A.P. Moeller concession of 1962 (as amended in 1963)
2. After commencement of commercial production of one hydrocarbon, concessionaire has 5 years to begin commercial production of associated hydrocarbons. This is renewable	2. Five-year rule obtains, if one hydrocarbon is in production
3. Concession becomes void if no exploration/ exploitation for two consecutive years	3. Same as with 1950, but if concessionaire can prove that production is economically undefensible, it can retain rights for another five years
4. All materials associated with salt dome must be exploited within 1.5 years of discovery. Failing this concession is revoked. Otherwise, concessionary rights cover 10,000 hectares around place of discovery	4. Not applicable
5. Before exploitation begins, equipment, plans and financing arrangements must be approved by Minister of Public Works	5. Same as in 1950

b. National production company

1. Upon commercial exploitation a Danish-based company will be founded on the following conditions:
   a. The concession for the raw material concerned is transferred to the company
   b. There will be an initial capitalisation of at least 6 million Dkr by Dapco
   c. The Danish Government will acquire 'participatory interest' with 5 per cent of the shares of the company which are transferred to it free

No provisions made for state participation, nor for a production company to which the concessionary rights should be transferred

		Dapco concession of 1950	A.P. Moeller concession of 1962 (as amended in 1963)
	2.	All monies expended on exploration by Dapco since the 1930s plus 3.5% interest will be transferred through the company to Dapco (this is for royalty provisions — see below)	
c. National provisions	1.	With the exception of unavailable expertise, 90% of the employment of Dapco shall be of Danish nationality	None
	2.	Re. production of raw materials from production company, Danish state empowered to purchase up to 50% of output at a reasonable price, for national reasons	
d. Information	1.	DGU authorised to receive most technical information	Essentially same as in 1950, but in Protocol, only 'original data' mentioned. Concessionaire insists this does not include economic assessments
	2.	Information Minister deemed necessary for general business control	
e. Auditing accounts	1.	Concessionaire pledged to give full accounts within three months of end of fiscal year. (Dapco had no partners)	Six-month deadline. Concessionaires alone responsible for their accounts. Shell, Gulf, Texaco, Chevron not required to submit accounts ('Bistandsyder')
V. Royalties			
a. Hydrocarbons	1.	7.5% until exploration expenditures plus 3.5% interest is repaid Dapco through producing company, and	For hydrocarbons: 7.5% royalty on real value, 12.5% after 5 years for hydrocarbons exploited on land; 5% royalty on real value, 8.5% after five years for hydrocarbons from Continental Shelf
	2.	10% thereafter	
b. Salts	1.	Best qualities: 2.00 Dkr per metric ton	All other resources: 8.5% for resources on land (sea area); 6% for Continental Shelf. Basis for assessment is price at place of production
c. Calcium	1.	1.00 Dkr per metric ton	
d. Other	1.	7% of value at place of production	
VI. Leasing fees		None	None
VII. Relinquishment		None	None
VIII. Petroleum tax regime		None	None

TECHNICAL APPENDICES TO CHAPTER 8

Appendix 8A: Assumptions behind the Production of Gorm/Vern Oil, 1972 and 1978

Investment expenditures for Gorm/Vern were considerably less in 1972 than they were in 1978. This was in part due to the overall increases in capital expenditures associated with the North Sea, but also to the addition of a $90 million reinjection system for Gorm/Vern in 1978. Such a reinjection system increases overall oil recovery by 2.8 million tons.

Overall capital expenditure, operation expenditures, amounts of oil recovered are listed in Table I.

	1972	1978
Capital expenditures	$56 million*	$188.8 million
Operations cost *per annum*	$1.5-2 million*	$11 million
Oil recovered	20.5 million mt	23.3 million mt
Gas produced	4.1 billion m^3	1.4 billion m^3
Field life	21 years	25 years

*Without rejection, the $90 million capital investment and increased operations costs.

Table II shows the production, capital expenditure and operations profiles for Gorm/Vern in the years mentioned.

Table II: Production Profiles of the Gorm/Vern Field (1972 and 1978)

	Gorm/Vern in 1972		
Year	Production (10^3 mt)	Operating costs	Capital investment
1970	—	—	7.0
1971	—	—	21.4
1972	—	—	25.0
1973	1,994	2.0	2.6
1974	1,994	2.0	—
1975	1,994	2.0	—
1976	1,824	2.0	—
1977	1,526	2.0	—
1978	1,359	2.0	—
1979	1,211	2.0	—
1980	1,095	2.0	—
1981	967	2.0	—
1982	884	2.0	—
1983	829	2.0	—
1984	753	1.7	—
1985	667	1.7	—
1986	598	1.7	—
1987	511	1.5	—
1988	489	1.5	—
1989	455	1.5	—
1990	392	1.5	—
1991	367	1.5	—
1992	351	1.5	—
1993	272	1.5	—

Table II *(contd.)*

| | Gorm/Vern in 1978 | | |
Year	Production (10^3 mt)	Operations costs	Capital investment
1978	—	—	28.3
1979	—	—	75.5
1980	—	—	85.0
1981	1,994	11.0	—
1982	1,994	11.0	—
1983	1,994	11.0	—
1984	1,967	11.0	—
1985	1,744	11.0	—
1986	1,506	11.0	—
1987	1,276	11.0	—
1988	1,183	11.0	—
1989	1,053	11.0	—
1990	985	11.0	—
1991	936	11.0	—
1992	780	11.0	—
1993	693	11.0	—
1994	651	11.0	—
1995	622	11.0	—
1996	530	11.0	—
1997	495	11.0	—
1998	489	11.0	—
1999	485	11.0	—
2000	408	11.0	—
2001	337	11.0	—
2002	304	11.0	—
2003	299	11.0	—
2004	299	11.0	—
2005	270	11.0	—

Sources (both Table I and Table II): J.D. Davis, B.A. Svendsen with T.S.F. Knudsen and K.L. Lau, *Dansk Naturgas — Problemer og Muligheder i 80'erne* (Åarhus, Denmark: Forlaget Politica, 1978), pp. 149-52; DeGolyer and MacNaughton, *Rapport om Tilvejebringelsen af et Beslutningsgrundlag angående Produktion af Naturgas fra Cora, Dan, Vern og Bent felterne i den danske Nordsø Sektor* (1 May 1978), Table 8.

Note that the IRRs in the text are those for oil alone. In addition to the income from oil, there will be a considerable income from natural gas. The net amount of natural gas remaining after reinjection will be used to ease peak load demands from the natural gas fields.

Appendix 8B: Assumptions behind the Production of Skjold/Ruth Oil

Investment expenditures for Skjold/Ruth were announced in public as being in the 200 million Dkr range — approximately $32.7 million in 1977 prices. This figure undoubtedly covered the expenses of well-completion, loading systems, and perhaps some of the conversion expenses for the jack-up involved. Operations costs, in contrast, are quite high. This reflects the assumption that the jack-up would be leased and that operating expenses would be higher than normal. No public data exist as to how capital expenditures would be allocated. The author therefore has evenly divided them over the investment period — a common practice in the oil industry when no detailed breakdowns are available.

Table III: Production Profile of the Skjold/Ruth Field (1977, 1979)

Year	Production (10^3 mt)	at $14/bbl. (1977) Operations costs ($m)	Capital investment ($m)
1977	—	—	16.35
1978	—	—	16.35
1979	365	11.4	—
1980	730	22.9	—
1981	730	22.9	—
1982	730	22.9	—
1983	730	22.9	—
1984	730	22.9	—
1985	730	22.9	—
1986	500	17.1	—
1987	250	8.6	—

Table III *(contd.)*

Year	Production (10^3 mt)	at \$22/bbl. (1979) Operations costs[a] (\$m)	Capital investment[b] (\$m)
1979	—	—	19.36
1980	—	—	19.36
1981	363	12.5	—
1982	730	25.2	—
1983	730	25.2	—
1984	730	25.2	—
1985	730	25.2	—
1986	730	25.2	—
1987	730	25.2	—
1988	500	18.7	—
1989	250	9.5	—

Notes:

a. In 1979 prices (allowing for 5 per cent *per annum* rise in real costs).

b. In 1979 prices (allowing for yearly 10 per cent rise in real costs).

INDEX

access provisions 21, 30, 32-3, 70-2, 155-9, 161, 210-11, 219-20, 222-32; area rental payments 70-2, 220-1; assignments 70-2, 220-1; definition 30; and Denmark 155-9, 161, 210-11; and discretionary provisions 30, 32-3, 89, 216-22; 'jointness' 72-6; policy alternatives 222-32; and relinquishment 70-2, 219-20
Adda 160, 162, 182
Allied Chemicals 58
Alwyn 94, 104, 105
Amethyst 94
Amoco (Standard Oil of Indiana) 77, 148-9, 182-3, 186, 227
Andrew 94
Ann 94
Anne 160, 162, 167, 171-2
area rentals 70-2, 220-1
Argyll 4, 12, 43-7, 94, 105, 223
Arne 160, 171
Arpet 56
assignments 30, 76-8, 164-7, 216-17; and access 30; British policy 77-8; Danish policy 78, 164-7; and the development decision 76-7; Netherlands policy 77-8, 217; Norwegian policy 77; policy alternatives 216-17
auction systems 82, 222-30, 232n13; and high cost fields 222-30, creating demand 222-5, and discretionary incentives 227-8, and natural gas 228-30, and the state 225-30 passim
Auk 12, 43-7, 94, 105, 107-8, 109, 113-14, 213, 241, 245-6; and Petroleum Revenue Tax 107-8, 109, 113-14; sensitivity 43-7, 213

Balogh (Lord) 104
Beatrice 12
Bent (Roar) 12, 160, 171, 185, 193-203 passim
Beryl A 12, 94, 105, 109, 112-13, 245, 248
Big Dotty 27
Blair, J.M. 27
blocks 64-5, 70-5, 219-20

bounded rationality 19, 26-34, 36n9, 48-55, 162-84, 207-11; contractual restraints 29-34; corporate preferences 48-55 passim; and the Danish Underground Consortium 162-84 passim; oligopoly behaviour 27-8; organisational procedure 26-7, 36n9; and Parento efficiencies 207-11; political activity 28-9; see also contract, institutional factors
Brae 44, 224
Brent 11, 12, 110, 147
British Electric Traction 224
British Gas Corporation 95-7, 122-50, 184, 188, 201-3, 223, 228, 229; and Dansk Olie og Naturgas (DONG) 186, 188; and de facto monopsony power 95-7, 122, 126-7, 148, 201-3, 228; initial South Basin negotiations 122-48, and load factor 134-5, and Minister of Power 126-8, prices 129-33, price escalation 139-43, production profiles 135-8; and marketing versus rent captor roles 128, 133, 144, 146, 148-50; renegotiating South Basin contracts 144-6, 147-50, Brent gas 147, drilling activity 144-5, fuel competition 144-6, trade offs 147-50; Rough field 186, 223, 229
British National Oil Corporation (BNOC) 24, 59, 77-8, 85, 100, 117, 216-17, 227
British Petroleum (BP) 36n1, 56, 58, 64-5, 215, 224
Browne, C. 195
Buchan 12, 215, 224
Burmah Oil 58, 59

Canada 219
carried interest see participation
Century Power and Light 224
Cheung, S. 79
Chevron (Standard Oil of California) 56, 58, 78, 82-3, 162-81 passim, 198

Christiansen, A. (Minister of
Commerce) 198
Claymore 12, 94, 105, 109, 113,
245, 246
Compagnie Française Petrolière
(CFP) 41, 57, 77, 212
Conoco (Continental Oil Company)
149
Continental Shelf Act of 1964 126-7
contract 21-34, 64-9, 82-6, 95-7,
210-12; access provisions 21-30,
32-3; discretionary provisions 21,
30, 31-4, 64-9, 210-12; and
natural gas 95-7; and oil 95-7;
property rights 29-31; rent
capture 19-21; and transaction
costs 69, 82-6, 210-12,
participation 85-6, royalties 82-3,
taxes 84-5; *see also* Denmark,
Great Britain
Cora (Tyra) 12, 159, 160, 171-2,
185, 188-92, 193-203; dispute
over reserves 188-92; and natural
gas negotiations 193-203 *passim*
Cormorant S 12, 56, 94, 105, 107-8,
109, 113; and Petroleum Revenue
Tax 107-8, 109, 113
crude oil 94-7
'crude-long' companies *see* oil
companies
'crude-short' companies *see* oil
companies
Cyert, R.M. 27, 209

Dam, K. 31, 82, 85, 89, 129
Dan (Abby, M- structure) 12, 82-3,
155, 159, 160, 162, 168-83, 190,
213; development decision
168-83 *passim*, and Gorm (Vern)
174-5; and royalties 82-3, 159
Danish Natural Gas Company 159,
161n6, 185-7, *see also* Danish Oil
and Natural Gas Company
(DONG)
Danish Oil and Natural Gas Company
(DONG) 25, 159, 186, 195-203,
228-9; monopsony 186, 228-9;
and natural gas negotiations
193-203 *passim*; *see also* natural
gas negotiations: Denmark
Danish Underground Consortium
(DUC) 25, 78, 82-3, 155-61,
163-76, 181-3, 185-203, 225
and concession 155-61; and Dan
168-74; and Gorm 174-6; group

behaviour 163-6, 182-3,
exploration activity 182-3,
Moeller, A.P. 167-8, reassignment
of interests 163-4, 165, 166, and
'sole risk' 164, 166, 168; and
natural gas 185-203; political
environment 81-2; and royalties
82-3
Dansk Boreselskab *see* Moeller, A.P.
Dansk Naturgas *see* Danish Natural
Gas Company
Dansk Olie og Naturgas *see* Danish
Oil and Natural Gas Company
(DONG)
Deep Sea Venture 77-8
De Golyer and MacNaughton 58, 59,
63, 162, 178, 188-90, 202-3, 223;
Danish reserves 162; and natural
gas negotiations 188-90, 202-3;
Skjold 178
Dell, S. 104
Denmark 17, 24-5, 78, 155-9, 167,
168, 190, 192, 207-32, 252-4;
assignment policy 78;
concessionary terms 78, 157-9,
167-8, 192, 252-4, 'commercial
production' 157-8, 252-4,
enforcement 159, Protocol of
1971 167, Protocol of 1976 168,
192, reinterpretation 158-9; and
Great Britain 24-5, 155-6,
207-32 *passim*; high-cost fields
17; and natural gas 159, 190, 192
Deny, L. 41, 42
Department of Energy 100, 110, 115,
117, 214
Department of Trade and Industry
100, 102
Department of Treasury 102, 105
development decision 15-16, 19-21,
65-7, 67-8, 162-81, 188-90, 194,
202; bargaining process 67-8;
context 15-16; Cora 188-90,
194, 202; corporate preferences
65-7; Dan 162-81 *passim*; Gorm
173-6 *passim*; present value
19-21; Skjold 177-9
discretionary provisions 20, 30, 31-4,
78-89, 119, 155-6, 158, 201-2,
207, 210-16; definition 30, 31;
and development decision 78-88
passim, 207, 212-16; discretionary economic incentives 79-82,
86-8, 89, 119, 155-6, 158, 201-2,
210-16, and access provisions 89,

155-6, 158, costs 79, 82, 86-8, 119, 210-16, and discrimination 79, 82, 89, 167-8, 201-2, effectiveness 79, 82, 212-16; *see also* access provisions, contract, participation, royalties, taxes
Dow Chemical 224
drilling programme 30
Dudgeon 93, 94
Dunlin 12, 94, 105, 109, 113, 245, 247

Ekofisk 11, 12, 77, 147, 151n29, 186-7
Elf-Acquitaine 35-6, 77
Errol, F.J. 116
Esso (Exxon) 1, 35-6, 57, 61, 64-5, 116, 157, 182, 227
'farm in' *see* assignments
'farm out' *see* assignments
Folketing (Danish parliament) 188
Forties 11, 12, 43-7, 60, 110, 111, 114, 121n13, 245, 247; and Petroleum Revenue Tax 110, 111, 114, 121n13; sensitivity 43-7, 213
Frigg 35, 43, 63, 141-2, 147, 212
Fulmar 177
Furutbotn, E. 29

GAO 224
Gas Council *see* British Gas Corporation
Gasunie 123, 198
Getty Oil 58
Gorm (Vern) 12, 159, 160, 162, 163, 171, 172, 174-7, 180-3, 210, 215, 255-8; and development decision 163, 171, 172, 174-6, 180-3 *passim*; reserves 12, 160, 162
Great Britain 14-16, 19-21, 24-5, 29, 65-8, 89, 93, 99, 162-81, 188-90, 194, 202, 207-32; and Denmark 24-5, 29, 155-6, 207-32 *passim*; high-cost fields 17, 93, 99; licensing policy 72-7, 89, 102-3, 116-17, assignments 77, exploration rates 72-7, favouritism 89, 116-17, Fourth Round 102-3, *see also* participation, Petroleum Revenue Tax, royalties; and

OECD/Europe 14-15
group behaviour *see* Danish Underground Consortium, oil companies
Gulf Oil 36n1, 77, 78, 82, 157-8, 162-81, 186, 188, 227; and Danish Underground Consortium 82, 158, 162-81 *passim*, 186, 188; and Rough 227
'guyed wire' platforms 35
Gwen 160, 162

Hamilton Brothers 223
Haylar, R.F. 84
Heather 12, 43-7, 94, 104, 105, 109, 111, 113, 114, 117-18, 120, 121n13, 213-14, 242, 245-6; and Petroleum Revenue Tax 109, 111, 113, 114, 117-18, 121n13; sensitivity 43-7, 213-14
Hewett 12, 56, 97, 125, 148
high-cost fields 17-19, 41-7, 87-8, 94-5, 98n3, 122-4, 149, 159-60, 162-3, 188-91, 237-40; Danish sector 159-60, 162-3, 188-91, 239; definition 17-19, 41-7, 87-8, 122-4, difficulties 17-19, 87-8, 122-4, and investment sensitivity 43-7, and 'marginal' fields 19; and Netherlands sector 240; and Norwegian sector 239-40; and UK sector 94-5, 98n3, 149, 237-8
House of Commons 99, 100, 102-3
Hutton 94, 104, 105

Indefatigable 12, 125, 130, 133-4, 148-9
Independents 48-55 *passim*, *see also* oil companies
Indonesia 209
Inland Revenue 102-3
institutional factors 19-21, 28, 46-55, 162-84 *passim*, *see also* access, contract, discretionary incentives, natural gas negotiations
intertemporal Pareto efficiencies 208-12
Iran 28

Jensen, E. (Minister of Commerce) 192
Jensen, G. 202

Kearton (Lord) 116, 148
Kemp, A.G. 245

Labour Party 100
Leman 12, 97, 123, 130, 148, 149
licensing policy *see* access, contract,
    discretionary provisions
Little Dotty 94
Lulu 162

Majors 48-55 *passim*
March, E. 27, 209
market values *see* auction systems,
    user costs
Maureen 94, 105
Meade, W. 213
Mexico 28
Ministry of Commerce (Denmark)
    177, 186, 187, 192, 198
Ministry of Justice (Denmark) 192,
    194
Ministry of Power (UK) 126-7, 130
Ministry of Public Works (Denmark)
    168
Mobil 35
Moeller, A.P. 82, 157-9, 161n3,
    163-8, 178-9, 187, 190-3, 198,
    215-16; Danish concessionaires
    157-9, 190-2, 215-16; and Danish
    Underground Consortium 163-8,
    198; and formation of the Danish
    Natural Gas Company 187; Skjold
    field 178-9
Moeller, M.M. 187
Montrose 12, 56, 94, 104, 105,
    107-8, 109, 113, 245, 247; and
    Petroleum Revenue Tax 107-8,
    109, 113
Morecombe Field 186, 229
Morgan, J. 42
Murchison 12, 63

National Coal Board 227
National Westminster Bank 224
natural gas 30, 94-7, 98n5, 122-46,
    186-8, 190-203, 249-51; and
    crude oil 94-7; discretionary
    provision 30; market price versus
    cost price 96, 98n5; negotiations
    (Denmark) 186-7, 190-203, *ab
    platform* versus landed prices
    193-7 *passim*, 199, 201-3,
    concessionary conflict 190-2,

contracted amounts 196-7,
    198-200, load factor 195, 197,
    199, marketing 194-5, pipeline
    200-1, right of first refusal
    192-3, taxes 199-200; and UK
    186, 201-3, *see also* Danish Oil
    and Natural Gas Company;
    negotiations (UK) 122-46, 187-
    8, 201-3, 249-51, contracted
    amounts 124, and Denmark
    187-8, 201-3, escalation clauses
    126, 139-43, European markets
    123-4, institutional interests
    122-4, load factor 124, 126,
    134-5, model assumptions
    249-51, negotiation procedure
    126, 130, and oil products 123,
    132-3, 135, 144-6, penalties 124,
    prices 124, 129-33, renegotiations
    see British Gas Corporation; *see
    also* British Gas Corporation,
    Danish Oil and Natural Gas
    Company
Nederlandse Aardolie Maatschappi
    (NAM) 76, 123, *see also* Esso,
    Gasunie, Royal Dutch/Shell
Netherlands 17, 74-9 *passim*, 86-7,
    216-21, 240; area rentals 220-1;
    assignment policy 77-8, 216-17;
    blocks 74-6, 219; high-cost fields
    17, 240; licensing process 218-19;
    operating costs deductible 79;
    royalties 86-7
Nigeria 28
Nils 162
Ninian 11, 12, 58-9, 63, 110
Noergaard, I. (Minister of Commerce)
    196
Norsk Hydro 77
North Arne 160
Norway 14-15, 17, 22-4, 35, 37n17,
    77, 83, 87-9, 210, 216, 218-20,
    223, 226, 239-40; assignments
    77; high-cost fields 17, 22-4,
    239-40; licensing policy 89;
    and OECD/Europe 14-15; oil tax
    35, 37n17; participation 88;
    royalties 83, 87, 88
Norwegian Oil Consortium (NOCO)
    77

Occidental 58, 67
Odell, P.R. 58, 60, 67
Odin 35

Offshore Pollution Liability Agreement (OPOL) 102, 120n2
oil companies: bounded rationality 26-9, 207-11; contractual relationship 29-35; differing preferences 48-55; group interaction 56-68, extended group 60-3, immediate group 56-60, 68n7; *see also* individual corporate entries
Oil Tax Act of 1975 *see* Petroleum Revenue Tax
Organization of Economic Cooperation and Development (OECD) 11-12, 14, 16-17
Organization of Petroleum Exporting Countries (OPEC) 209

participation 30, 85-6, 90n9, 155
Petroleum and Submarine Pipelines Act 77, 112
Petroleum Industry Advisory Committee (PIAC) 101-2
Petroleum Revenue Tax (PRT) 35, 79, 95-7, 99-121, 214, 215; chronology 99-100; and high-cost fields 79, 95, 116-21; increases 35, 100, 116-18, 215; Oil Tax Act 100-21, and loopholes 84-5, 103, negotiations 99-121, oil allowance 103, 106, 108-10, 117, proposed rates 105, 106-8, 117, 'tapering provision' (CAPEX) 103, 106, 111, 112, 115, 118, 121n13, and UKOOA 100-21 *passim*, 'uplift' 85, 103, 106-7, 110-11, 117; transaction costs 103, 119; *see also* discretionary provisions, Great Britain, taxes, United Kingdom Offshore Operators Association
Petronord 77
Peyovich, S. 29
Phillips 77, 186
Piper 12, 58, 67, 104
Placid 78
Pleasance, R.T. 84
Prices Commission 146
Progressive Conservative Party 100, 118

Ravlin, F. 157
relinquishment 64-5, 70-2, 156-9, 161, 216, 219-20; and area rental payments 70-2; Danish concession 156-9, 161; rates 64-5, 216, 219-21
rent capture legislation *see* discretionary provisions, participation, royalties, taxes
rents 18, 20-1, 36n6
Reynolds, J. 104
Riggs Bank Status Report on North Sea Drilling 1977 94, 175, *see also* Browne, C.
risk pooling and spreading strategies 212, 232n3
Robinson, C. 42
Rosing, K. 60
Rotterdam spot market 132-3, 139-41
Rough 12, 130, 147, 149, 186, 223, 229
Royal Dutch/Shell 36n1, 56, 57, 61, 64-5, 82-3, 149, 162-81 *passim*, 198, 223; activity 64-5, 182; and Danish Underground Consortium 82-3, 162-81 *passim*, 198; Leman 149
royalties 33, 78, 79, 82-3, 86-7, 90n5, 111-12, 214-15; comparison 33; discretionary refunds 78, 214-15; sliding scale 79, 86-7; transaction costs 82-3, 86-7, 90n5, 111-12, British 83, 90n5, 111-12, Danish 82-3, Dutch 86-7, Norwegian 83, 86-7
Ruhrgas 186, 198

Sampson, A. 158
Saudi Arabia 11-12
Schloctern 11
Scram 94
Scurry Rainbow 78
Seagram Distillers 224
Shawn 94
Shell Transport *see* Royal Dutch/Shell
Siebens 224
Skjold (Ruth) 12, 160, 162, 177-9, 180-3, 210, 215, 258-9; and development decision 177-9, 180-3; reserves 12, 160, 162
Social Democratic Party (Danish) 168, 187, 192, 194
South-east Indefatigable 227, 230
Statfjord 11, 12, 63
Statoil 85
Sullivan, R.L. 126, 138

tanker-based field producing
systems 35
taxes 34, 83-5;
comparison in North Sea 34;
interest payments 84-5;
transaction costs 83-5;
'X-company' 84; *see also*
discretionary provisions,
Petroleum Revenue Tax
Tehran-Tripoli Agreements 102
'tension leg' platform 35
Tesoro 78
Texaco 56, 78, 82-3, 162-81 *passim*
Thatcher, M. 118
Thistle 12, 94, 105, 109, 112, 113,
245-6; and Petroleum Revenue
Tax 109, 112, 113
Thomson Newspapers 58, 224
Trans Canada Pipeline 197
Tricentrol 224
Tuck, C.E. 100, 103

Ultramar 224
Union Oil of California (Unocal) 47,
77
United Kingdom Offshore Operators
Association (UKOOA) 93,
99-120, 210, 243-8; and Oil Tax

Act 103-20, 243-5, 246-8,
'marginal' field representations
104-10, 112-15, oil allowance
108-10, 'tapering provision'
(CAPEX) 111, 'uplift' 110-11,
and royalties 111-12
United Kingdom Offshore Operators
Committee (UKOOC) 101, *see
also* United Kingdom Offshore
Operators Association
United Kingdom Oil Industry
Taxation Committee (UKOITC)
99, 101-2
United States of America 28, 82, 84,
209, 226, 232n13
unitisation 60-3
user costs *see* market values, rents

Valhall/Hod 12, 77, 183
Van Dyck Oil 78
Viking 12, 56, 97, 125, 127, 130,
146-9 *passim*

Walter Levy and Associates 197
West Germany 123, 186-7, 210
West Sole 12, 94, 97, 130-4 *passim*,
148

For Product Safety Concerns and Information please contact our EU
representative GPSR@taylorandfrancis.com Taylor & Francis Verlag GmbH,
Kaufingerstraße 24, 80331 München, Germany

Printed and bound by CPI Group (UK) Ltd, Croydon, CR0 4YY

08/05/2025

01864406-0006